# An Uncertain Legacy

## Essays on the Pursuit of Liberty

*foule*

*edited by*
*Edward B. McLee*

**ISI**

*Intercollegiate Studies Institute*
*Wilmington, Delaware*

*Library of Congress Cataloging-in-Publication Data*

An uncertain legacy : essays on the pursuit of liberty / edited by
    Edward B. McLean.—Wilmington, Del. :
    Intercollegiate Studies Inst., c1997.

       246pp., 15.2 x 22.8 cm.
    ISBN   1-882926-15-3
       1. Liberty. 2. Liberalism. 3. Montesquieu,
Charles de Secondat, baron de, 1689-1755—Contributions in
political science. 4. Political science—Europe—History.
5. Political science—United States—History. I. McLean,
Edward B.

JC585 .U53 1997     97-072119
323.44—dc21       CIP


Published in the United States by:

Intercollegiate Studies Institute
3901 Centerville Road • P.O. Box 4431
Wilmington, DE   19807-0431
http://www.isi.org

Manufactured in the United States of America

# Contents

# Introduction

EDWARD B. MCLEAN

W estern man's pursuit of liberty has been constant. Indeed, the concept of liberty is central to Western political thought and history. The following essays, which were the first of the Goodrich Lecture Series at Wabash College, examine the concept of liberty as it has been understood from antiquity through the twentieth century. Since they were delivered, some of the essays have been modified, but the original thrust of the lecture series has been preserved. It is fitting that these lectures focused on this concept which was so important to Mr. Pierre Goodrich, in whose honor this lecture series was created. Mr. Goodrich founded Liberty Fund Inc., a foundation given over to the programmatic and philosophic study of society made up of free and responsible individuals. The value of such studies reflects Mr. Goodrich's understanding of the difficult problems raised in advancing and defending human liberty.

These essays examine the meaning given to the concept of liberty in selected periods of Western history. They demonstrate that Western man, in the pursuit of liberty, has concerned himself in every historical epoch with this concept as he attempted to define, implement, and, most importantly, understand it.

Free will, that quality which characterizes the uniqueness of human beings, is evidenced in their acts, behaviors, and choices. However, this fact does not mean that human behavior, thought, and choice have unchanging purpose or content since such free choices are within the power of the individual and are conditioned by the circumstances in which individuals operate. Consequently, historical examination of this concept provides an outline for the inquiry made regarding the nature of liberty—its definition, its implementation, and its value.

Professor Rufus Fears's essay opens this unique collection by examining the concept of liberty in Republican Rome and its transformation from the period of the Republic to the Empire. In the Republic, liberty was a religious tenet reserved exclusively for Romans. Juridically protected, it was considered necessary to preserve Roman morality. After the collapse of the Republic, the concept of liberty remained as a rhetorical support for the emperor, but its substantive meaning had changed.

One development in this period, however, enhanced both the value and future success of liberty, for:

> Out of the political wasteland of the collapse of the Roman Republic there came birth as well as death. There was death for a narrowly defined ideal of republican Liberty based upon a concept of collective political authority. Yet in hard and bitter agony there was also the birth of a new and more noble conception of Liberty. It was this more exalted, more inclusive vision of Liberty which would be invoked so many centuries later by a bold group of men willing to justify revolution by an appeal to the self-evident truth that all men are created equal and endowed by their creator with the inalienable right to Liberty.

The idea of liberty received its greatest impetus and universal appeal from Christianity, which breathed life into it by revealing its connection with the providence of God. The implications for this revelation were refined in the course of the Middle Ages and are here examined by Professor Ralph McInerny.

McInerny observes that in modernity, liberty is considered as "immunity from obstacles and impediments," so that one may fulfill the choices made by his own will, while in the Middle Ages scholars believed liberty's proper meaning referred to one's capacity *for* something. Medievals maintained that since man chooses deliberate actions he is different from other living things and must be held responsible for those actions. Man alone knowingly directs himself to the good.

The good man seeks to act in accordance with a good which is not self-determined, but exists independently of his choosing. In order to achieve that good, man is compelled to make choices to pursue the good in proportion to his being and to conduct himself well in that pursuit. The full goodness men should pursue is the ultimate good—God, who "is not just another good thing."

Therefore, the authentic meaning of man's liberty, which requires him to act in ways that serve his true good, contrasts sharply with modern notions that goals and means are good because they are desired. The medieval conception of rights bears no resemblance to modern beliefs and the claims derived from them. When these claimed rights conflict, force is the only resolution. As McInerny demonstrates, the modern shibboleths of pluralism and tolerance—honorable and meaningful in their own ways—have practical value *only* if they are made operative within a context that allows prudent and constructive meaning to be ascribed them. To embrace relativism is to bring about the end of liberty generally and of free society particularly.

The sixteenth century witnessed the emergence of philosophies of liberty opposed to those found in antiquity and the Middle Ages. Professor George Martin addresses the sources and nature of these changes.

The clearest sixteenth-century defender of the older concepts of liberty was Richard Hooker, who maintained that liberty, properly exercised, requires men to act in conformance with the traditional social, political, and religious orders, which enable them to serve ends proper to their being. Mankind's true end is to "live virtuously" so that he may approach God.

Shakespeare also believed that liberty, obtained through right reason, was necessary for the acquisition of virtue. For both men, genuine liberty was found in a community based on tradition and right reason. While Shakespeare believed familial institutions best provided such a condition and Hooker looked to the use of positive law, both men resisted the radical transformation of society through religious zealotry. "[B]oth men," Martin writes, "would affirm [liberty], but liberty within the context of authority."

Such views were challenged by those who denied that liberty was a means by which men served ends that were properly human. Pico della Mirandola illustrates this "spirit of the Renaissance." He maintained that man is "liberated from superstitions and unnatural social restraints,...[and]...could recover the lost image of God within himself." Machiavelli identified liberty as man's self-assertion in the fulfillment of his own aspirations and desires. Both rejected the idea that liberty was to be used by men to accommodate themselves to a higher order. Rather, liberty allowed individuals to pursue their desires absent objective external measures of rightness or purpose.

Luther's and Calvin's views contributed further to the development of more modern ideas of liberty. The individuality of conscience and the self-determination of the right exercise of liberty espoused by both men created conditions in which "men...cannot live peacefully together except under conditions of religious freedom or tyranny."

Professor Timothy Fuller focuses on the writings of Thomas Hobbes. Fuller maintains that Hobbes has left us two legacies that most affect the degree to which we understand and value liberty. The first relates to the "estrangement" of people under the impersonal rule of the state; the second rejects the idea of the rule of law in the belief that a repudiation of such formalism ends the estrangement of individuals from one another.

In the seventeenth-century, liberty was seen as freedom from restraint; thinkers rejected the previously held belief that liberty is to be used to achieve the good. The seventeenth-century liberal concept of liberty, Fuller maintains, would be "hard pressed to defend itself in light of the necessary indeterminacy that liberty in this sense seems to require." Furthermore, Hobbes's notion of liberty is descriptive of the value of liberty in the modern affairs of man.

Dean William B. Allen, a scholar of Enlightenment thought, maintains that Montesquieu's concept of liberty is compatible with that found in antiquity and the Middle Ages. Allen considers the Enlightenment's impact on America during the Revolutionary period. He notes that the oft-stated idea that Americans' attitudes relied mainly on certain "Whiggish" notions of the "rights of Englishmen" is only partially correct, for one must acknowledge Montesquieu's influence.

Montesquieu's ideas contrast sharply with those of Rousseau who, Allen argues: "opened the modern assault on nature as a moral standard and natural rights as a source of political principles." Rousseau argued that man is separated from other living creatures by historical developments rather than human nature—a relativistic fallacy which provides the foundation for those elements of modern thought directly opposed to the ideas of human liberty advanced by Montesquieu. Jefferson temporarily employed Rousseau's idea that the absence of constancy in man's history reveals liberty as a matter of development rather than a principled right. Although Rousseau's influence overshadowed Montesquieu's in European thought, the latter's influence in America was substantial. Daniel Fowle, who advanced the notion that legislative authority and power derived from the liberty of the people, the exclusive guardians of their

Constitution, was particularly influenced by the illustrious Frenchman.

Professor George Carey contrasts the Founders' idea of liberty with those of modern scholars. He observes that modern views are numerous and diverse compared to the period of the Founding, when there was general agreement regarding the meaning of liberty. For the Founders, the maintenance of liberty required the rule of law to protect against arbitrary and capricious government. Rights provide protection against oppressive government action, and the rights protected by the law must be considered in terms of "civil" and not "natural" liberty. Civil liberty could not be so expansive that it would permit licentiousness nor so restrictive that it would lead to subjection to an oppressive government.

The colonists believed England had deprived them of their liberty, since men should only be subject to laws to which they assented, and a virtuous people would determine the extent of liberty sufficient to serve the common good. Such virtue results from the operation of the extended society—families, education, and religion—which induces morality and enables men to restrain their unruly and selfish passions.

Contemporary conceptions of liberty, Carey argues, illustrate the full implication of Popper's notion of an open society, and are revealed in the relativism that characterizes contemporary American notions of morality, manners, responsibilities, and duties. For Carey, the U. S. Supreme Court has been the primary means by which our understanding of liberty has been turned away from the views of the Founders. The Court has constructed a "national standard" for free speech that provides only the weakest and ineffectual restraints on it, even as they developed a whole panoply of "rights" that include deviant behaviors and lifestyles. Society is even required to view each individual as a separate moral universe devoid of allegiance to any conception of the common good. This new definition of liberty flows naturally from the concept of equality. To assure this linkage governmental programs are created to achieve greater equality—primarily economic equality. This linkage of liberty and equality further defines the common good as best served by autonomous individuals who are permitted to act in conformance with their own notions of morality without reference to those of the community of which they are a part.

In contrast, Carey observes, the Founders did not believe liberty should be so defined as to become detrimental to the common good. Liberty's value is anchored in virtue and protected by deliberative self-government. The Founders would reject utterly the contemporary view of free speech, for their commonsense view of the world and man's place in it, which required acceptance of his responsibilities and duties, rejects the view of individuals as isolated atoms who can be restrained *only* when they threaten physical harm to others.

Leonard Liggio examines the concept of liberty in eighteenth-century French thought. France's mercantilist economic system involved massive intrusions of state power into the economy of the country. However, this use of state power was opposed and challenged by those who exalted human reason and held an optimistic view of human nature. Archbishop Fenelon and Abbé Fleury, for example, maintained that although human nature involved original sin, men could still make moral choices and act in conformance with God's plan for the universe, and both believed that a market economy provided men with the chance to act morally. Opposition to such views was obvious in Rousseau's idea of the "general will." In accepting an active and intrusive state, Rousseau's thought, Liggio notes, "became a virulent source for the creation of the modern bureaucratic state," the emergence of which was supported by both Jacobin thought and ideas supporting enlightened despotism.

Liggio contends that the most significant French theorist in this period was Benjamin Constant, whose break with Enlightenment ideas laid the foundation for nineteenth-century liberal thought and who, therefore, "speaks to and for modern man." Constant rejected all ideas of system building; rather, he believed that religion is necessary for human liberty since it provides a moral bulwark against state oppression. In contrast to ancient liberty, which related only to man's participation in collective decisions, modern liberty, Constant maintains, is a product of commercial society and is based on Christian thought and human rights. Consequently, he criticized Rousseau's belief in the rightness of collective decisions and pointed out that such ideas were erroneous, dangerous to liberty, and would lead to all manners of despotism.

Professor Jeffrey Wallin examines the concept of liberty in the period before the War between the States and in the latter part of the nineteenth century. Since the issue of slavery was not resolved at the time of the Founding, it would occupy all discussions about liberty in the first half of the century. Wallin argues that the Republic's founding was based on the belief in the equality of men, government with the consent of the governed, and government action for the common good. In this context, government could succeed as long as everyone obeyed its rightful acts. Such a premise, however, suggests two possible dangers: that those who hold power act only in their own interest; and that those out of power reject their obligation to those in office. These dangers surfaced in the early part of the nineteenth century when the issue of slavery pitted the belief in the equality and rights of man against the obligation of obedience to laws made by those in power in the South.

The industrialization in the second half of the nineteenth century that transformed the very nature of American society again raised questions about the nature of liberty. The great concentrations of wealth which affected government and society posed a major challenge to the Republic's ability to deal effectively with ensuing problems. Response to this issue instituted the growth of a powerful national government which, in theory, would protect both the market's role of creating and distributing wealth as well as the public interest.

John Gray's essay provides an examination and critique of contemporary liberal concepts of liberty and focuses particularly on the thought of F. A. Hayek. Hayek is considered in many circles as the definitive writer in the "classical liberal" tradition, a school of thought most frequently assumed to reflect the most thoroughgoing and complete definition of liberty in the context of modernity. Gray sees significant problems in using Hayek's formulations as a foundation for liberal thought and particularly for liberty. What Gray considers to be the "instability" and "incoherences" of Hayek's formulation are attributable to one "single conception," i.e., Hayek's "idea of a spontaneous order in society." Gray acknowledges some value in this belief for the examination of economic activity, but he believes Hayek stretched it beyond credibility in his attempt to construct a complete social theory based on his "illicit generalization from [these] market processes and exchanges to legal rules, political institutions, and cultural traditions."

Such attempts diminish greatly the value of Hayek's thought as well as the theories of the Virginia School and John Rawls, who maintain that "market institutions can be legitimated by an appropriate constitutional framework or contract whose justice has sufficient general acceptance to assure support for liberal institutions." This legalism ignores the fact that liberal regimes are fostered by particularistic cultural traditions which sustain the liberal policies of a civil society. Talismanic ideas such as those presented in these various versions of liberalism cloud and distort a proper understanding of liberal thought, institutions, and practices. Gray asserts that "prudence and wisdom" require an abandonment of the classical liberal infatuation with a "universal...doctrine of liberty," and an understanding that the existence of "free peoples" is only one form of life among many alternatives that reflect complex and disparate cultural sources.

Certainly Gray's essay provides a challenging conclusion to this collection. The record set forth in this book demonstrates the magnitude of the task required for the defense of liberty. As the title *An Uncertain Legacy* suggests, liberty can, in effect, disappear. Given shifts in the cultural values of a society, it can be replaced by either benevolent or malevolent despotism in which the concept of liberty describes a condition of serfdom or worse. Liberty cannot be defended unless one understands what it is and what it is not.

The long historical struggle to obtain and secure liberty is one of the great contributions of the Western world. As typified by the struggles that resulted in the collapse of the Soviet Empire, history proves that the task of providing circumstances wherein men can enjoy liberty fully is not a matter of merely pronouncing that it shall be so. A long arduous journey faces all of us in meeting this challenge, and whatever the problems abroad, our attention must not turn from the threats to our own liberty. Such awesome tasks present challenges and opportunities as well as danger. Honor and duty require our meeting the task resolutely and realistically. Fictions will neither advance nor defend liberty. Thus one of the chief contentions of the book is that the fruits of man's centuries-long struggle for liberty are by no means guaranteed into the twenty-first century.

The need for a careful examination of the history of liberty is clear. Recent American history reveals trends destructive to both the American constitutional order and to individual liberty. The cumulative effects of these developments are not unlike a *coup d'etat*. The absence of a vigorous, committed, and steady resolve by the populace to restore a Republic characterized by virtue and devoted to preserving liberty has had disastrous results. Today we live in a non-constitutional regime, where, as in the days of the Roman Empire, many people claim only those liberties granted by their present rulers. They hope, as did the Romans, to be ruled by an Augustus, yet they know they may be dealt a Caligula. It is hoped that *An Uncertain Legacy: Essays on the Pursuit of Liberty* will continue the renewal of interest in the nature, value, and protection of human liberty so that we may live fully as human beings.

# Antiquity: The Example of Rome

### J. RUFUS FEARS

L iberty is the definitive attribute of the American republic.[1] The doctrine of Liberty is evoked in the two fundamental documents of the political creed of the American People. In the Declaration of Independence, Liberty is the God-given and inalienable right of all men, a self-evident truth which justifies revolution. In the Constitution, Liberty appears as a blessing, the secural of which justifies the ordination and establishment of new articles of government. At that most critical moment in the history of the republic, Abraham Lincoln adapted Liberty to the fundamental mystery of Christianity, commemorating his countrymen who had sacrificed their lives so that a nation might be saved, that a people might have a new birth of freedom.[2] In its grim struggle with a savage tyranny, Franklin Roosevelt rallied the free world with a commitment to four freedoms. Throughout the course of our history we Americans have observed a marked tendency to regard ourselves as, in the words of Herman Melville, "a peculiar, chosen People; the Israel of our time, we bear the ark of the liberties of the world."[3] Small wonder that the statue of the goddess of Liberty, holding her torch aloft as a beacon of hope to an oppressed and suffering humanity, serves as the most profound symbol of our republic. The very coins which we carry invoke Liberty, paradigmatic statements of the sacrifices which our forefathers have undertaken to secure Liberty.[4]

In what follows, I shall discuss the experience of Liberty in another republic, in another age. *Libertas Populi Romani*—the Liberty of the Roman People: for a traditionalist like M. Junius Brutus, director of the Roman mint in 54 B.C., Roman Liberty was synonymous with republican government; Liberty was coterminous with the republic of the Roman People, its constitutional forms and its laws.[5] *Libertas Populi Romani*: for Brutus that single phrase embodied the ideal and the reality of four and one half centuries of historical development. The Roman nation came into being as a place of refuge, an asylum for outcasts, men driven from their native lands by poverty, by oppression, by crime. Some free, some slaves, they had come to Rome asking nothing but a fresh start.[6]

In the beginning kings had ruled Rome; for 254 years after its foundation Rome remained a monarchy until that fateful day in 509 B.C. when Brutus' great ancestor, L. Junius Brutus, rallied the Roman People to the battle standard of Liberty. In an act of revolutionary violence, the Roman People declared their independence, their republic, and their Liberty, dissolving those political bonds which had connected them to their lawful monarch. The king was driven into exile, the implements of constitutional republican government established, and the Liberty of the infant republic successfully defended against the tyrant and his foreign mercenaries.[7] From that hallowed date, the history of Rome had been the story of the achievements of a free people governing themselves under the institutions of Liberty.[8] The achievement of that People was unparalleled. Once a small city-state by the Tiber, surrounded by hostile and aggressive foes and without any marked advantages of geography or natural resources, Rome had conquered the Mediterranean world. In the year 54 B.C. Rome was absolute mistress of all she surveyed. Her military might was unchallenged, her economic power unprecedented. All Italy was now gathered into the protecting fold of Roman citizenship; the remainder of the Mediterranean world, from Syria to the Pillars of Hercules, lay under the domination of the Roman People. In this very year, 54 B.C., the legions of the republic, under the leadership of C. Julius Caesar, were augmenting the imperium of the Roman People, subduing Gaul and making armed forays into Britain and Germany.

Ecumenical imperial power, unchallenged military supremacy, unparalleled material affluence—these were the achievements of the Roman People under the Liberty of the republic. It was this tradition of Liberty which M. Junius Brutus evoked on the silver coinage struck during his one-year tenure as director of the mint. The Roman was acutely sensitive to the coinage as a medium of propaganda or image making.[9] Coins represented the most frequent point of physical contact which the ordinary citizen had with an organ of his government in everyday life. The Roman consciously and carefully exploited this point of contact by the employment of an elaborately refined pictorial script of remarkable brevity and profundity. The Roman coinage of any one year presented a kaleidoscope of obverse and reverse types, each bearing a concisely formulated message and enabling the government and individual monetary magistrates to inform and to persuade the political constituency. Fully in the tradition, Brutus used the typology of the coins issued under his direction to present a bold declaration of political principle; like any good politician and with more reason than most, Brutus equated his personal beliefs and his announced political principles with the traditions of the republic which he served.[10]

The obverse portrait personifies the goddess Liberty. The idealized form of divine beauty contrasts forcefully with the stark historical realism of the reverse portrayal of Brutus' illustrious progenitor: L. Junius Brutus, father of Roman Liberty and institutor of the republic, that paradigmatic figure of Roman virtue to whom the People awarded the honor of serving as the first duly elected consul of the republic.[11] As holder of this office, as chief executive of the Roman People, great Brutus is portrayed on the coin; he is accompanied by attendants of his rank who bear the fasces, that bundle of rods and an axe which symbolized the awesome executive authority of the supreme magistrate of the Roman People: his power to chastise, his power to execute.

The simple obverse legend renders explicit the political message of the coin: *Libertas*. The imagery of Brutus' coin, this fascinating and evocative historical document, commemorates the ideal of Liberty on four levels: as religious form, as historical motif, as political catchword, and as constitutional and juridical concept. On each of these levels the notion of Liberty functioned in the political life of the Roman republic. Each represents one approach, one point of access leading the modern student to a clearer understanding of that complex of ideas which for the Roman of the republican epoch was inherent in the conception of Liberty. In the imagery of the obverse Brutus both commemorates and invokes the goddess Liberty: may she watch over, guide, and protect the Liberty of the Roman People. The personification of Libertas as a goddess was more than allegory. To the Roman, Liberty was an actual goddess of the first magnitude, a supernatural power who bestowed upon the Roman People the benefit of political liberty. Liberty was fully incorporated into the pantheon of the gods of the Roman state. She possessed a temple and a feast day, April 13. In cult action she was closely associated with Jupiter, the supreme divine patron of the republic:[12] one nation under god with Liberty and Justice for all. The deification of social and political conditions which, like Liberty, were of powerful significance to the community was characteristic of the religious mentality of Roman polytheism.[13] Deification meant immortality. By recognizing Liberty as a godhead, the Roman ritually secured permanence for the central ideological construct of his state, elevating the blessed condition of Liberty beyond the sphere of the profane and into the sphere of the sacred, the sphere of absolute reality and eternity.[14]

Thus, for the Roman, Liberty lived beyond history. Yet, at the same time, like every Roman god, she manifested her miraculous blessed power within history.[15] In the imagery of the reverse of our coin, Brutus dramatizes a single event, the origins of Liberty, to remind the Roman People of the totality of their historical experience of Liberty and of the sacrifices which Romans in the past have made in order to maintain their freedom. At the same time, Brutus recalls that it was his ancestor who led the Roman People to Liberty. Brutus declares his full acceptance of his family's ancestral guardianship of Liberty.[16] The coin of Brutus was more than a commemorative medal. Its message was aimed squarely at the realities of political life at Rome in the year 54 B.C. The coin declares *Libertas* as the rallying cry of Brutus and such political associates as M. Porcius Cato: we are the best men; we are the party of constitutionalism, the sons of Liberty; our opponents are demagogues, traducers of Roman Liberty. The coin was meant as more than an exercise in slogan making and electioneering. It conveyed a grim warning to M. Licinius Crassus, to Gnaeus Pompeius, surnamed the Great One, to C. Julius Caesar, and to the multitudinous supporters of those three colossi who did bestride the world of politics at Rome, menacing the traditional balance of power and the traditional workings of the electoral process. For five years now these three men had exercised an unofficial but *de facto* domination of the political scene, based upon an overwhelming combination of prestige, wealth, patronage, political power, and military resources. Such domination threatened to leave no room within Rome's wide walls for the traditions of Liberty represented by Brutus, Cato, and the party of best men.[17]

The threat to republican Liberty was a very real one. The domination of this triumvirate was but a symptom of the cancer eating away at the Roman republic. Amidst unchallenged military supremacy and unprecedented material affluence, the body politic of the Roman People was desperately ill. The wealth of

the empire, its opportunities and its burdens, had brought grave
social and political problems which the constitutional machinery
seemed unable to solve. In the old days of the republic the
forefathers of the current generation seemed willing to endure
any sacrifice, no matter how great: by violent revolution and
appeal to force of arms they had won Liberty; by peaceful means
they had secured the political franchise and the full protection of
the laws for every Roman citizen, regardless of the circumstances
of his birth; by martial prowess they had driven the savage
Carthaginian from their homeland and had carried the victorious standards of Rome to the far corners of their world. Now,
rich, successful, and safe from any foreign threat, the Roman
People seemed oblivious of the meaning of the word "sacrifice"
and bent upon self-destruction. Factionalism was rife; private
interest groups vied with one another to secure their own
immediate advantage at the expense of the commonwealth as a
whole. Political leaders seemed concerned only with their own
aggrandizement; the People, a feckless mob, willing to vote for
any demagogue who promised material benefits. As the historian Tacitus would later describe the age, it was a time when the
republic wore itself out in factious strife and discord; there was
no common purpose among the People, no unity in the Senate,
no order in the courts, no regard for competence or propriety
among the elected officials.[18] In the year 54 B.C. the situation
was assuming crisis proportions. The supporters of great Pompey
spoke openly of making him dictator "to clean up that mess in
Rome."[19] In the electric atmosphere of this year, Brutus issued
his clarion call for Liberty.

By portraying his ancestor in the guise of consul, Brutus
further defined his idea of Liberty by associating it with the
constitutional and legal forms of traditional republican government. For the traditionalist of the republican epoch, Liberty was
a juridical concept, defining a nexus of rights which rested upon
the positive laws and institutions of the commonwealth.[20]

In its most basic sense *Libertas* denoted the status of a *"liber,"* a free man. The existence of slavery as a recognized legal institution lent a particular clarity to the Roman notion of Liberty. Under Roman republican law, to be a slave was to be completely under the domination of a master; the slave was entirely without rights, entirely without legal recourse.[21] The Roman People as a corporate body and the individual citizen possessed Liberty, freedom from involuntary servitude and freedom to exercise specific rights and to assume specific duties. Under this ideal of Liberty the Roman People, as a corporate entity, was its own master, free from internal domination by a monarch or by a political faction and free from subjection to any foreign power; the Roman People was thus free to exercise its sovereignty, free to determine its destiny, free to follow those laws and customs which represented the Roman way of life. As an individual, the Roman was free from the impositions of slavery; as a citizen he was free from arbitrary exactions of fellow citizens, including magistrates. He was free to enjoy a variety of rights: free to elect his own occupation, free to marry the woman of his choice, free to own slaves and to dominate his wife and children. As a citizen, he was free to participate in the assembly, free to vote, free to hold public office, free to serve in the army.

The Liberty of the individual citizen was protected from despotic power by concrete legal and constitutional provisions. Fundamental to the Liberty of the individual citizen was the office of the tribune of the People, which provided the ordinary Roman with a bulwark against arbitrary exactions by the State. Ten tribunes were elected annually; the doors of their houses stood open day and night, an asylum in which the common man might find refuge from overzealous officers of the State. Such was the power of the tribune, exercised on behalf of the Roman People, that by his veto alone he could bring the entire machinery of the Roman state to a halt. Of equal significance was the citizen's right of appeal to the People against a capital sentence imposed by a magistrate in peace or in war.[22] In the eyes of the Roman of the republican epoch, the office of the tribune and the right of appeal were the two supreme citadels of Roman Liberty.[23]

The right of appeal was equally an affirmation of the principle of popular sovereignty. The absolute power of life and death over a fellow citizen resided not with the chief executive, not with a supreme court, but with the assembled body of all Roman citizens. As its very name indicates, the *res publica Populi Romani* was quite literally the commonwealth of the Roman People. It was a polity in which sovereignty was vested in the People. *Senatus Populusque Romanus*: the Senate and the People of Rome. For the sympathetic observer like Polybius, the cause for the extraordinary success of the Roman state lay in the excellence of its constitution.[24] Fundamental was its harmonious balance between the People and the Senate, between the ideal of popular sovereignty and the necessity of guidance by those best suited to govern: the rich, the well-born, and the able.

The Roman of the republic would not have been flattered to have his government described as a democracy. For the Roman, freedom and Liberty were not synonymous with democracy. Extreme democracy meant license, not Liberty. Plato's unflattering portrait of extreme democracy was quoted with approbation in Cicero's treatise on the commonwealth.[25] Under democracy there is a dangerous superfluity of Liberty. Fathers cease to exercise authority in the home with the result that the parents come to fear their children and the children lose all respect for their parents. To such a degree does license replace Liberty in a democracy. Teachers fear their pupils and flatter them; pupils scorn their teachers. The young affect the gravity of age; and old men revert to juvenile pranks to win the favor of children. Slaves conduct themselves with freedom; and wives enjoy the same rights as husbands. Even dogs and jackasses live in such an atmosphere of freedom that they expect humans to yield them the right of way. Ultimately, under this extreme form of democracy, the citizens become so sensitive and effeminate that, if the least restraint is applied to them, they are enraged and cannot endure it. Finally, they begin to ignore the laws, and so are completely without any master. Such unbridled license was, for the Romans, the foulest corruption of Liberty and the breeding ground of tyranny. Dictatorship would inevitably follow such democratic extremism; and slavery was the ultimate fate of a people which refused to recognize the limits of its freedom.[26]

To avoid such dire consequences, the Roman tempered *Libertas*. As the sovereignty of the People was limited by the overriding moral authority of the Senate, so the Liberty of the individual was tempered by the Law. The supreme authority of the Law prevented Liberty from becoming license. Cicero's striking metaphor underscores the centrality of the Law to the Roman concept of Liberty. "The laws are the foundation of the Liberty which we enjoy; we are all the Law's slaves so that we may be free."[27] Law was king in republican Rome; and in this epoch the Roman People recognized only two masters: Jupiter, divine guardian of the community, and the Law.

For Cicero the Law is integral to the very definition of the State. It is essential in his view that there be at least one element in the State which affects all citizens in the same way. The Law provides this element. There will never be equality for all citizens in terms of intelligence, talent, character, and wealth.[28] But all may share equally in the Law. Indeed, the essential qualities of the Law are two; that it be just and that it apply equally to all, granting special exemptions and dispensations to no one.[29] It was this idea of equality before the Law which provided the most significant point of identification between *Lex* and *Libertas* at Rome. Again, to quote Cicero, "True Liberty can only exist where there is equality before the Law."[30] No Roman citizen was so humble that he was not afforded the full protection of the Law; none so great that he stood above the Law.[31] The antithesis of *Libertas* was *regnum*, the state of affairs in which a single individual, because of wealth or birth or political power, stood above the Law.[32]

It is in this identification with equality before the law that we find ourselves particularly in sympathy with the traditional Roman concept of Liberty. There is much in it which would not be acceptable to many modern Americans. Roman Liberty condoned slavery and denied political rights to women. Liberty meant equality before the Law; it did *not* mean egalitarianism.[33] Rome possessed an aristocracy; nobility was conferred through public service; the consulship bestowed nobility upon its holder and his descendants; such a nobility was, of course, not a closed caste; it was, if you will, aristocracy by plebiscite. The magistracies were in theory open to all citizens; but, in point of fact, the nobility dominated politics in republican Rome. Newcomers to the ranks like Cicero believed equally in government by aristocracy, an aristocracy of merit rather than of birth. For a noble like Brutus, an essential aspect of Liberty was the right of his class to political preeminence.

Thus only in a very limited sense did traditional Roman Liberty embrace the ideal of equality. Nor did Liberty imply fraternity, the brotherhood of man. For the Roman of the republican epoch, Liberty was *not* an innate faculty of man; it was *not* an inalienable right bestowed upon man by his creator. The Roman *did* believe that all men by nature strive for Liberty; few, however, obtain it or are worthy of it.[34] In the words of Cicero, while other nations are capable of being slaves, Liberty is the characteristic property of the Roman People.[35] Far from proving that all men are free, the laws of nature provided the Roman with the justification for denying Liberty to other people. For the Roman, his wars were justified in the Aristotelian sense; wars were undertaken in self-defense, and they established Roman rule over people who would benefit by it and over nations which deserved to be enslaved.[36] The enslavement of others was not merely consistent with Roman Liberty; the security of the Liberty of the Roman People frequently demanded it. "Freedom for the pike is death for the minnows."

The Roman's idea of civil liberty was narrowly restricted. Our own constitution includes a Bill of Rights. Most of the freedoms guaranteed by the First Amendment would not have been included by the Roman under his definition of Liberty. Freedom of assembly was limited. Neither freedom of speech nor freedom of religion was guaranteed. The republic possessed an established religion; to be a Roman citizen was to participate in the civil religion of the commonwealth. For the Roman there could be no question of separation of Church and State. The state religion permeated every aspect of public life, providing the very basis of the social order.[37]

Finally, the republican idea of Liberty countenanced what might seem to us a remarkable degree of interference in the private lives of citizens. The right of the State to supervise the morals of its citizens was officially recognized.[38] Thus, the Roman government made various efforts to curtail flagrant consumerism, limiting, for example, the amount which a citizen might spend on dinner or the amount of gold jewelry which a woman might possess. Inevitably, such attempts ended in failure.[39]

Such sumptuary laws were not infrequent in ancient society. Nor was Rome unique among ancient republics in its conviction that on occasion the good of the commonwealth requires the censorship of ideas and beliefs. Thus, the most radical democracy in history, Athens of the fifth century, prosecuted, convicted, and exiled the philosopher Anaxagoras on grounds of impiety because he taught that the sun was a red-hot mass of metal.[40] Even more telling, the Athenian People tried and executed Socrates on account of his beliefs; the official charge stated that he did not believe in the gods of the State.[41]

To summarize, the traditional concept of Liberty under the

Roman republic was far removed from John Stuart Mill's classic dictum that "liberty consists in doing what one desires."[42] Indeed, in his very approach to Liberty the Roman of the republic was at variance with a prevailing attitude in modern democratic liberalism; the Roman did not perceive the fundamental issue as the reconciliation of the freedom of the individual with the dictates of society—in the words of Mill, the question of how to make the fitting adjustments between individual independence and social control.[43] The traditional republican concept of Liberty would not have agreed with Frank Knight's assertion that "the law itself is coercive, and being a restriction of individual freedom, largely by the will of others, it is justified only when it adds more to freedom in some way than it directly subtracts." Republican Liberty was equally at variance with Mill's contention that "the despotism of custom is everywhere hostile to the spirit of liberty."[44] For the Roman of the republican epoch, Liberty was entirely consistent with the dictates of the Law and custom of the commonwealth of the Roman People. The necessary prerequisite of Liberty was the renouncement of self-willed actions. Consequently, genuine Liberty could be enjoyed only under the Law. The freedoms, personal and private, which constituted *Libertas*, were conceived of as the rights not of the isolated individual but of the citizen within the organized community of the Roman state. The state, the laws, and the customs and traditions of the Roman People were central to the realization of Liberty. The Roman of the republic would have agreed with Hegel in affirming that

> law, morality, and government represent the positive
> reality and completion of freedom. Society and the
> state thus provide the very conditions in which free-
> dom is realized; the limitations imposed by duty and
> law limit the premeditated self-will of caprice and

passion and thus provide the indispensable proviso of emancipation.[45]

Again, with Hegel the Roman could have agreed that it is only in duty that the individual acquires his substantive freedom. Certainly, in its traditional sense, Roman Liberty encompassed obligations as well as rights. To be a Roman citizen, to be possessed of Liberty, was to undertake a burden of political responsibility: to vote, to participate in the assembly of the Roman People, to serve in the army, and (if commensurate with one's ability and status) to hold public office. In short, the Liberty of the individual received its deepest meaning only within the larger context of the community as a whole.

With its connotation of service to the laws and traditions of the Roman People, Liberty thus provided the central ideological construct for the republic, a political myth to justify and to rationalize the institutions and policies of a commonwealth based fully upon a concept of collective political authority. The continuity of any government rests ultimately upon such a myth of supernatural character, upon a legitimization beyond military, economic, and socio-political bases of power. Such a political myth or ideology is essential to any society. Borrowing from Tallcott Parsons, we might define ideology as a system of belief held in common by members of a collectivity, a system of ideas that is oriented to the evaluative integration of the community.[46] In these terms, ideology forms the matrix of social behavior and provides the principal means for attaining social solidarity. Through ideology a given state of affairs can be rationalized, legitimized, and perpetuated. Such a political myth binds a group of people together, taps their sentiments and emotions, and directs their energies towards specific objectives.[47]

The last generation of the Roman republic—the age of Caesar, Cicero, and Brutus—witnessed the collapse of a political mythology based upon the traditional concept of Liberty as the reflection of a commonwealth rooted in an ideal of popular sovereignty, representative government, and collective decision making. Within a generation after Brutus' coinage of 54 B.C. with its clarion call to the traditions of republican Liberty, monarchy was an established fact at Rome. It was because Caesar was ambitious of monarchy that Brutus slew him. The assassination of Caesar merely prolonged the death agony of the republic. The work of Julius Caesar was completed by his adopted son and heir, C. Octavius, known to history as Augustus, "the sanctified one."[48]

In 27 B.C. Augustus solemnly claimed to have restored the republic. It was a pious political fiction, useful and well received. In a superficial sense it was true. As under the old republic the Senate met and the traditional magistrates, duly elected by the People, carried out their functions.[49] In point of fact, Rome had become and would remain throughout its history a hereditary military dictatorship. All real power—military, political, and financial—rested with Augustus. Prudent, pragmatic, providential, in his career and character he is living refutation of Lord Acton's dictum that all power corrupts and absolute power corrupts absolutely. Augustus improved with age. He died in 14 A.D. after a long and peaceful reign of forty-five years, old and full of honors, truly loved and revered by his people, whom he had served so well; his power passed, with the assent of the Senate and the People, to his heir Tiberius. The commonwealth of the Roman People had become, in fact, the private estate of a king. The title "king" was avoided, ill-omened and unnecessary. Men spoke of Augustus as *princeps*, with the implication that he was simply the leading citizen, who guided the commonwealth and kept it on an even keel. His absolute power rested upon clearly articulated and legally transmitted constitutional and juridical forms. Yet despite its constitutional facade, despite the moderation and profound sense of public service with distinguished Augustus and the vast majority of his imperial successors, the commonwealth of the Roman People was now properly a *regnum*—a despotism; albeit an enlightened despotism, it was the antithesis of the republican concept of Liberty. Now one man, because of his power, stood above the Law of the commonwealth.[50] Compliance with the law was the hallmark of a good emperor; but such compliance was voluntary. If the emperor obeyed the law it was because he chose to obey.[51] The emperor replaced the corporate body of the People as the sovereign of the Roman commonwealth; monarchy replaced the ideal of collective political authority. The two supreme citadels of republican Liberty—the powers of the tribune and appellate jurisdiction—were now vested in the emperor. The emperor became the font of law; like an Egyptian pharaoh of old, his mouth was effective utterance. Such power had not been usurped. It was legally bestowed upon the emperor by the organs of the republican government, by the Senate and the Roman People. In the words of the imperial jurist: "Any decision of the emperor has the force of law because the Roman People have by legal decree surrendered to him all their power and authority."[52]

It was a political fiction which conveyed a higher truth. Over the course of several generations the Roman People *did* effectively resign their sovereign power and invest all real power in the hands of the dictator. Our sources permit us to trace in relative detail the events surrounding the collapse of republican government and the establishment of the monarchy of the Caesars. However, we cannot answer the question why the Roman People were unable or unwilling to solve their admittedly grave social, political, and economic problems by means of their traditional republican institutions. We cannot explain why at the height of empire, with unchallenged military supremacy and unprecedented material affluence, the Roman People permitted the emasculation of their republican institutions and embraced with fervor the political mythology and reality of dictatorship.

A post mortem of the body politic of the Roman republic offers clues, not certain answers; material for speculation, not finality. Most suggestive is the spiritual malaise which we encounter again and again in our sources for the period. In the late republic pessimism and brooding premonitions of despair replaced that sense of mission and destiny which was so marked a feature of policy and public imagery in the great age of the republic. With unparalleled confidence in themselves, their leaders, and their institutions, the Romans, immediately upon the conclusion of the bloody and debilitating war with Hannibal, embarked upon a bold new program of imperial expansion in the East. The coinage of this age, the late third and second centuries B.C., proclaimed this spirit of manifest destiny. The gods have bestowed upon the Roman People a divine mandate for world dominion. Thus, on the coin struck in 205 B.C., Jupiter is represented as the divine patron of Rome, who has foreordained victory and empire without limit for his chosen people. For writers who witnessed the last generation of the republic, for Sallust and his younger contemporary Livy, the great achievements of the Roman People in the golden age of the republic served but to highlight the bleakness of the contemporary scene. For Sallust, the Roman had achieved unparalleled preeminence through unity, labor, and a profound respect for law and justice.[53] But the vigor of these earlier generations now seemed exhausted; luxury and idleness had demoralized the Roman; and avarice and the lust for power had engendered every form of evil in the body politic, destroying honor, integrity, and every other virtue. "I do honestly believe," writes Livy,

> that no country has ever been greater or purer than Rome or richer in good citizens and of noble deeds. But in recent years wealth has made us greedy, and self-indulgence and sensual excess have so debilitated

us that we seem to be courting death, death as individuals, death as a nation.

Having considered the way in which Rome's empire was acquired, Livy asks his reader to:

> trace the progress of our moral decline, to watch first the sinking of the foundations of morality as the old ways were allowed to lapse, then the rapidly increasing disintegration, then the final collapse of the whole edifice, then the dark dawning of the modern day when we can neither endure our vices nor face the remedies needed to cure them.[54]

As Livy knew, that remedy was dictatorship, the replacement of collective decision making by the rule of a single charismatic leader. The elixir of monarchy was swallowed with alacrity by the Roman People and by their subjects in the far-flung provinces of the empire. Fervent and sincere was the wave of popular enthusiasm which greeted the monarchy of Augustus, bringing to an end a generation of almost unabated civil war and the accompanying social and economic disruption. Nowhere is this enthusiasm more forcefully expressed than in a decree enacted by the confederation of Greek cities in the Roman province of Asia.[55] Its purpose was to establish the birthday of Augustus as the day on which the new year began. In the words of the decree, Augustus is a god; he is the divine saviour. The nativity of Augustus brought good tidings of great joy for all people. The decree continues its praise of Augustus by proclaiming that Providence, which divinely orders our lives, has created the most perfect good for our lives by sending Augustus into the world so that all mankind might be saved. Divine Providence has thus blessed contemporaries and posterity with a saviour who put an end to war and established peace, a saviour who surpasses all who came before or will come in the future.

Men were sincere in calling Augustus a saviour. He was not a saviour in the Christian sense; he did not offer men eternal life; such was not his function. His salvation was of *this* world; the paradise to which he led humanity was one of material benefits enjoyed not in the sweet by-and-by, but here and now. The millennium had dawned; the advent of Augustus brought a golden age of peace and prosperity for all mankind. Such was the message of Augustan propaganda. In a brilliantly conceived and orchestrated publicity campaign the finest artistic and literary talent was employed to proclaim the good tidings of peace on earth and good will toward men.[56]

As must be true for any effective propaganda, the publicity campaign of Augustus was inordinately successful because there was substance behind the imagery. The promises which Augustus held out of peace and prosperity, of efficient and responsive government, of justice and mercy, of law and order—these were fulfilled. And at all levels of society the population of the Roman world saw the monarchy of Augustus as a necessary good, as the prerequisite for the enjoyment of orderly life and material prosperity.

> ...Who gives us peace shall ruler be
> ...anew the realm directed,
> Each one secure and sheltered stand,
> And in a fresh-constructed land
> Justice and peace be mated and perfected.[57]

In this brave new world, Liberty sprang from the union of Peace and Justice. The monarchy of Augustus and his successors did not mean the extinction of the ideal of Liberty at Rome. As juridical concept, as historical motif, as political catchword, as divine form, Liberty remained one of the most vital elements in the political imagery of the imperial age.[58] However, like old Proteus in the *Odyssey*, Liberty underwent a startling and profound metamorphosis.[59]

The keynote for Liberty under the new order was struck on this coin, issued in 28 B.C., thus at the beginning of Augustus' reign. On the obverse Augustus claims the title *Vindex Populi Romani Libertatis*, "Defender of the Liberty of the Roman People."[60] In the imagery of the reverse, Augustus' defense of Liberty is symbolized not by the personification of Liberty but by Peace: *Pax*. Under her feet the goddess tramples the sword of civil war;[61] in her hand she holds the caduceus, the magic wand which makes our wishes come true.[62] According to the message of the coin, Augustus has championed the Liberty of the Roman People by bringing Peace. In Augustan propaganda, Liberty was thus from the outset intimately associated with Peace, the primary ideological motif of the new order.[63]

Throughout his life Augustus insisted that he had been the true defender of Liberty. In his last days, in 14 A.D. at the age of seventy-six, he composed a remarkable public account of his accomplishments. His final statement to the Roman People and to history was inscribed on two bronze pillars erected in front of his mausoleum.[64] Copies were set up throughout the empire, and our best preserved text was inscribed on the walls of the temple erected to Augustus in Ancyra, modern Ankara, Turkey. In his first sentence Augustus reminds the Roman People of his championship of Liberty. In this version of history, Augustus has rescued the Liberty of the Roman People from the tyrannical excesses of a corrupt and self-serving oligarchy: Brutus and his self-styled party of good men. The domination of these oligarchs threatened with extinction the Liberty of the commonwealth and the Liberty of the ordinary citizen. Propaganda certainly, but it was a propaganda which most men chose to believe and upon which many acted. Having assassinated Caesar, Brutus and Cassius found that their call to Liberty evoked no real response among the People.[65] It was Caesar whom the common man deified, and it was on an ever growing wave of popular enthusiasm that his son Augustus rose to monarchy. Perhaps the cynical Sallust was correct: only a very few men really want Liberty; what the vast majority want is a just master.[66]

It was the central theme of imperial propaganda that under monarchy one had the best of both worlds: a just master *and* Liberty. Once again there was substance to the imagery. The fundamental guarantees of the Liberty of the ordinary citizen under the Roman law remained fully in force under Augustus and his imperial successors. The citizen still possessed the right of appeal, received protection against arbitrary exactions of magistrates, and was guaranteed equality before the Law. The emperor now assumed the role of supreme guardian and enforcer of these freedoms: it was a role which Augustus and the overwhelming majority of the emperors fulfilled with remarkable and commendable efficiency, thoroughness, and fairness. [67]

As under the republic, so under the monarchy Liberty represented an ideal of the state. Once the definitive attribute of a true republic, Liberty was now held to be the peculiar property of legitimate kingship.[68] Under the rule of a good king men find the truest form of Liberty, the truest form of democracy. Under a good emperor every element in society receives its due; government is in the hands of those most worthy and capable of handling the business of ruling. In the same way, service in the army for pay is reserved for those who are the strongest physically, the most needy, and the best adapted to military life. The ordinary citizen is thus free to live as he chooses, to do as he wishes. He has the security and the leisure to pursue his own aims, his own career. In this view, widely voiced by the intelligentsia, what men once called democracy, actual government by the People, was in fact the bitterest form of servitude: tyranny of the majority. By subordinating all to the passions of a mob, men wrought the destruction of the commonwealth. Now, in place of the tyranny of mob rule, a true and universal democracy has been established because one man, capable, honest, and just, governs and provides for the welfare of every member of the community. Through his beneficent and competent exercise of power, the wealth of the rich is rendered secure while the poor receive financial and other needed assistance. This is the meaning of true equality: the resources of the community are divided so that every member receives his proper share. This is the meaning of true Liberty: the undisturbed freedom to enjoy the benefits of such rule. By bestowing such benefits upon his subjects the good monarch is the defender of Liberty.

This equation of Liberty with the blessings of monarchical rule was not limited to panegyrists and other publicists of the imperial regime. Across a broad spectrum of Roman society men viewed the emperor as guarantor and guardian of their Liberty. In these terms Philo, a hellenized Alexandrian Jew and one of the most brilliant intellects of the age, celebrated the Liberty which Augustus had given to the world. Augustus found the world enslaved, oppressed by the fetters of civil discord. By calming the storms of war, by curing the ills which beset Greek and foreigner alike, by bringing order out of chaos, Augustus rescued all the nations of the world and gave them Liberty.[69] No less revealing, on a more popular level, is this anecdote told of Augustus. At the close of his life Augustus was sailing through the Gulf of Puteoli, near Naples. The sighting of the imperial bark was the occasion for a spontaneous demonstration of genuine affection by the passengers and crew of a merchant ship recently arrived from Alexandria. Putting on white robes and garlands and burning incense, they prayed for Augustus, saying that they owed to him their lives and their opportunity to sail the seas; because of you, they shouted, we enjoy prosperity; because of you we enjoy Liberty.[70]

Under the traditional republican concept of Liberty, freedom carried the burden of political responsibility. Liberty was the obligation to participate in the political life of the community. Now Liberty was freedom *from* the responsibilities inherent in the collective decision making process of a republican government which rested upon the concept of popular sovereignty. Now all real political power lay with one man, the emperor, to whom all agencies of government, all persons, citizens and provincials alike, looked for authority and guidance. By his enlightened despotism, the emperor provided the security and opportunity for men to live free lives. Under the emperor the dominant popular definition of Liberty was "freedom to do what one wants."[71] The freedom of the isolated individual became a predominant aspect in the popular idea of Liberty. It was a conception of Liberty which bears a strong resemblance to what Isaiah Berlin calls the most common use of the term "Liberty" today: Liberty is the absence of obstacles to the fulfillment of men's desires.[72]

In the imperial age, as today, there was a strong tendency to regard economic opportunity and security as an essential adjunct of Liberty. We have noted how the merchants from Alexandria intimately associated the ideal of Liberty with the economic opportunity to earn a good living through mercantile enterprise. From their perspective, the emperor provided for freedom by clearing the sea of pirates and, in general, by creating a favorable atmosphere for trade.

In short, under the empire Liberty could be viewed as an absence of obstacles to the individual's enjoyment of desired opportunities and privileges. Furthermore, it was the recognized duty of the government by positive means to secure these opportunities.

Even those who, like the historian Tacitus, bemoaned the extinction of the old republic and its tradition of Liberty nonetheless recognized the necessity for monarchy.[73] The annals of the late republic and the early principate offer proof enough that men did not want liberty, testaments aplenty to the eagerness with which they sought servitude.[74] All that one could hope for was the good fortune to live under the rule of a good and just prince like Trajan, who protected Liberty and bestowed its blessings upon all elements in a society.[75]

"Bestowal" is the key word, for Liberty was now a gift which a gracious master of his own free will bestowed upon his subjects. *Libertas Populi Romani* was reduced to a mere slogan. The true sense of Liberty was now rendered by the phrase *Libertas Augusti*. Liberty was now manifest in the person and deeds of the emperor. He alone could give it, he alone could restore it.[76] Once so long ago the Roman People had boldly seized Liberty by revolution and war, assuming to themselves the awesome burdens and responsibilities of self-government. Now, like children, at each imperial accession they eagerly awaited to see whether their new master would be just and good like Augustus or Trajan, or a perverted monster like Caligula or Domitian. Such was the fate of a people who had abandoned republican Liberty.

In his *Civilization and Its Discontents*, Freud pointed to the psychological aspect of ideology.[77] Ideology performs the function of wish fulfillment; it affords protection and security to the individual; it controls instinctual behavior and relieves man of his sense of guilt; it counteracts man's sense of alienation from society. The bestowal of the title "Father of the Fatherland" upon Augustus and his successors had significance far beyond the honorific.[78] It bespoke the collapse of a commitment to collective political authority, with its demands for collective decision making and its concomitant anxieties and political strife, all hallmarks of the vivid civic life of the Greek polis and the Italian city-state. It bespoke a society eager to seek refuge and find salvation in a great father figure who could nourish and foster all who came to his bosom, relieving them of all anxiety and responsibility, all necessity for decision.

Liberty in moderation and with careful restrictions is the boon which a wise father grants his children. The mind of the average Roman and the imagery of imperial propaganda conceived the boon of Liberty in quite concrete terms. Liberty was freedom to share in the munificence of the emperor. *Libertas Augusti* came to be equated with *Liberalitas Augusti*:[79] a primary manifestation of imperial Liberty was the shower of gifts which the emperor freely poured upon his people, including donations and welfare benefits.[80] It is not anachronistic to term the government of the Roman emperors a welfare state. Both the ruler and the governed believed it to be a primary responsibility of the State to provide for the social welfare of the individual citizen. Such provisions encompassed well-conceived programs of assistance to needy children as well as the regular supply of foodstuffs to citizens, including grain, wine, oil, and meat. Under the republic the Roman People had deified Liberty. Now they sought to assure immortality for these welfare benefits by invocation of Annona Augusti, the goddess of the imperial Dole.[81] Such regular provision of foodstuffs was complemented by spectacles, such as gladiatorial games and chariot races. A busy mind and full stomach were pillars of imperial Liberty.[82] Furthermore, it became customary for the emperor, at his accession and in commemoration of other notable events during his reign, to distribute sums of money to the People. The right to participate in the various gratuities dispensed by this elaborate system came to be regarded as a key element in the Liberty of the average citizen. This view is dramatically represented on a gold coin struck under the emperor Antoninus in the year 153 A.D.[83] The goddess Liberty, or rather Liberality, is portrayed holding a cornucopia; from it she pours a stream of coins into the out-stretched toga of a Roman citizen. The emperor watches be-nignly over the seventh such manifestation of Liberty in his fifteen years of rule.

Such gifts of money were a very concrete manifestation of the salvation which the emperor offered his people. From this perspective and in a very real sense, the Roman People had abandoned the insecurity of republican Liberty for the security of imperial Liberty. By freely accepting servitude to the emperor, the Roman People enjoyed the fruit of material prosperity and found temporal salvation. This intellectual construct was not without its effect upon that most redoubtable Roman citizen, Saint Paul. For Paul, man's response to the divine gifts of Liberty and salvation, indeed, the very means of his receiving them, must be the free acceptance of servitude to God: "But now being made free from sin and become servants unto God, ye have your fruit unto holiness and the end, everlasting life."[84]

In the imagery of imperial propaganda the emperor is a messianic figure, bringing salvation to mankind and liberating humanity from the forces of evil. The emperor is a Herculean figure, his life one of unremitting sacrifice to bring to all the children of god the blessings of imperial rule: security, civilization, common law, prosperity. In his own imagery the emperor is quite literally *Salus Generis Humani*, the saviour of the human race.[85]

This vision of the universality of the imperial mission provided the framework for the most positive and the most seminal development in the concept of Liberty under the emperors. The republican ideal of Liberty was a narrow and exclusive one. Liberty was the peculiar possession of the Roman People. Other nations could endure slavery; indeed, many such foreigners were by nature slaves. Now, in an age which equated Liberty with imperial beneficence and which found salvation in acceptance of the emperor as the common father and saviour of the human race, Liberty and Equality came to be commonly regarded as the innate faculty and natural right of all mankind.[86]

Alexander the Great had dreamt of a world in which all nations might be united in harmony and brotherhood, working together as though they were all members of one family.[87] With good reason emperors like Trajan, Hadrian, and Caracalla invoked Alexander as the historical archetype for their civilizing mission.[88] Under the emperors the far-flung, disparate, and supranational empire of Rome was transformed into a true commonwealth. Under the emperor Caracalla in 212 A.D. this development received its ultimate expression in the decree bestowing Roman citizenship upon all freeborn inhabitants of the empire: from the forests of Germany to the sands of the Sahara, from the mists of England to the deserts of Syria, there was one law, one citizenship for all.[89] In the words of her most enthusiastic panegyrist, Rome had made one city of what was once a world.[90]

In this quite literal fashion, the ideal of Liberty inherent in imperial citizenship received a form of universal validity. However, still more profound in its historical significance was the clear articulation in Roman philosophical and legal thought of the doctrine that all men, foreigners as well as Roman citizens, slaves as well as freemen, are by nature free and equal.

This was a revolution in human thought. Aristotle had defended slavery on the grounds that it was a natural and reasonable institution which was justified by a fundamental inequality among men.[91] For Aristotle, mankind is fundamentally divided into two groups: one capable of exercising reason, one lacking this capacity. The former is by nature free, the latter naturally slave. It was a proposition which Alexander, the pupil of Aristotle, rejected;[92] and in the generations following Alexander, Stoic philosophers propounded a theory of the natural equality of all men.[93] In this view, all men possess reason; and because all men are thus fundamentally equal, one law and one government can suffice for all men. In the Roman tradition this concept was developed by Cicero.[94] There is no resemblance in nature so great, no equality so complete as that which exists among men. Since in their possession of the faculty of learning all men are equal, there is no race of men which cannot attain to virtue. A century later Seneca gave even clearer articulation to

the belief that Liberty and Equality are innate faculties belonging to all men.[95] As they share the same creator, so slave and
master share the same nature. It is fortune, not nature, which
makes man a slave; slavery is only external, it affects only the
body; the mind can never be given into slavery. In the high tide
of the imperial epoch, Roman jurists like Ulpian and Florentinus
emphatically stated that slavery is a violation of natural law, for
by nature all men are free and equal.[96] However, it is in the
Christian Fathers that we find the fullest development of this
principle. Thus Lactantius insists that God, as the common
creator of all men, wished them to be all equal.[97] In the sight of
God no one is slave, no one is master. God is the father of us all,
and we are all free. Lactantius' words echo Saint Paul's ringing
declaration of Christian equality: "Ye are all sons of God,
through faith in Jesus Christ. There can be neither Jew nor
Greek; there can be neither bond nor free; there can be neither
male nor female; for they are all one in Christ Jesus."[98]

Christian writers like Origen and Tertullian saw the hand of
God in the coincidence of the birth of Jesus with the establishment of the monarchy of Augustus.[99] In this view, the ecumenical empire of Rome was an instrument of God preparing the way
for the universal kingdom of Christ. In fact, with the conversion
of Constantine, the imperial destiny of Rome and the evangeli-
cal mission of the Church became one. Roman Liberty was there
to witness the birth of this momentous union. In the imperial
propaganda of Constantine, Liberty took her place beside the
new faith. The imagery of the Constantinian coinage proclaimed the gospel that in the universal power of Christ lay the
hope of the Roman People and their Liberty.[100]

From the republic of Brutus to the Christian empire of
Constantine, we have come a long way in our search for Roman
liberty. Out of the political wasteland of the collapse of the
Roman republic there came birth as well as death. There was
death for a narrowly defined ideal of republican Liberty based

upon a concept of collective political authority. Yet in hard and bitter agony there was also the birth of a new and more noble conception of Liberty. It was this more exalted, more inclusive vision of Liberty which would be invoked so many centuries later by a bold group of men willing to justify revolution by an appeal to the self-evident truth that all men are created equal and endowed by their creator with the inalienable right of Liberty.[101]

## ENDNOTES

1. In an earlier version, *Roman Liberty: An Essay in Protean Political Metaphor*, (Bloomington, 1980), this paper was delivered as the first *Distinguished Faculty Research Lecture* at Indiana University on February 11, 1980 and published and distributed by the University in that same year. In a revised form, it was subsequently, in 1985, delivered as part of the Goodrich Lecture Series at Wabash College. Copies of my *Distinguished Faculty Research Lecture* have long since been exhausted; and the current publication has provided a welcome opportunity to revise the text and notes to reflect scholarship and discussion on this theme between 1980 and 1996. The most careful perusal and consideration of that scholarship has left me all the more convinced of the validity of my thesis and of the need for a large-scale history of the idea of liberty in the Greco-Roman world, which is objective, scholarly, and yet aimed at a broad audience.
2. In the words of Robert Lowell, the "Gettysburg Address is a symbolic and sacramental act," joining "Jefferson's ideals of freedom and equality...to the Christian sacrificial act of death and rebirth." Cf. A. Nevins, ed., *Lincoln and the Gettysburg Address* (Urbana, Illinois, 1964), pp. 88-89; Garry Wills, *Lincoln at Gettysburg: The Words that Remade America* (New York, 1992).
3. H. Melville, *White Jacket* (New York, 1892), p. 144.
4. A thoughtful study in the history of the idea of Liberty in the United States is M. Kammen, *Spheres of Liberty: Changing Perceptions of Liberty in American Culture* (Madison, Wisconsin, 1986).
5. There is a considerable body of scholarly literature dealing with the concept of Liberty at Rome. Much of it requires a knowledge of the classical languages and a close familiarity with Roman history and political institutions. Of these, the best remains C. Wirszubski, *Libertas as a Political Idea at Rome during the Late Republic and Early Empire* (Cambridge, 1950). A. Momigliano's review of Wirszubski in *Journal of Roman Studies* 41 (1951), pp. 146-153 is in itself a significant contribution to the subject. Although almost fifty years old, Wirszubski's analysis of the significance of Liberty in the Roman republic and the continuation of this republican tradition under the empire has not been superseded by more recent studies such as J. Bleichen, *Staatliche Ordnung und Freiheit in der römischen Republik* (Kallmunz, 1972) and P.A. Brunt, *The Fall of the Roman Republic and Related Essays* (Oxford, 1988), pp. 281-350. Derivative in approach and content

from Wirszubski, Brunt adds nothing to our understanding of the history of Liberty at Rome.

The weakness of Wirszubski's approach is his neglect of the highly creative developments which the idea of Liberty underwent in the imperial age and which I discuss in the current paper. The best balanced large-scale study of the idea of Liberty in both the republican and imperial age is the excellent but infrequently cited doctoral dissertation of A. Sylow, *Libertas und Liberalitas* (Diss. Munich, 1972). In the same way, the best general guide to the idea of Liberty in Greece, Rome and early Christianity is the 1972 German encyclopedia article of D. Nestle, "Freiheit," *Reallexikon fur Antike und Christentum* VIII, pp. 270-306.

A study of the Greek concept of Liberty (*eleutheria*) and its history and transformation should be an essential complement of any study of Liberty in the Roman world. The best treatment of the concept of Liberty in classical Athens is Mogens H. Hansen, "The Ancient Athenian and the Modern Liberal View of Liberty as a Democratic ideal," in Josiah Ober and Charles Hedrick, eds., *Demokratia: A Conversation on Democracies, Ancient and Modern* (Princeton, 1996) pp. 91-104. Two other essays in that same collection are also relevant: Robert W. Wallace, "Law, Freedom, and the Concept of Citizen's Rights in Democratic Athens," pp. 105-119; and Ellen M. Wood, "Demos versus 'We the People': Freedom and Democracy Ancient and Modern," pp. 121-137. The most detailed discussion of freedom in Greece is K. Raaflaub, *Die Entdeckung der Freiheit: Zur historischen Semantik und Gesellschaftsgeschichte eines politischen Grundbegriffs der Griechen* (Munich, 1985). With his social science jargon and his Marxist constructs, Raaflaub elaborates upon the thesis of Max Pohlenz, *Greichisch Freiheit* (Heidelberg, 1955), English translation as *Freedom in Greek Life and Thought* (Dordrecht, 1966). For Pohlenz and Raaflaub the social institution of slavery was fundamental to the development of a concept of liberty in ancient Greece.

The work of Pohlenz and Raaflaub is formative for the approach to the history of freedom in antiquity and the Middle Ages taken by Orlando Patterson, *Freedom* vol. I, *Freedom in the Making of Western Culture* (Basic Books, 1991). Patterson builds his study of liberty on the thesis of Pohlenz and Raaflaub that slavery was "the decisive factor explaining the social invention and the nature of freedom in ancient Athens" (Patterson, p. xiv). Patterson's concerns and biases are sufficiently indicated by the fact that he devotes one sentence to *Magna Carta* and an entire ten-page chapter to slavery and cannibalism among the Tupinamba tribe of Brazil. All this in an effort to prove that "it is no accident that the first and greatest mass democracies in the ancient and modern worlds—Athens and the United States—share this evil in common: they were both conceived in, and fashioned by, the degradation of slaves and their descendants and the exclusion of women" (Patterson, p. 405).

It is with considerable pleasure that we turn from such contemporary efforts at rewriting the history of liberty to Lord Acton's classic lectures, *The History of Freedom in Antiquity* and *The History of Freedom in Christianity*, in *Selected Writings of Lord Acton*, ed., J. Rufus Fears (Liberty Fund Inc., Indianapolis, Indiana) pp. 5-53 and to Herbert Muller's literate and erudite three volume history of liberty, *Freedom in the Ancient World*, *Freedom in the Western World*, and *Freedom in the Modern World* (New York, 1961-1966).

6. Livy 1.8. Livy's history of Rome from the time of the city's foundation (*ab urbe condita*) is a fudamental document for the political and moral restoration of the Roman nation undertaken by Augustus. Like the emperor [Augustus]...Livy was a moralist. His primary purpose was not an objective recording of Rome's history; as explicitly stated in his preface, the aim is inculcation of political virtue through historical example: to use the lessons of the past as a guide to the present. The modern student, seeking to understand the ideal of Liberty in Rome of the first century B.C., asks not whether Livy's version of early Roman history is accurate in fact. Rather he asks what was the *image* of Roman history prevalent in the last generation of the Roman republic. For this Livy is our primary source.

7. Livy, 1.39-2.20. The Greek and Latin authors cited in the following notes are most conveniently consulted, in translation, in the *Loeb Classical Library* (London-Cambridge, Mass.).

8. Livy 2.1.

9. J. Rufus Fears, *Princeps A Diis Electus: The Divine Election of the Emperor as a Political Concept at Rome* (American Academy in Rome, 1977), pp. 199-205.

10. For the coins and their date of issue see M. Crawford, *Roman Republican Coinage* (Cambridge, 1974) I, pp. 455-466.

11. Livy, 1.60.

12. Ovid, *Fasti* 4.623-624; Livy, 24.16.19; *Res Gestae Divi Augusti* 19; A. Degrassi, ed., *Inscriptiones Italiae* XIII ii 440. Cf. Stylow, *Libertas und Liberalitas* (above. n. 5), pp. 5-8. The temple of Libertas, on the Aventine Hill, is represented on a coin type of C. Egnatius; the stylized representation would suggest the temple contained statues of both Libertas and Jupiter; Crawford, *Roman Republican Coinage* I, p. 405 no. 89 1/2.

13. Cf. J. Rufus Fears, "The Cult of Virtues and Roman Imperial Ideology," *Aufstieg under Niedergang der römischen Welt*, II xvii, ed. W. Haase (Berlin-New York, 1981), pp. 827-948.

14. On the "rite of passage" from the profane to the sacred, see M. Eliade, *The Myth of the Eternal Return*, trans. W. Trask (New York, 1954), pp. 17-18.

15. I discuss at length the conceptual framework in which the Roman understood divine power in my "Cult of Virtues" (above n. 13), pp. 833-869.

16. Along with our denarius, Brutus also had struck a second type, Crawford, *Republican Coinage* I 455 no. 2. The obverse head of L. Junius Brutus is complemented on the reverse by a head of C. Servilius Ahala. Through his mother Brutus was descended from this Servilius Ahala, who murdered the demagogue and would-be tyrant Sp. Maelius; cf. Livy 4.13-14. Marcus Brutus' admiration for these two ancestors who refused to tolerate tyrants is well attested; cf. Cicero *Brutus 97; Letters to Atticus* 13.40.1; *Philippics* 2.11; Plutarch, *Brutus* 1.

17. L. Taylor has written a lucid and evocative study of *Party Politics in the Age of Caesar* (Berkeley-Los Angeles, 1949). Good biographical accounts include M. Gelzer, *Pompeius* (Munich, 1959); *Cicero* (Wiesbaden, 1969); and *Caesar: Politician and Statesman* (Cambridge, Mass., 1968); J. van Ooteghem, *Pompée le Grand* (Brussels, 1954); F. Adcock, *Marcus Crassus, Millionaire* (Cambridge, 1966). R. Syme, *The Roman Revolution* (Oxford, 1939) is a classic account of the collapse of the republic and the establishment of the Augustan principate. For recent approaches, Walter Eder, "Republicans and Sinners: The Decline of the

Roman Republic ansd the end of a Provisional Arrangement," in *Transitions to Empire*, eds. Robert Wallace and Edward Harris (Norman, Oklahoma, 1996) pp. 429-62.

**18.** Tacitus, *Dialogue on Oratory*, p. 40.

**19.** Cicero, *Letters to Atticus* 4.18.3; *Letters to Quintus* 3.4.1; 3.8.4; 3.9.3; Cassius Dio 40.45.4-5.

**20.** For what follows, see, in general, Wirszubski, *Libertas* (above n. 5), pp. 1-65.

**21.** Cf. W. Buckland, *The Roman Law of Slavery* (Cambridge, 1908), pp. 1-396, esp., pp. 1-9.

**22.** Controversy over the character of *provocatio-appellatio* is discussed by A. Lintott, "Provocatio," *Aufstieg und Niedergang der romischen Welt*, I ii, ed. H. Temporini (Berlin-New York, 1972), pp. 226-267.

**23.** Livy 3.45.8.

**24.** Polybius 6.2-57, pp. 2-57, esp. 11-18.

**25.** Cicero, *On the Commonwealth* 1.43, paraphrasing Plato *Republic* 562c-563e.

**26.** Cicero *On the Commonwealth* 1.44. Cf. A. Dermience, "La notion de libertas dans les oeuvres de Cicéron," *Les etudes classiques* 25 (1957), pp. 157-167.

**27.** Cicero *For Cluentius* 53.146. Cf. J. Bleicken, *Lex Publica. Gesetz und Recht in der römischen Republik* (Berlin-New York, 1975), pp. 423-432.

**28.** Cicero *On the Commonwealth* 1.25; 1/32; *On Laws* 1.4; 2.5; *On Duties* 2.21.

**29.** Cicero *On Laws* 2.5; 3.19; *On the Commonwealth* 1.32. I am much indebted to the excellent discussion of G. Sabine and S. Smith in the introduction to their translation *On the Commonwealth* (Columbus, Ohio, 1929), pp. 52-56. See also Cicero, *De Re Publica:* Selections, ed. James E. G. Zetzel (Cambridge, 1995) pp. 1-28.

**30.** Cicero, *For Plancius* 13; cf. *On Duties* 1.34; 2.24: *On the Commonwealth* 1.45. Cf. G. Ciulei, *L'équite chez Cicéron* (Amsterdam, 1972); H. Dieter, "Der Justitia-begriff Ciceros," *Eirene* 7 (1968), pp. 33-48.

**31.** Livy 38.50 is instructive.

**32.** The contrast is dramatically implied in Livy 2.15.

**33.** Cicero, *On the Commonwealth* 1.27.34. Cf. Wirszubski, *Libertas* (above n. 5) pp. 12-17.

**34.** Caesar *Gallic Wars* 3.10.

**35.** Cicero *Philippics* 6.7.

**36.** Aristotle *Politics* 1333b; cf. Cicero *On the Commonwealth* 3.23, 25.

**37.** These points might usefully be elaborated with individual examples. As good polytheists the Romans had no objection to private worship of deities lying outside the established pantheon. However, Roman Liberty did not guarantee to citizens or to foreigners unfettered practice of such private religion. The state possessed the right, indeed, the duty to suppress any private cult which it deemed injurious to public order. Thus in 186 B.C. the senate passed a decree severely restricting the opportunity for foreigners and Roman citizens to worship the Greek god Bacchus (Livy 39.8-19; E. Warmington, *Remains of Old Latin* (Cambridge, Mass., 1935-40), IV pp. 254-259. In 139 B.C. Jews were expelled from Italy for the crime of proselytizing and thus attempting to corrupt the morals of the Roman People (Valerius Maximus 1.3.3; cf E. Smallwood, *The Jews Under Roman Rule* (Leiden, 1976), pp. 128-129.

The Roman ideal of Liberty did not guarantee freedom of speech. In 161 B.C. Greek rhetoricians and philosophers were as a group expelled from Italy (Suetonius *On Famous Rhetoricians* 1). In 139 B. C. astrologers suffered the same fate because, in the view of the Roman government, they were confusing shallow minds by false interpretations of the stars and by other deceptions contrived for illicit financial profit (Valerius Maximus 1.3.3). Book burning was consistent with Roman Liberty; in 181 B.C. the state formally consigned to the fire certain books which were judged to be subversive of orthodox religious ritual (Livy 40.29; Pliny *Natural History* 13.27.84-7). Nor was academic freedom a pillar of Roman Liberty. In 92 B.C. magistrates issued a stern warning to young men who squandered their time by studying under Latin teachers of rhetoric: "Our forefathers determined what they wanted Roman children to learn and what schools they should attend; innovations in the customs and principles of our forefathers do not please us or seem proper" (Suetonius, *On Famous Rhetoricians* 1).

38. The power was invested in the magistracy of the censorship, an office which, in the great days of the republic, was regarded as the pinnacle of a career of public service. The best discussion of the censors' supervision of public morals remains T. Mommsen, *Römisches Staatsrecht* II (Leipzig, 1887), pp. 375-384.

39. An interesting collection of such sumptuary laws is preserved in Aulus Gellius, *Attic Nights* 2.24. See also Macrobius 3.17. General discussions of sumptuary legislation at Rome include E. Savio, "Intorno alle leggi suntuarie romane," *Aevum* 14 (1940) pp. 174-194; and J. Bleicken, *Lex Publica: Gesetz und Recht in römischen Republik* (Berlin-New York, 1975) pp. 169-172. Tacitus, *Annals* 3.52-55 comments upon the character and cause of personal extravagance under the empire. Among modern treatments of imperial luxury, L. Friedländer, *Darstellungen aus der Sittengeschichte Roms* (Leipzig, 1920) II, pp. 266-383 remains unsurpassed. Social and economic implications of personal wealth at Rome are considered by I. Shatzman, *Senatorial Wealth and Roman Politics* (Brussels, 1975), pp. 94-98; and F. Kolb, "Zur Statussymbolik im antiken Rom," *Chiron* 7 (1977), pp. 239-259. In general, see E. Baltrusch, *Regimen Morum* (Munich, 1988).

40. Diogenes Laertius 2.3.12.

41. Plato, *Apology* 24b.

42. J. S. Mill, *On Liberty*, chapter 5, p. 152 in *Utilitarianism, Liberty and Representative Government* (London, 1910).

43. Mill, *On Liberty*, chapter 1, pp. 68-69. There is a wealth of material, usefully arranged, in M. Adler, *The Idea of Freedom* (New York, 1958).

44. F. Knight, *Freedom and Reform* (New York, 1947), p. 196; Mill, *On Liberty* chapter 3, pp. 127-128.

45. G. W. F. Hegel, *Sämtliche Werke, Jubiläumsausgabe* (Stuttgart, 1961) vol XI, *Vorlesungen über die Philosophie der Geschichte*, pp. 70, 74; English translation as *Lectures on the Philosophy of History* by J. Sibree (London, 1884), pp. 40, 43; Hegel, *Sämtliche Werke, Jubiläumsausgabe* (Stuttgart, 1964) vol VII, *Grundlinien der Philosophie des Rechts* section 149, p. 230; English translation as *Philosophy of Right* by T. Knox (Oxford, 1945), p. 107.

46. T. Parsons, *The Social System* (Glencoe, Illinois, 1951), pp. 348-359.

47. The best introduction to the nature of political mythology is G. Brand, *Welt, Geschichte, Mythos, und Politik* (Berlin-New York, 1978).

**48.** For the name "Augustus" and its meaning, see Suetonius, *Augustus* 7; Cassius Dio 53.16.

**49.** M. Hammond, *The Augustan Principate* (Cambridge, Mass., 1933); 2 ed. with bibliographical appendix surveying the scholarly literature 1933-1967 (New York, 1968), is a masterly study of constitutional aspects.

**50.** Cassius Dio 53.17-18.

**51.** Pliny, *Panegyric* 65.1.

**52.** Ulpian, *Digest* 1.4.1.

**53.** Sallust, *Catiline* 7-13.

**54.** Livy *praef.* The translation is adapted from that of A. de Sélincourt in his Penguin edition of the first five books of Livy, *The Early History of Rome* (Harmondsworth, Middlesex, 1961).

**55.** Text and commentary in U. Laffi, "Le iscrizioni relative all'introduzione nel 9 a.C. del nuovo calendario della Provincia d'Asia," *Studi classici e orientali* (1967) pp. 5-98. Translation of relevant parts in N. Lewis and M. Reinhold, *Roman Civilization* II (New York, 1955), pp. 64-65.

**56.** Vergil's *Aeneid*, Horace's *Roman Odes*, Livy's history, and the Altar of Augustan Peace—each in its own medium celebrated the Augustan political achievement. Subtly persuasive, each is a propaganda document of consummate skill, the product of genius, capable of elevating temporal and limited themes into statements of timeless and universal significance.

**57.** The translation of Goethe's *Faust*, lines 10279-84 is that of Bayard Taylor. These sentiments which Mephistopheles attributes to "die Tüchtigen," would have struck a responsive chord in the hearts of many capable and wealthy Italian and provincial supporters of Augustus.

**58.** General studies of the concept of Liberty in imperial political thought and imagery include Wirszubski, *Libertas* (above n. 5), pp. 97-171; L. Wickert, "*Princeps*," A. Pauly, G. Wissowa and W. Kroll eds., *Real-Encyclopädie der classischen Altertumswissenschaft* XLIV, pp. 2080-2098; Stylow, *Libertas und Liberalitas* (above n. 5), pp. 18-98; and R. Klein, ed., *Prinzipat und Freiheit* (Darmstadt, 1969), a collection of fourteen articles by various authors treating aspects of this theme from the Augustan age to the later Roman empire. Excellent as these are, the best introduction is M. Hammond, "*Res Olim Dissociabiles: Principatus ac Libertas. Liberty under the Early Empire*," *Harvard Studies in Classical Philology* 67 (1963), pp. 93-113, an erudite and perceptive essay. Patterson, (above n.5) pp. 203-90, makes extensive use of Hammond's essay.

**59.** *Odyssey* 4.351-570.

**60.** H. Mattingly, *Coins of the Roman Empire in the British Museum* I (London, 1923), p. 112, no. 691. Cf. G. Walser, "Der Kaiser als Vindex Libertatis," *Historia* 4 (1955), pp. 353-367; R. Scheer, "Vindex Libertatis," *Gymnasium* 78 (1971), pp. 183-188; D. Mannsperger, "Appollon gegen Dionysos: Numismatische Beiträge zu Octavian Rolle als Vindex Libertatis," *Gymnasium* 80 (1973), pp. 381-404.

**61.** The image of civil war in Roman literature is the subject of P. Jal's stimulating monograph, *La guerre civile à Rome* (Paris, 1963).

**62.** For the caduceus as the symbol of Peace (*signum Pacis*), see the story of the Roman message to Carthage in Aulus Gellius *Attic Nights* 10.27.3: the Carthaginians were to signify their desire for war or peace by choosing either the spear or the caduceus.

The caduceus, the insignia of the modern day physician, is perhaps best known as the attribute of Mercury, with whom Octavian was identified (as in Horace's *Ode* 1.2, with commentary by R. Nisbet and M. Hubbard, *A Commentary on Horace: Odes Book* 1 (Oxford, 1970), pp. 34-36; and T. Gesztelyi, "Mercury and Augus-tus," *Acta Classica Universitatis Scientiarum Debreceniensis* 9 (1973), pp. 77-81. However, the caduceus was also of primary importance for the Romans as the symbol of the general conception of a golden age and its characteristic qualities of good fortune and fertility (Felicitas) and peace and civic harmony (Pax et Concordia). On Roman coins the caduceus appears as the attribute of the goddess Felicitas, while a caduceus was physically incorporated into the structure of the temple of Concordia Augusta dedicated in the Roman forum by Tiberius in 10 A.D. In general see E. Samter, "Caduceus," Pauly, Wissowa, Kroll, eds., *Real-Encyclopadie*...(above n. 58) V, pp. 1170-1171; A. Alfoldi, "Der neue Weltherrscher der vierten Ekloge Vergils," *Hermes* 65 (1930), pp. 369-384, esp. p. 379; J. Crome, "Kerykeia," *Mitteilungen des Deutschen Archäologischen Instituts, Athenische Abteilung* 63/64 (1938-1939), pp. 114-126, esp. pp. 124-126; N. Brown, *Hermes the Thief* (Madison, 1947), pp. 15-17. The association of the caduceus with the divining rod was already to Jakob Grimm, *Deutsche Mythologie* (Berlin, 1875-1878), pp. 815-816.

**63.** My views on Augustus are developed at length, with full citation of the sources and scholarly literature, in three studies, all published in *Aufstieg und Niedergang der romischen Welt* II xvii, ed. W. Haase (Berlin-New York 1981): "The Cult of Jupiter and Roman Imperial Ideology," pp. 56-66; "The Theology of Victory at Rome," pp. 804-812; and "The Cult of Virtues and Roman Imperial Ideology," pp. 884-889. Karl Galinsky, *Augustan Culture* (Princeton, 1996) is a detailed study of the Augustan Age, with excellent bibliographical notes.

**64.** A convenient translation of the *Res Gestae Divi Augusti* is Lewis and Reinhold (above n. 55) II, p. 9-19. The best commentary is that of J. Gage, *Res Getae Divi Augusti* (Paris, 1950).

**65.** Immediately after the assassination the conspirators showed their daggers and bloody hands to the crowd and summoned their fellow citizens to Liberty: Plutarch, *Brutus* 18. At their decisive battle with Antony and Octavian, at Phillippi in 42 B.C., the forces of Brutus and Cassius took "Libertas" as their watchword; Cassius Dio 47.42.1-43.1. Slightly earlier in 42 B.C., the coinage of Brutus gave a dramatic statement to the cause for which Caesar was assassinated: the reverse type portrays the symbol of Liberty (the Liberty cap or *pileus*) between the two daggers; the grim legend commemorates "the Ides of March" (*Eid.Mar.*); cf. Crawford, *Roman Republican Coinage* (above n. 10) I, p. 518 no. 508/3. The coin is mentioned by Cassius Dio 47.25.

**66.** Sallust, *Historiae* 4.69.18; cf. Cassius Dio 47.39.2-5.

**67.** The point is forcefully argued and fully documented in M. Hammond, *The Antonine Monarchy* (The American Academy in Rome, 1959).

**68.** For the following panegyric to monarchy, see Cassius Dio 52.14, writing in the early third century A.D., thus after more than two centuries of monarchical government at Rome. Born of a distinguished Greek family in Nicaea (modern Isnik in Turkey), a senator and twice consul (205, 229 A.D.), and author of a detailed history of Rome, Dio is himself a vivid testament to those policies of just administration, tolerance, and assimilation which transformed the city-state of Rome into a world state or, better, a true universal commonwealth of free citizens under one rule. These sentiments are forcefully expressed in the *Panegyric to Rome* delivered ca. 143 A.D. by another Greek from Asia Minor, Aelius Aristides (section 60): "Neither sea nor intervening continent are bars to citizenship, or are Asia and Europe divided in their treatment here. In your [Rome's] empire all paths are open to all. No one worthy of rule or trust remains an alien, but a civil community of the World has been established, as a Free Republic [demokratia] under one man, the best man, ruler and teacher of order; and all come together as into a common civic center, in order to receive each man his due"; edited with translation and commentary by J. Oliver, *The Ruling Power* in *Transactions of the American Philosophical Society* n.s. 43,4 (1953), p. 901. See further C. Starr, "The Perfect Democracy of the Roman Empire," *American Historical Review* 58 (1952), pp. 1-16; and J. Bleicken, *Der Preis des Aelius Aristides auf das romische Weltreich, Nachrichten der Akademie der Wissenschaften, Göttingen*, Philol. Hist. Klasse (1966).

69. Philo, *Embassy to Gaius* 21.143-47.

70. Suetonius, *Augustus* 98.

71. This Stoic definition of freedom is cited in Cicero, *On Moral Duties* 1.20.70 and *Paradoxes of the Stoics* 34. Popular acceptance of this definition of freedom in the imperial epoch is suggested by its appearance in Epictetus 2.1.23, 4.1.1 and more explicitly by its detailed examination and refutation in Dio Chrysostom, *Oration* 14.3-8.

72. Isaiah Berlin, *Four Essays on Liberty* (Oxford, 1969), xxxviii; as Berlin emphasizes, this definition of freedom does not represent his position.

73. Discussions of Tacitus on the theme of Liberty include Wirszubski, *Libertas*, (above n. 5), pp. 160-167; W. Jens, "Libertas bei Tacitus," *Hermes* 84 (1956), pp. 331-352; W. Liebeschuetz, "The Theme of Liberty in the *Agricola* of Tacitus," *Classical Quarterly* 16 (1966), pp. 126-139. Wirszubski, pp. 124-171, offers an illuminating discussion of the continued conflict between Liberty and Caesarism in the early imperial age. The careers of Roman Stoics like P. Clodius Thrasea Paetus, condemned to death under Nero, and Helvidius Priscus, executed by Vespasian, illustrate this very different aspect of the history of Liberty at Rome. For such upper class Roman critics martyrdom was the price, willingly paid, for their adherence to a "republican" concept of Liberty. For them "Libertas" served as a battle cry, and Cato the Younger, Brutus, and Cassius as heroes. Reconciled to the necessity of a *princeps* and even seeing positive benefits in monarchy, their position was often not directed against the principle itself but against tyranny which used its absolute power not to benefit its subjects but to destroy all personal freedom and security. Good studies of this so-called "senatorial opposition" to the principate include G. Boissier, *L'Opposition sous les Césars* (Paris, 1905); R. MacMullen, *Enemies of the Roman Order* (Cambridge, Mass., 1966), pp. 1-94; T. Adam, *Clementia Principis* (Stuttgart, 1970), pp. 56-82; and Adalberto Giovannini, ed., *Opposition et resistance a l'empire d'Auguste a Trajan* (Geneva, 1987).

74. Tacitus, *Annals* 1.7; Tacitus returns again to this theme, which underscores his emphasis on the moral degeneration of the Romans under the early principate; cf. *Annals* 2.32; 3.57; 4.28; 14.12; *Histories* 2.37; 4.42; *Agricola* 1-2.

**75.** In the view of Tacitus, *Agricola* 3, it was the achievement of Nerva and Trajan to inaugurate a new golden age, in which Liberty and monarchy were to become truly compatible. D. C. A. Shotter, "Tacitus' View of Emperors and the Principate," in *Aufsteig und Niedergang der römischen Welt*, ed. W. Haase II. 33.5 (Berlin-New York, 1991) pp. 3263-3331.

**76.** Implied by Tacitus, *Agricola* 3, this is explicit in Pliny's *Panegyric to Trajan* 66: "You [Trajan] order us to be free and so we are free." The sense of Pliny's references to the restoration of Liberty (58, 78) is rendered on an earlier coin type of Galba issued after the fall of the tyrannical Nero (68 A.D.). Rome, personified as a warrior goddess, watches on as the emperor raises up the kneeling figure of Liberty; the legend reads *Libertas Restituta* (Liberty Restored). Mattingly (above n. 60) I p. 358 no. 258.

**77.** S. Freud, *Das Unbehagen in der Kultur* (Vienna, 1930) esp. pp. 20-39; English translation as *Civilization and its Discontents* by J. Strachey (New York, 1962), pp. 21-32.

**78.** For its history as a title of the Roman emperors, see Hammond (above n. 67), pp. 87-89.

**79.** Stylow, *Libertas und Liberalitas* (above n. 5) pp. 58-98; H. Kloft, *Liberalitas Principis* (Cologne, 1970).

**80.** D. van Berchem, *Les distributions de blé et d'argent à la plèbe romaine sous l'empire* (Geneva, 1939); Z. Yavetz, *Plebs and Princeps* (Oxford, 1969), esp. pp. 133-138.

**81.** She first appears interestingly enough on the coinage of Nero; Mattingly (above n. 60) I, p. 220 no. 127.

**82.** "Bread and circuses" in the more familiar words of Juvenal, *Satires* 10.81.

**83.** Mattingly (above n. 60) IV, p. 33 no. 216.

**84.** *Romans* 6:22: cf. J. Cambier, "La liberté chrétienne selon Saint Paul," *Texte und Untersuchungen zur Geschichte der altchristlichen Literatur* 87 (1964), pp. 315-353; K. Niederwimmer, *Der Begriff der Freiheit im Neuen Testament* (Berlin, 1966).

**85.** See J. Rufus Fears, "Optimus Princeps—Salus Generis Humani: The Origins of Christian Political Theology," in E. Chrysos, ed., *Studien zur Geschichte der römischen Spätantike: Festgabe fur Professor Johannes Straub* (Athens, 1989), pp. 88-105.

**86.** For a brief but excellent discussion of this development to which I am much indebted, see A. Carlyle, *Political Liberty* (Oxford, 1941), pp. 1-11.

**87.** For our purpose it is enough that writers of the Roman imperial period, such as Plutarch *On the Fortune or the Virtue of Alexander 329-330*, believed that Alexander "wanted to make one law and one form of government for all mankind and to declare that all men were one nation, one people." W. Tarn, *Alexander the Great* (Cambridge, 1950) II, pp. 339-449, eloquently argued that in historical fact Alexander himself was the first to proclaim the idea of the brotherhood of man and to attempt to achieve this ideal. More recently and with different emphasis, H. Stier, *Welteroberung and Weltfriede im Wirken Alexanders des Grossen* (Oplanden, 1973) has defended the historical veracity of Plutarch's description of Alexander's aim. It might be added that, as Diodorus of Sicily 18.4.4 indicates, it was Alexander's intention to carry out a massive program of population transferrals within his empire, so that through familiarity and miscegenation the various peoples under his rule would be induced into living together in harmony and in friendly kinship. This would suggest that Plutarch, Tarn, and Stier are nearer to understanding the historical Alexander than the polemics of E. Badian, "Alexander the Great and the Unity of Mankind," *Historia* 7 (1958), pp. 425-444, would allow.

88. Fears (above n. 9), pp. 249-250.

89. In *Digest* 1.5.17, Ulpian is quoted to the effect that "all living in the Roman world were made Roman citizens by the constitution of the emperor Caracalla." In an ironic vein Cassius Dio, who despised Caracalla, associated this decree with the emperor's admiration for Alexander (77.9). A papyrus from Egypt (Giessen, Papyrus no. 40) is generally considered to contain a Greek version of the actual edict; for a translation see Lewis and Reinhold (above n. 55) II, pp. 427-428. The best general discussion of Caracalla's decree, the *Constitutio Antoniniana*, is A. Sherwin-White, *The Roman Citizenship* (Oxford, 1973), pp. 279-287, 380-393. C. Sasse, *Die Constitutio Antoniniana* (Wiesbaden, 1958) is a detailed treatment. For recent attempts to date the decree to 213 or 214 rather than 212, see P. Herrmann, "Überlegungen zur Datierung der *Constitutio Antoniniana*," *Chiron* 2 (1972), pp. 519-530. H. Wolff offers an exhaustive examination of *Die Constitutio Antoniniana und Papyrus Gissensis* 40.1 (Diss. Cologne, 1976). Andrew Lintott, Imperium Romanum: Politics and Administration (London-New York, 1993) pp. 161-67 is a brief survey of the spread of Roman citizenship.

90. This sentiment, which we have already noted in Aelius Aristides *Panegyric to Rome* 60 (above n. 68), is best known in the words of one of the latest and most enthusiastic pagan panegyrists to Rome, Rutilius Claudius Namatianus, whose fervid praise to Rome forms the centerpiece (lines 47-164) of his poetic description of *His Voyage Home*, written some seven years after Alaric's sack of Rome in 410 A.D.: "You [Rome] have created a common fatherland for the far-flung and disparate peoples of the earth.... You have made a city out of what was once a world" (lines 63,66).

91. Aristotle, *Politics* 1253b-1255b.

92. Plutarch, *On the Fortune or Virtue of Alexander* 329b.

93. G. Watson, "The Natural Law and Stoicism," in A. Long ed., *Problems in Stoicism* (London, 1971), pp. 216-238, is a good introduction.

94. Cicero, *On Laws* 1.10, 12.

95. Seneca, *On Benefits* 3.19, 20, 28.

96. *Digest* 1.5.4; 50.17.32.

97. Lactantius, *Divine Institutes* 5.15. The best introduction to the idea of Liberty in early Christianity is Nestle, "Freiheit," *Reallexikon fur Antike und Christentum* VIII, pp. 280-304. Peter Garnsey, *Ideas of Slavery from Aristotle to Augustine* (Cambridge, 1996) is an excellent study of the ideas of both Liberty and slavery in Christian and pagan thinkers.

98. *Galatians* 3:28.

99. Tertullian *On the Pallium* 2; Origen, *Against Celsus* 2.30. The idea also appears in Hippolytus, *Commentary on Daniel* 4.9 and in Melito as quoted by Eusebius *Ecclesiastical History* 4.26.7. Cf. F. Dvornik, *Early Christian and Byzantine Political Philosophy* (Washington,1966), pp. 603-604.

100. After his victories by land and sea over Licinius in 324, a victory which his propagandists portrayed as the triumph of Christ over the demons and false gods

of paganism (cf. Eusebius *Life of Constantine* 2.1-42), Constantine issued two remarkable coin types: C. Sutherland and R. Carson, eds., *The Roman Imperial Coinage*, vol VII by P. Bruun (London, 1966), p. 572 no. 18-19. The reverse of no. 18 has a type of Victory on a galley; the legend celebrates "Public Freedom" (*Libertas Publica*). The reverse of no. 19 portrays the Christian emblem, the labarum, piercing a dragon, symbolic of paganism. The legend proclaims "Public Hope" (*Spes Publica*). The message of the coins is clear: by the will of God and with the active assistance of Christ, Constantine has destroyed the forces of the usurper and tyrant Licinius; Constantine has thus restored freedom to the Roman People; the Christian faith and the triumphant and beneficent power of Christ and of his earthly viceregent Constantine are both the present salvation of the Roman People from the demonic power of evil as well as their hope for future peace and prosperity.

**101.** Classical influence on the American Founding has been the subject of much recent scholarship. See, e.g., P. Rahe, *Republics, Ancient and modern: Classical Republicanism and the American Revolution* (Chapel Hill,1992); S. Wiltshire, *Greece, Rome and the Bill of Rights* (Norman-London, 1992); C. Richard, *The Founders and the Classics: Greece, Rome, and the American Enlightenment* (Cambridge, Mass., 1994). Jennifer T. Roberts, Athens on Trial: The Antidemocratic Tradition in Western Thought (Princeton, 1994) pp. 175-93; and J. Peter Euben, John R. Wallach, and Josiah Ober, eds., *Athenian Political Thought and the Reconstruction of American Democracy* (Ithaca, 1994).

# Medieval: The Grand Synthesis

## Ralph McInerny

U sed as we are to speaking of Liberty with a capital L, we tend to think of it as an absolute, some isolable object of desire and pursuit—perhaps more accurately as an inalienable right, along with life and the pursuit of happiness. Give me liberty or give me death. We have a Statue of Liberty, an immense personification of the value that others associate with America. In the wake of our own revolution, the French Revolution of 1789 enshrined *Liberté, Egalité, et Fraternité*. The association of liberty with revolution encourages the thought that it is a modern preoccupation, a modern value, something peculiar to these last times.

And so, in a way, it is. Whatever the views of those who brought about the American and French Revolutions, in the present time liberty is most likely to be thought of as immunity from obstacles and impediments, the sweeping away of whatever might prevent me from working my own will. As opposed to what?

By associating freedom with two prepositions—*from* and *for*—we can easily see the point I wish to make. The most easily grasped sense of freedom is freedom *from*—we want to be free from incursions into our lives on the part of state or neighbor. Underlying this is the notion that we ought to be free from all obstacles, and thus free to do what we will, with a minimum of restrictions. The minimum restriction is that any use of my freedom which impairs or impinges on the freedom of others is unjustified. For libertarians this minimum restraint may also be the maximum restraint allowed. Above all, the libertarian wants to be free from anyone telling him what he is free for.

Why are we free? We may be so used to thinking of free action as an absolute value that the very question strikes us as odd, as if to act freely were its own justification.

Any attempt to recapture the medieval conception of liberty does well to down present-day assumptions like these. There is a way in which the medieval conception will provide a kind of rationale for the libertarian, but not at the cost of denying that we are free *for* something. Free action is one way of achieving an end or purpose that is given. This is an assumption the medieval Christian shared with some Greek pagan thinkers. If you asked Plato or Aristotle what the good for man is, what perfects or completes or fulfills the human person, they would give you an answer.

If there is such a thing as the human good, we have freedom in order to achieve it. In short, if man is free he does not enjoy total freedom, as if he could decide what it is that perfects the kind of agent he is.

## Man as Moral Agent

The medieval Christian regards man as the image and likeness of God. Every creature is thought to intimate or reflect in some remote way the divine perfection, since every effect gives us a clue as to the nature of its cause. Thus a rock or cloud or horse will, each in its own way, say something to us about its ultimate source, but not very much. Man is called God's image and likeness principally because he has dominion over his own actions.[1] Man not only performs actions of the kind most other things do, such as falling, growing, breathing, digesting, etc.—

actions whose causes are not forms of awareness and desire. If on entering a room you step on a roller skate, career wildly among the furniture flailing your arms, bang into the wall and then go alley-oop through the open window, all this taking place on the 13th floor, you will willy-nilly plummet to the ground below. If, as you pass the 7th floor, someone should ask you why you are falling, you are likely to think the question inappropriate. You would not think it inappropriate if, having jumped from the high board at the pool, the same question were put to you by someone standing on a lower board. "I'm going for the gold!" you might cry. Your last words, alas, since the pool has not yet been filled with water.

Not every activity that can be truly ascribed to the human agent is ascribed or attributed to him as human. Falling when dropped is true of Joe, but also of rocks and just about anything else. So, when pushed from a plane at 12,000 feet, a man's falling is no more peculiar to him than is the simultaneous falling of his unfastened parachute.

> Joe falls.
> Joe has grown three inches.
> Joe's beard is growing.
> Joe is digesting.
> Joe feels hungry.

On and on. We can easily imagine circumstances in which all these sentences are true. But we can just as easily substitute for 'Joe' a noun designating some lesser being and still end up with true sentences. Activities which can *truly* be said of human persons but which are not *peculiar* to them are not what a medieval like St. Thomas Aquinas would call a human action. What is a human action? Well, whatever it is, it will be that thanks to which man is said to be created in the image and likeness of God. Human action, as such, is deliberate voluntary action. It is the sort of thing we do of which it is appropriate to ask: Why are you doing that? Actions that we are answerable for, responsible for—because they are actions we might not have performed, yet we did. We were not forced to do them. They did not take place just because of certain factors over which we had no control. We bring out specifically human actions of our own volition. We do them freely.

Here then is a sense of *freedom from*. There are two things which render an action less than human.[2] First, *ignorance*. You have to know what you are doing in order to do it, humanly speaking. It may be true that someone is wooing his mother yet also true that he is not doing that. If he does not know that Jocasta, the desirable widow, is his mother, it is not true to say, without qualification, that Oedipus is wooing his mother. Free action is conscious, deliberate action. Notice that a person can be consciously and deliberately performing action A and at the same time doing B, yet doing A is a human action and doing B is not. Oedipus pursues the widowed queen consciously and deliberately; as it happens, she is his mother but he does not know this. Thus, in wooing the queen he is in some sense wooing his mother. But since he does not know it, we would not, save as oblique warning, ask: Why are you serenading your mother?

*Violence* is another factor that diminishes or destroys the freedom of an action. A gust of wind picks me up and carries me out to the south forty. It is not true to say that *I* went from point A to point B. Why? The answer, my friend, is blowing in the wind. I did not *do* it. Physical violence, but also psychological pressure, threats, etc., can lead us to say that a person is not *doing* something in the full sense of the term.

The glory of the human agent is that, alone among cosmic creatures, he knowingly directs himself to a good. Man's relative autonomy, the fact that he can propose to himself a course of action and then pursue it or not as he wills, sets him apart, gives him mastery and dominion over his life.

Of course, no sooner do we begin to paint such a picture than we feel the qualifications forming in our mind. One need not be a pessimist to recognize limitations on his freedom. Not everyone is free to become a sculptor even though no one is stopping him—or a scratch golfer, a lyric poet, a basso profundo, etc., etc. Think of all the things that we are free to do but cannot do. Circumstances, genes, opportunity, on and on, exercise constraints on what we can do. The Romantic Agony consists in an unquenchable nostalgia for all the things I cannot do or be. If I marry Fifi, I am no longer free not to marry Fifi—or to marry Conchita. I am free to cast a stone or not, but once I have acted I am no longer at the point where I was free to do either. The Romantic kicks against this goad; he does not want any use of freedom to diminish or foreclose future possibilities definitively. The Romantic thinks he can always go back to Square One—so there he is, standing at the altar, sixty years old, marrying for the fifth time.

Most of us will recognize limits on *freedom from*—there are constraints on future choices which follow from earlier uses of freedom; there are limitations not due to the use of our freedom, or even to others' use of theirs. The acceptance of such constraints on our freedom is compatible with the claim that when we do act, we are free to do anything we wish. The classical view, and the medieval as well, will not accept that, except with qualifications. Whatever we choose, we choose as something good for us. But are we free to make anything our good simply by choosing it, or is our choosing constrained with respect to its objects as well?

The good for man is that which makes one a good human being. But how can we possibly say what will make one a good human person? Let us first recall the Greek approach to this seemingly unanswerable question. Some version of this approach shows up in medieval discussions.

Aristotle likens the question about the good man to those concerning a good eye, a good knife, a good golfer, etc. If you are asked whether Matilda is a good golfer, you are not likely to answer: Who is anyone else to decide such a question? Let Matilda decide for herself. You are unlikely to use this approach if the question asks whether Dr. Zhivago is a good brain surgeon or Dr. Novocain a good dentist or Jorge a good cook. These are functions with definable criteria for performing them well. We do not regard it as a relative or subjective matter. A surgeon who regularly kills his patients will be called a bad surgeon. A golfer who when he does not miss the ball hits it far too often, is a bad golfer. And so on.

If there is some definable function or work of man, then doing it well will make one a good man in much the same way that performing well the task of the golfer makes one a good golfer, and likewise with other tasks and functions. But does man have a function? Is there a human work that can be done well or badly with the result that the agent is thereby a good or bad person?

We have already answered the question. The distinctive human act is deliberate voluntary activity. Doing that well—this is the meaning of virtue: excellence of performance—is the human good. Aristotle adds, significantly, that if there are many such virtues or excellences, then the human good will consist in them all. I want here to suggest rather than argue for the position that dominated medieval moral theory. So allow me to put the matter summarily thus. If I deliberate about what actions I might take that will sustain my health, there are certain possibilities that are canceled out by the nature of the case. If in a desire to get more starch in my diet I decide to consume shirts newly returned from the laundry, I would be embarking on a course of action unlikely to preserve my health. A diet of broken glass is certain to endanger rather than preserve my health. Notice that this does not mean I lack the freedom to eat my shirt or consume broken glass, say in the privacy of my own home. What my freedom cannot establish, however, is that such ingestions should be good for me. In much the same way, if other courses of action can be shown to be good for me, fulfilling of me, the recognition of such truths does not remove my freedom to act contrary to them. But I am not free to make what is good for me bad for me or *vice versa*.

When the medievals speak of free will (their term is *liberum arbitrium*, free judgment) they tend to make it bear on means rather than ends, particularly when the end is the ultimate end of human persons, that is, that which is perfective of human persons. Man is not free to choose his end, his good, what is perfective of him. His freedom comes into play when it is a matter of selecting means to realizing this end. By and large, there is no tight logical connection between this or that course of action, as means, and human fulfillment, as end. Several courses of action might get one there, so one is free to take the one path or the other. What I have already said makes it clear that one is free to will the end or not to will it; but freedom does not extend to *constituting* something as the human ultimate end.

*Freedom and End*

Most of us already know the basic account of the good the medievals held, if only because we are acquainted with its classical version. There are certain character traits or virtues which make up the human good—temperance, courage, justice and practical wisdom. These are the cardinal virtues. You may be acquainted with the kind of arguments formulated to show that human fulfillment cannot terminally consist of wealth or honors or pleasure or power. Getting such lesser goods into their proper, subservient, place in our lives, the acquisition of the virtues, is the moral task.

Hand in hand with such arguments goes the realization that most of us pursue wealth and honors and pleasure and power most of the time. As we have already suggested, this means that we are free to act against our true good. Thus it seems that freedom extends to ends as well as to means.

Well, yes and no. Yes, in the obvious sense. Temperance may be a constituent or element of our true good, but most of us act intemperately. We are free to do so and we do. But such freedom cannot make intemperance our true good.

There is another sense in which we are not free to pursue anything other than our true good. If you imagine the numberless acts you perform, it is possible to say—and this is to make a very long story short—that there is one overarching reason why you do anything you do. This is seen from the fact that whatever we do we do under the assumption that it is good for us to do. To do A embodies the judgment that it is better to do A than not to do A. The only reason we can do anything is on the assumption that it is something good for us to do. You will, of course, think of lots of apparent counterexamples to this claim, and we can discuss them, but meanwhile let me go blithely on.

The notion that whatever anyone does he does under the assumption it is good for him—*sub ratione boni*—leads medievals to say that all men share the same aim in life: All men seek the good.

The obvious objection to this is that the agreement covers every manner and sort of disagreement, so what good is it? It turns out to be a very powerful observation nonetheless. If I do A, I must think that it is good for me to do A; if however doing A is bad for me and I come to see that, then I have a reason for not doing it. Then to go on and do it is an example of irrational behavior. But for a rational creature to engage in irrational behavior, shorts out its reason for being. Furthermore, I have a motive for not doing A. If my understood reason for doing A is that it is good for me, my abiding and inescapable desire to do what is good for me is a motive for not doing A—if I become convicted it is not good for me.

This is admittedly a swift way to put a very complicated

matter, but such is the nature of my assignment: to depict *grosso modo* the medieval conception of liberty. There is an ideal of human conduct, a recognition we can come to what fulfills the kind of agent we are. Like it or not, that is the human good. Furthermore, even if we act contrary to it there is a sense in which we cannot completely do so. This is true because no matter what we do we do as something good for us to do—however mistaken we may be about that.

A basic distinction is, then, between the notion or formality of goodness, on the one hand, and, on the other, the concrete types of action which are taken to embody that notion.

Thus far this is the Greek contribution. To it the medieval adds another distinction. No finite good, no collection of finite goods, can exhaust the goodness we seek. Any created good shares in goodness, participates in it—there is always a gap between the thing desired and the reason for desiring it. That is the point of Augustine's haunting remark: "You have made us for yourself, O Lord, and our hearts are restless until they rest in you." Only God is goodness; any other good thing is a limitation of or participation in goodness. God is not just another good thing. He is goodness itself. God is the only object who completely fulfills the notion of goodness. This is why the medieval will say that God is our ultimate end. Of course, simply to acknowledge that God is goodness does not necessitate that I subordinate all my other desires to my desire for God.

*Interim Summary*

Thus far I have done little more than recall things already well known to you and to underscore some obvious distinctions. (1) the distinction between freedom from and freedom for; (2) the distinction between our reason for doing anything and the many things that we do; (3) the distinction between the imperfect happiness attainable in this world and the perfect happiness that will be ours in the next life.

Given what a human person is, human goodness, perfection, or fulfillment can be had only within a limited range and we are not free to change that although, again, we are free not to pursue our true good. The negative and positive precepts which arise out of this conception of the human agent make up what the medievals call natural law.

One of the most striking contrasts between natural law theory and more recent political theories which will be familiar to you is that the former speaks rather of duties and little of rights, whereas the latter are preeminently theories of rights. This is a profound difference and reveals almost diametrically opposed views of what it is to be a human agent.

In the classical view, individuals are almost an abstraction. That is, you and I and other persons come into existence as part of a wider social whole, primarily a family. For a good number of years our existence is dependent upon others feeding and changing and warming and sheltering us. It is not simply that our private good was insured by this community; there are common goods which from the outset we recognize as our better good, more important than our merely private good. Chances are that this domestic society was an element in a yet wider one involving goods we share with many others. The point is clear. We cannot speak of what is good for humans without basing what we say on what it is to be a human person. To be a human person is not to be an isolated, autonomous individual, but a member of a community. Just as we only gradually achieve physical autonomy, so we only gradually achieve moral maturity, i.e., the ability to direct ourselves responsibly to what is perfective of us.

The natural law thus grounds itself unabashedly in the way things are[3] and, in its religious form, in the nature God has given us. Man is seen as part of the cosmos and as having, like it, though in his own peculiar way—he is made in God's image and likeness—a purpose and destiny. Within this framework we can speak of what is obligatory and what is not. The obligatory will be explained in terms of either a course of action prescribed because without it the end cannot be achieved or, conversely, an action prohibited because it always thwarts the end. It is my constitutive desire for the end or goal that gives obligation its force: duty arises out of desire for fulfillment.

The natural rights view of man rests on a quite different picture, at least for the most part. It begins with autonomous human units that have needs and desires and imagines them as entering into concert with one another. The motive for such social union is that the individual is better able to achieve his own desires by cooperating with others than on his own. But such agreements must be entered into cautiously. There must be a careful statement of the rights the individuals retain, and these amount to claims against others. What is happening as a result of such association is a domination of individual liberty. If I accept such restrictions it is only because the net effect will be the greatest practical amount of liberty. Thus, if I live alone, I do not have to recognize the claims of others on me, but I lose what I might gain from cooperation. Beneath this account, is a kind of calculation: how can I best achieve what I want? If I enter into a social arrangement it will be because I judge this to be in my own best interests.

The obvious casualty of this change of perspective is the common good. Not that the term is abandoned, but it comes to mean quite different things than it hitherto had. For example, the commonweal can be taken to mean the good of the collectivity, that is, the sum total of private goods. Or it can be taken to mean the greatest good of the greatest number. Or it can be taken to be an alien good—not my good, but the good of others.

There have been attempts to put these two traditions together, usually on the side of those who hold some version of the natural law view. Thus Jacques Maritain, in *Man and the State*[4], attempted a natural law account of rights theory and, more recently, John Finnis in *Natural Law and Natural Rights*[5] suggests a similar reconciliation. There can be little doubt that, within the context of natural law morality and its understanding of liberty and freedom, I can give an account of rights. I have a right to whatever is necessary for me to fulfill an obligation. Rights are thus connected with the good and with societal arrangements.

Things are quite different when we begin with isolated units and ask what rights they have. Even if rights talk begins when such units enter into community, rights as claims reside in characteristics of individuals independently of the societies without which they can neither exist nor mature. It is this that has made rights talk vulnerable to such criticisms as that of Alasdair MacIntyre in *After Virtue*.[6] MacIntyre simply denies that there are any natural rights—that is, rights understood independently of societal arrangements. You may think this criticism goes too far, but it is clear that it is aimed at what is most vulnerable in modern natural rights talk.

*Rights and the Good*

By far the most dramatic difference between medieval natural law talk (I do not mean to suggest that the view is no longer held today) and modern natural rights is that the latter has commended itself as a means of going around our different views as to what substantively the good is. The term pluralistic applied to modern liberal societies connotes a live and let live attitude toward substantive differences concerning the good. To his credit, Maritain confronted this head-on. He was writing in the atmosphere of the 1948 Universal Declaration of Human Rights. A question had to arise as to the significance of agreement to this declaration when the signatories held such radically different views as to the meaning of the rights in question. A whole succession of American ambassadors and delegates to the United Nations have lamented the fact that the only thing member states can agree on is words—meanings are another matter. So what is the point of signing onto a declaration of rights to democracy, self-determination, freedom of expression, and so forth, when the meaning of such terms can be completely equivocal? A merely verbal agreement scarcely seems worth the trouble. (This is an aspect of MacIntyre's rejection.) Maritain suggests that there is at bottom, almost unconsciously, a recognition of substantive goods which explains the verbal agreement. His argument is complicated and, at least at first blush, unpersuasive. But there can be little doubt that what he presupposes is just what many nowadays would take not to be presupposed by rights theory.

I can clarify what I mean by returning to my first distinction—freedom from and freedom for. It is far easier to understand rights talk as an insistence on freedom from, a rejection of restraints on my exercise of freedom. My freedom is basically freedom to do whatever I want to do—*because there is no other measure of the good than the fact that I want it.* That is, I do not desire X because X is good; rather, X is good because I desire it. In short, freedom is taken to be constitutive of the good. My wants and desires are givens, and they can differ wildly from yours. It is just because we do not want to get into an argument about what desires are good and what are not, that we as rights theorists tend to take the desires as simple givens. The task is then to accommodate such desires in a formal way. My rights are read in terms of what I want and there can be no discussion of that. The only restraint—and here we rejoin our first remark—has to do with whether my pursuit of what I desire interferes with others' pursuit of what they desire. This is not to be taken as a ranking of desires or as any substantive judgment of them. It is a purely formal adjudication of differences. Each desire receives, so to say, a value of 1.

Pluralism and tolerance and personal liberty are noble concepts—but only within a controlling context. When pluralism becomes moral relativism, when tolerance is destructive of the society within which tolerance receives its meaning, when personal liberty is taken to be a blank that can be filled with any object whatsoever, we are light-years distant from the sense such terms had for the Founding Fathers. The libertarian relativist's embrace of these grand old notions is a mortal one, involving the kiss of death. The eschewal of substance and the emphasis on mere form has been devastating both in the moral and political realms.

The glory of our own country is to be found in religious tolerance. But such religious tolerance was almost never associated with relativism in religious matters. Pluralism makes sense only if you have a plurality of substantive views. Religious liberty is so fundamentally important just because there is no way the assent of belief can be forced. The only thing that can be forced is a hypocritical adherence, and this is a parody of the freedom of the sons of God. Most importantly—and we see this in Vatican II's *Declaration on Religious Liberty*—the argument for religious liberty must be formed within a substantive religious tradition.

## ENDNOTES

1. See Thomas Aquinas, *Summa theologiae*, IaIIae, q. 1, a. 1.
2. The role of ignorance and violence in diminishing the responsibility of human actions as discussed by Thomas Aquinas, and any other medieval after the translation of the *Nicomachean Ethics*, is indebted to Aristotle.
3. Cf. *Summa theologiae*, IaIIae, q. 94, a. 2.
4. University of Chicago Press, 1951.
5. Oxford University Press, 1982.
6. University of Notre Dame Press, 1981.

# Sixteenth-Century Search

## George B. Martin

B efore I start to try to discuss the sixteenth-century conception of liberty, I need to enter several caveats that pertain to
the problem. The first is that I am a student of literature, not an
historian or political philosopher. Consequently, I see the age
through the *feelings* authors had about their age, and as a rule I
draw on my knowledge of the background only to illuminate the
text or to recognize the social, political, or intellectual conditions
that the texts embody. It is not usually my intention to attempt
to summarize the intellectual and social history of the age.

The second caveat is that I draw my own conception of
liberty—and consequently the presentation of liberty I recognize
in the sixteenth century—primarily from my experiences as a
twentieth-century, Southern American. What have we come to
call "The Enlightenment Project" does not loom so large for me
as it does for many historians of thought. I speak instead from the
concrete experiences of the world around me in order to define
what I mean by liberty. To that end I am going to start, then, with
a statement by Ezra Pound and anecdote from my personal
world.

Somewhere, Pound says that "a slave is someone waiting to be
freed." Pound was a master of the epigram, which is to say he
could cram a whole lot of thought, tradition, and feeling into a
few words. In this line, I would suggest that he was being more
Classical than Christian, more Machiavellian than Calvinist, to

use sixteenth-century figures. Lest we misunderstand how I read the lines, I want to turn them around and say, "Somebody waiting to be freed is a slave." And to illustrate in very contemporary terms what I think the lines mean, I would like to relay the story of my father-in-law.

This story's significance came to me the other Sunday when my wife and I were riding out in the country to visit her father on his farm. We had just seen a production of *Death of a Salesman*, and I was thinking about this lecture and the revival of the play and how different Willie Loman's life is from my father-in-law's. Putting them in contrast, I also thought about how rich the fruits of freedom are. My father-in-law grew up in the boll weevil belt of South Carolina on a subsistence farm, had little more than a grammar school education, and spent most of his life working in a cotton mill boiler room. He learned early on that nature is brutal, and that work, if you let it, will brutalize you. He raised five children—two boys and three girls—on the philosophy that children are like chickens: if you feed them too close to the back door they will never get out and scratch for themselves. All of them are devoted to him, and they have, by anybody's standards, turned out well. He is ninety-three now; his wife has only recently died. He retired, resentfully, when he was sixty-five, to a farm that was little more than a weed and briar patch when he bought it—the image in many ways of the world he had left nearly seventy years ago. He cleaned it up with a used bulldozer, put in fescue pastures, and now runs upward of two hundred head of beef cattle on it. He tends it by himself mostly. I do not know anywhere a more self-satisfied man. He will die a man who through his thrift and industry has had the absolutely best life he can imagine. He has the feeling that his life has turned out well, that he has things as he always wanted to have them and that he made them that way himself.

Seeing how people make money now, how seemingly separated from thrift and industry wealth is, I am not sure that the

America still exists that produced my father-in-law. Our cultural idea of Miller's death play as our tragic image of ourselves and the American dream does not, I think, bode well. I prefer the image of America that my father-in-law's life gives: the America that gave an overall-wearing Low Country boy the courage and hope it took to leave what could never have been more than a bare subsistence income in order to work in the mills for such wages as he could get. He saved his money, lost it all in the bank crash, made it and saved it again, until he got enough together to build some houses for people on weekends and in the evenings. He did not walk into the jungle and come out a rich man. Instead, he had the confidence and faith that industry and prudence would yield the way of life he wanted. America had somehow taught him that. He had what the old Romans called *virtu*, that quality of character that overcomes *fortuna* and enables a man to feel that his life is his own creation.

I communicate this story in reference to Pound's definition of a slave because it demonstrates something about what I think liberty is: *the opportunity to have as much control over one's life as one's innate ability, prudence, courage, wisdom, and temperance will permit.*

At its most basic level the story tells of self-mastery—the ability to subjugate passions to the achievement of rationally determined and approved ends. That is the kind of freedom that is primary, that is included in what the old Romans meant by *virtu* and is expressed in triumph over *fortuna*. Hannah Arendt, whose teachings in such matters I follow very closely, argues that we can divide the human condition up into the activities of labor, work, and action, and that it is only in the area of action—civil life we can call it—that the term freedom means anything. Labor, by which she means the activity of maintaining the animal being, and work, by which she means creating and acquiring objects that will outlast us and reduce the amount of labor required for our maintenance, are not free activities inasmuch as they are things we *have* to do in order to live. To the extent that we allow our appetites to bind us to such activities, I would argue, we do not have the capacity for freedom she assigns to the active, or civic, life.[1]

On other levels this story speaks of a social system that will allow a man proceed in the world, despite the handicaps of his origins, and of an economic system that lets a man keep and invest the fruits of his industry and shrewdness. It speaks of a political system whose designers respected and wanted to cultivate the kind of virtue my father-in-law has, and who perceived that this kind of virtue is synonymous with political, social, and economic freedom. These, I would argue, are *freedoms of circumstance*, to use for my purposes Stanley Hook's term, freedoms which men create and sustain for themselves and future generations through their laws and institutions.

Finally, implicit in my father-in-law's story is a religious belief that does not despise or decry the material benefits of this world, that tends to see material success as an outward sign of God's love and blessings, that requires a reasonable amount of charity from a man—my father-in-law has always tithed—but also says that a man should use his God-given abilities to be self-sufficient. This, too, is an aspect of liberty, of social and religious freedom.

To be interested in this liberty, these freedoms, in relation to the literary works of any age is to be interested, in large part, in how artists *felt* about their age. How they felt is significant, I would argue, because discussions of things like liberty emerge out of feelings. People who do not feel constrained by existing conditions, people who feel they are living meaningful, fruitful lives do not tend to argue about whether they have true liberty or not. People who feel that an hereditary absolute monarchy assures their rights as individuals and as groups to pursue their own interests and exercise fully their talents do not want a revolution. Only when they have acquired a new sense of themselves and of life's possibilities that exceeds the traditional order, or when they feel that someone or some government is abridging or usurping their traditional rights do they begin to want to change the social order and begin to talk about liberty.

Discussions of liberty take on a particular form under such circumstances. In *Richard II*, for example, Shakespeare as a conservative confronts the convergence of these two conditions that produce discontent and give rise to revolution. On the one side he has Richard II, who in confiscating Bolingbroke's land and goods has violated a subject's rights and, as York warns him, the very covenant upon which his kingship rests. In such a case, Bolingbroke's return home to claim his inheritance under English custom is justified. On the other hand, Bolingbroke is one of Machiavelli's "new men," an opportunist who feels no ethical restraint in assuming the kingship. Both are usurpations, violations of the authority that Shakespeare would maintain as the basis of his society, and in order to counter them, he has to have Hal, Henry V, revalidate the ideal of Tudor kingship. In doing so he begins a process of reiteration and articulation of old values that gives them a new cast and a currency greater than they originally had. His Henry V becomes not just an example of what kingship before the violation has been, but also what Shakespeare sees it must be if the ideal is to survive.

Shakespeare's primary interest in the history plays is, then, the preservation of authority—as opposed to violence and persuasion—as the primary form of power. He knew that he lived at the end of an age of transition, a time when the medieval world was ending and the modern world was beginning. On the basis of Hamlet's "What a piece of work is man" soliloquy, I assume he knew Pico della Mirandola's "Oration on Man," the document that, I would argue, summarizes and articulates the Renaissance spirit. It embodies the belief that man, liberated from superstitions and unnatural social restraints, freed, as it were, from the ignorance of the past, can so develop his intellectual facilities that he can recover the lost image of God within himself. If the original Eden was lost through man's sin, if man was eternally separated from his original destiny, he could find the potentiality within himself, within his history and through the development of his own powers, to overcome that loss and to create the new Eden. He could become man as he was originally intended to be. In case you have forgotten it, I want you to cite a part of it.

According to Mirandola, man is a "great miracle" because, on the testimony of ancients, he:

> is the intermediary between creatures, the intimate of the gods, the king of lower beings, by the acuteness of his senses, by the discernment of his reason, and by the light of his intelligence the interpreter of nature, the interval between fixed eternity and fleeting time, and (as the Persians say) the bond, nay, rather, the marriage song of the world, on David's testimony but little lower than the angels. [He is this also because God made Adam to be more than even angels].... Neither a fixed abode nor a form that is thine alone nor any function peculiar to thyself have we given thee, Adam, to the end that according to thy longing and according to thy judgment thou mayest have and possess what abode, what form and what functions thou thyself shalt desire. The nature of all other things is limited and constrained within the laws prescribed by Us. Thou constrained by no limits, in accordance with thine own free will, in whose hand We have placed thee, shalt ordain for thyself the limits of thy nature. We have set thee at the world's center that thou mayest from thence more easily observe whatever is in the world. We have made thee of neither heaven nor earth, neither mortal nor immortal, so that with freedom of choice and with honor, as though the maker and molder of thyself, thou mayest fashion thyself in

whatever shape thou shalt prefer. Thou shalt have the power to degenerate into the lower forms of life, which are brutish. Thou shalt have the power out of thy soul's judgment, to be reborn into the higher forms, which are divine.[2]

This enthusiasm, this feeling that everything is within the reach of modern man, could go in a lot of ways. Erasmus, you will recall, set his life to the great project of educating noble men and princes. In his *Enchiridion* he wrote, as many a Christian moralist before him had, that life is warfare between the soul of man and the forces of evil. Our weapons in the war are prayer and knowledge—knowledge of Scriptures, of pagan authors, and of the Church fathers. The battleground is ourselves, the conflict between the inner man and the outer man. In regard to the outer man, we are no more than dumb beasts, but in regard to the inner man, because we have reason and the eternal laws engraven in us, "we are capable of divinity, that is we may climb in flight above the minds of the very angels themselves and become one with God."[3] What is potentially very radical in Pico's humanism has been modified or reexpressed in terms that are consistent with traditional Christianity. His humanism has become a means of trying to conserve traditional authority, both religious and political. Others, like Thomas More and Elyot, followed his lead in attempting to educate princes and noblemen to the range of human possibilities. But none of these men could think beyond the contemporary political order nor imagine a society that was not basically an extension of the family. Instead, they were content with the contemporary political order and the opportunities it offered them, finding in the educating and advising of a prince adequate and satisfying political roles for themselves. Although they were well-schooled in Greek democracy and in Roman republicanism, and although they thought man had a natural virtue which he could express in social and political forms, they continued to think mostly in terms of the medieval monarchy as an extended form of the family. Erasmus, for example, writes: "The good prince ought to have the same attitude toward his subjects, as a good *paterfamilias* toward his household—for what else is a kingdom but a great family? What is the King if not the father to a great multitude?"[4] More, although making his persona a bit of a strawman, says in his *Utopia* "For from the prince, as from a perpetual wet spynge, commethe amonge the people the floode of al that is good or evill."[5] And More's *Utopia*, for all its seemingly revolutionary intent in its projection of a republic without private property, turns out to be a reduction of men to a congenial form of slavery. Even though *Utopia* is a society formed out of classical virtues, it does not have the dimensions of the *polis* or the Roman republic. It is too entirely utilitarian to admit the leisure and the degree of social liberty that the Greeks saw as the active life, and plainly what More is after is a state that fosters economic equality but not Greek *arete* or Roman *virtu*. Shakespeare was in deep sympathy with these humanists' desires to shore-up the old, medieval order. Although his history plays are the most overt assertion of his love for English monarchy and his belief that the health and well-being of the nation are expressed in the prince, as the feasting and harvesting imagery of *Macbeth* demonstrates, he thought in that later play of the nation as being, ideally, an organic unity of reciprocal relationships grounded in nature. Kingship, he seemed to think, is grounded in natural law as surely as parenthood is. A violation of kingship is a violation of that authority that will ultimately result in the people's loss of liberty until the bloody restoration of the true king.

Shakespeare was, however, also very much aware of the emergence of a new kind of man whose energies exceed the old prescriptions of the Chain of Being. From the spirit of Pico, this new man developed a sense of himself and of life's possibilities that the old system did not recognize. In part, that form of humanism was as much a reaction against the corruption of the Church as the Reformation was. These humanists railed against the abuses and attacked or ridiculed scholastic theology as violently as did Luther or Calvin. They became, in increasing numbers, what Luther had despised so in Erasmus: religious skeptics. That skepticism, allied with the nominalism that was so much in the air, undercut all notions of universal and natural law. They began to deny the essential dogmas of the Church and the immortality of the soul as superstitions that ill befit an educated and enlightened man. Where Aquinas had sought to ground society in an idea of virtue that was included in the knowledge of God, they began to think of virtue as a personal and social end. In Rabelais' "House of Liberty," where the only law is "Do what you will," the humanism—in its faith in the idea of individual virtue in the educated man—begins to approach the conception of liberty John Stuart Mill expresses.

But the more permanent and ultimately pervasive expression of this frequently atheistic humanism came from Machiavelli's much discussed idea of *virtu*. Professor Pocock has outlined the history of the term for us:

> The *baraka, mana, or charisma*...of the successful actor thus consisted both in the quality of personality that commanded good fortune and in the quality that dealt effectively with whatever fortune might send; and the Roman term for this complex characteristic was *virtu*.... A term which originally, and largely remained, part of the ethos of a political and military ruling class, *virtu* became assimilated to the Greek *arete* and shared its conceptual development. From the meaning of "civic excellence"—some quality respected by other citizens and productive of leadership and authority over them—*arete* had been refined by Socrates and Plato to mean that moral goodness

which alone qualified a man for civic capacity, which could even exist without it and render it unnecessary, and which at the highest levels of Platonic thinking, rendered existence and the universe intelligible and satisfactory. *Arete* and *virtu* alike came to mean, first the power by which an individual or a group acted effectively in a civic context; next, the essential property which made a personality or element what it was; third, the moral goodness which made a man, in city or cosmos, what he ought to be. This diversity of meanings was carried by "virtue" and its equivalents in various languages down to the end of Old Western thinking.[6]

Herein, of course, lies the basis for the kind of liberty my father-in-law's life expressed. Men like Harrington in the next century would recognize this and make it a large part of their republicanism. But Machiavellism did not translate easily into Shakespeare's assumptions about the organic, mutually reciprocal nature of the human community. Machiavelli, disbelieving in any natural law that sustained kingship and wanting to see the reestablishment of old Roman republicanism, advocated a policy on the part of the prince to achieve these ends that seemed to Shakespeare's age barbarous. Machiavellism became a synonym for malicious ambition, and the liberty in civic life Machiavelli was trying to achieve no more than immoral advantage through ruthless behavior.

We can see this fairly clearly in the shocking audacity of Marlowe's *Tamburlaine*. Medieval accounts of tragedy, such as Chaucer's "Monk's Tale" and early Elizabethan warnings to princes, such as *The Mirror for Magistrates*, were all predicated on the principle that man is subject to fortune and that he who rises with Fortune's wheel will surely fall when his place on the wheel reaches its apex. This conception of tragedy, called *de casibus*, intended to instruct men not to value the things of this world and be constant for death. It was, therefore, in its didactic intention synonymous with the aims of such morality plays as *Everyman*. In *Tamburlaine* and *Dr. Faustus* Marlowe inverted this order, to present us first a man who does not fall from Fortune's wheel, who continues to rise until old age and death finally overtake him, and then a man who in order to obtain his aspirations and escape human limitations barters his soul to the devil.

These "overreachers" embody Machiavellism without its re-deeming social and political ends. They are merely ambitious for power. Consequently, Machiavelli's virtuous man who would master fortune and give direction to his own life becomes Shakespeare's Edmund, the bastard son of Gloster in *King Lear*, a man for whom the law of nature is the survival of the strongest and for whom virtue means ruthless strength to overcome the conditions that fortune presents him.

And yet, despite his fears about the Machiavellian man, Shakespeare perceived how applicable Machiavellian politics were to the new age. His Henry plays, which are very much about the nature of monarchy and society, are his articulations in terms of the traditions of his own people of his own version of Machiavellism. Shakespeare, having observed Elizabeth's po-litical acumen, having observed her capacity to generate patriots and to identify the nation with her person, appreciated the role that political genius played in acquisition of power through the establishment of kingship as an authoritative entity. He did not need to read Machiavelli, for he had, in his lifetime, seen the greatest of Machiavellians operating to consolidate her power while, at the same time, assuring the liberty of her subjects. He knew the forms that power takes—authority, violence, and persuasion—and he knew that liberty is consistent with only one of these—authority—for it is the only form of power that derives its basis from the liberty and virtue of the people. He knew that the beliefs that had traditionally sustained the power of a king and had given him his authority were disappearing. (This disappearance of the traditional virtue of a people is an oft repeated theme in Shakespeare—in his Roman plays as well as his histories.) His Richard II, for example, despite the absolute loyalty of old men like York and John of Gaunt, cannot command the younger generation by his person—Mowbrary and Bolingbroke defy him in the quarrel and Bolingbroke's opportunism feels no moral or ethical restraint. The old metaphors—the king as the father, the king as the head in the body of the state—will not hold things together. Violence, the rule of Henry IV, and "policy" which includes violence and persuasion become the sources of power. The Prince Hal, Henry V, if he is to rule successfully, must make certain public gestures toward traditional sources of authority—the law in the person of the Chief Justice and the Church—and he must become an institution, a public being who can excuse insults against his private person but not treason toward his kingship. He must translate the ambitions of private men from the raw struggle for power into either patriotism or treason. Hal, in trying to solidify his power and his hold on the kingship through a war with France, knows that he must induce his soldiers to feel that his cause, his heroism, his kingship expresses the finest parts of their lives. He must reestablish kingship as an authoritative entity in the nation. He knows that in a very important sense his people have to live through him, that they have to feel that his cause is their cause. He must recover the sense of nationhood that his father destroyed when he usurped the throne.

A great deal of what Shakespeare is articulating in his presentation of the monarchy and his fear of ambitious men is simply an expression of what is often called the Tudor constitution. Deeply loyal as old York is to Richard II, and as willing as he is to leave judgment of Richard's actions to God, he still warns Richard that in confiscating Gaunt's lands and Bolingbroke's inheritance he is violating the legal tradition by which he is king.

He implies that kingship involves a covenant with the people, a covenant embodied in the laws of custom and usage in England. A king who violates those laws violates that covenant and gives Bolingbroke the legal excuse to return from exile and to gather supporters to claim what is rightfully his own. And Hal insists upon the Church's approval on legal grounds of his invasion of France. Even Bolingbroke, as he usurps the kingship, wants to move within the laws of England.

Shakespeare's basic conservatism was complemented by that of his contemporary, Bishop Richard Hooker. Now to my own way of thinking, no political thinker of consequence has been as neglected or ignored in histories of and courses on political thought as Richard Hooker. I suspect that most college libraries do not contain more than half a dozen books on him. In my opinion, his *Laws of Ecclesiastical Polity* is the first major document in the history of conservative thought, and therein, I suspect, lies the cause of his being disregarded. For what Hooker sought to do was to preserve what he thought Western civilization in general and England in particular had obtained in the way of religious, social, and political order (he was one of the last men who could think of such things as being aspects of each other). Consequently, he had nothing new, in itself, to add to the history of political thought. His learning was vast and totally assimilated to a world view, and he saw his role to be using that vast learning to meet the challenge of those who would overthrow that order. He was the first thinker of note to understand the nature of Puritanism and its dangers. Calvinism, he recognized, had opened the laws that had traditionally governed man and insured his liberty up to the scrutiny and criticism of the ignorant, with the result that rational discourse about matters of religion and politics was becoming almost impossible. Puritan zeal, religious enthusiasm in the literal sense of the term, born of one's experience with the Scriptures, threatened to all but shove reason out as a basis of reconciliation between disagreeing but well-meaning men. The absolute confidence the radical Protestant had in his beliefs derived, he believed, from the inspiration of the Holy Spirit in his reading of the Scriptures, would brook no disagreement. "Reason," Luther had said, "is the Devil's whore." To the suggestion that statements in Scripture might be metaphorical, he replied, "If my God tells me to eat dung, I'll eat dung." In charity, Hooker felt the need to speak rationally to such people, so that "posterity may know that we have not loosely through silence permitted things to pass away as in a dream."[7]

Now, what Professor McInerny pointed out in the previous essay, concerning the Middle Age's conception of liberty, is true also of the Christian humanists that Hooker followed: they thought not so much in terms of liberty in itself as in terms of the ends that a man should live for. They accepted as paramount the Middle Age's division between authority, which resided with the Church, and power, which resided with the Monarch. Sir Thomas More, you will recall, believed in this division so strongly that he lost his head rather than assent to Henry VIII's assumption of the authority of the Church into the power of the Crown. We err, however, if we see More's refusal as an exercise and plea for religious freedom or rebellion against the power of the Crown. The More who went to the scaffold is the same More who in the King's name persecuted those English Protestants who refused to take the sacraments, although it would seem that in the midst of these persecutions he had a premonition of how they might in time redound on his own head. And Erasmus, while he certainly hoped for the reformation of the Church, continued to insist upon the authority of the Church in directing princes' rule of their subjects.

> I tell you that all is the commonwealth's. The king is
> but your servant and minister. Wipe away your tears,
> and turn to the Lord your God....What is a king? A

king exists for the sake of his people: he is an outcome from nature in labour; an institution for the defense of material and temporal interests. But inasmuch there are interests beyond the temporal, so there is a jurisdiction beyond the king's. The glory of a king is the welfare of his people; and if he knew himself and knew his office, he would lay his crown and kingdom at the feet of the priesthood, as in a haven and quiet resting-place.[8]

Reformation leaders did not depart so radically from the Middle Age's conception of freedom as is sometimes allowed. While forming his essay *On Christian Liberty*, Luther later recognized that the most basic point of disagreement between him and the Roman Church was aimed at reconciliation with the Pope. In the essay he is arguing for the orthodoxy of his opinion by demonstrating how his idea of justification through faith as opposed to works does not exclude free will, ultimately, nor good works as an aspect of worship. The paradox with which he begins the essay—that a "Christian is perfectly free lord of all, subject to none," and a "perfectly dutiful servant of all, subject to all"— would have been acceptable to Aquinas once it was clear what Luther means by a Christian. Nor would Aquinas find much to quarrel with in Luther's assertion that faith gives fallen man access to the Word of God, and the Word of God access to righteousness and freedom. Just as Luther does, he would have said that obedience to God is true freedom, and he would have assented that freedom is, in some way, made possible by grace.

Where Luther departs from the Middle Age's tradition and where he forces Erasmus to respond reluctantly to his teachings is in the exclusiveness of his language. At the core of Luther's religious opinions is his religious experience, an experience born out of the despair, his nominalism and his disdain for the authority of a corrupt Church they brought him to. Unlike

Erasmus, who found in his will the freedom that allowed him "to apply himself to what concerns his salvation, or to turn deliberately aside from it," Luther found that he was corrupt throughout, that his will was in bondage to his self-love, and that he was not free, until through faith he had experienced the healing power of God's grace and found, through his gratitude and love for God for His forgiveness, deliverance from himself. Where Aquinas had spoken of the Church as the authority that guides man into virtue and knowledge of God, Luther now found that authority in his own immediate experience of the Scriptures. "It is clear then," he would argue, "that a Christian has all that he needs in faith and needs no works to justify him; and if he has no need of works, he has no need of laws; and if he has no need of law, he is free from the laws." "All of us who believe in Christ," he would say further, "are priests and kings."[9] While Luther was quick to insist that this did not mean we are earthly kings, that it did not mean we were outside the civil laws and the power of magistrates or that Christians should live outside of society, as the Anabaptists would argue, his convictions about Christian freedom would seem to point that way. The man who undergoes the kind of conversion Luther has undergone, who has discovered in his own experience the authority of God speaking, has indeed become a man unto himself, an individual in the most modern sense of that term, who can act with confidence and hope out of the strength of his own conscience. While, as the history of Luther and Calvin testify, the conviction of such men is so strong that they have trouble extending the same authority to other men, trouble believing that their experience of God is not the only authentic one, it does, once received as the basis of authority, create men who cannot live peacefully together except under conditions of religious freedom or tyranny.

Although Lutheranism had its immediate political effect in Germany, its most powerful effect was in the Swiss republics. The political effect has its origins in the difference between

Luther and the early Swiss reformer, Zwingli. Where Luther's thought originates in the question, "how can I be saved," Zwingli's thought arises out of his patriotism, out of the question, "How can my people, my nation, be saved?" His theology—he refused to call it Lutheran despite his basic agreement with Luther about the authority of the Scriptures—, therefore, applied to man's political and social relationships to an extent that Luther did not envision for his own. For him, as for Luther, man's "self-seeking, self-love," his "persistent affection for himself," is what alienates him from God and his fellow man. What he sought to create in Zurich and throughout Switzerland was a new society based on the Scriptures' revelation of Christ and the common bond of men who have experienced that revelation. The Word, he argued must be preached publicly; it must be made to dominate all men, believers and unbelievers, because it alone is valid and it alone can make a human society viable. This led him to introduce into Protestant thought the idea of the "watchman" or "over-seer," who is to keep the "mischievous goats under control." This as a function of the clergy is not in Luther, but it appears as an important aspect of Oecolapadius, Bucer, and Calvin, and it leads to the creation of a class of clerics who feel authorized by Scripture and their relationship with Christ to dominate all phases of human society.

Calvin brought what was implicit in Zwingli to full theological and social statement. Where Lutheran thought admitted the idea of Christian liberty and even moved later, under the influence of Melanchthon, toward essential agreement with Erasmus, Calvin made no such admission. For him, Scripture revealed the absolute power and glory of God, the power that was in His Law and the glory that was in His salvation of man through Christ. That law served not as a basis for freedom, not as a covenant through which God could freely enter into love and friendship with His creature man, but as a judge which convicted man and revealed the totality of his depravity. Although Calvin admitted that God permitted man freedom in the Garden, lest he convict God of originating evil, he denied that man had any freedom after his fall. Consequently, man was totally alienated from God and from his fellowman; he was a prisoner of his own conceit, and personal liberty was only an illusion that revealed how ignorant he was of his true condition. It was only through the glory of God—the regenerative power revealed in the Scriptures—that man could enter into relationship with God. Those Scriptures revealed that all was of God, that His will was absolute, and that those He chose to deliver from the despair of alienation, He chose. Those He chose could, by the illumination of the Holy Spirit, feel that choice working in them as the image of God within themselves, converting their will to His will (which in any case would be done). This working of God's will was Providence, which man, if he was not to live in alienation from God, must accept.

It was for Hooker, confronting those Puritans who had returned from the Genevan exile during the reign of Mary intent upon reforming the English church and society along Genevan lines, to perceive the dangers that Puritanism posed for liberty. If Shakespeare was frightened by the Machiavellians and the implications of Machiavellism, Hooker was frightened by the "Geneva men" and the implications of Calvinism. The same "Englishness" that lived in Shakespeare's bones, the same trust in English laws and institutions to preserve individual liberty, lived in Hooker's bones and resonates through his wonderful prose the way it resonates through Shakespeare's history plays.

All creation, he argued, is under the law, the Eternal Law which God has set down for Himself and through which He does all things, the Law of Natural Agents through which God rules irrational creatures, the Law of God for man, known through reason and confirmed by Scripture, and Positive Law by which in compliance with the Law of God for Man nations govern themselves. To attempt to organize society along purely biblical lines—to extend the laws for governing Israel to England on the basis that all behavior ought to be brought under the prescriptions of Scripture—was to ignore the role that reason played in the discovery of laws and experience has played in their enactment and maintenance. Positive laws exist because men do not always follow the Law of God, because reason is not always forceful enough to restrain them in their appetites. This Positive Law was enacted law, and it varies from country to country. Men enact it because when they enter into society they find they must restrain human depravity. To that end, they find they must have governments, and these governments enact laws. "Submission to government is voluntary, and the laws are valid only if the whole people assent to them."[10] But once men have become subjects of a government, they are not at liberty to dissolve it or disobey its Positive Laws. They may change these laws as new needs arise, but they must recognize that they are "the general and perpetual voice of men" and "as the sentence of God himself." Herein lies the continuity and the authority that society requires to maintain liberty and develop virtue among its people. The form of government best for the maintenance of liberty and virtue among people varies, according to the history of the people.

I hope that from these brief outlines of two significant sixteenth-century figures' responses to the advent of the modern world, you can get some sense of how the sixteenth century felt about liberty. With the exception of a few "advanced thinkers" like Rabelais, no one thought of liberty as being a good in itself. Although many saw that liberty was necessary to virtue—that it was derived from and obtained through right reason—no one thought a free life was necessarily a good life. Shakespeare, who wanted to retain what he thought was best in English life, looked to the familial, as the monarchy incorporates it in a nation's history, as the first line of defense against Machiavellism. He feared a world without authority as being purely opportunistic and ultimately self-destructive. Consequently, liberty meant something to him only in the context of authority. Hooker looked not so much to the authority of the familial as to the idea of Positive Law to define liberty. In this law he heard both the voice of reason and of human experience, speaking as the democratic voice of history, which is as the voice of God. Consequently, in resisting the authority of the "inner voice" of the Puritan reformer for the voice of Positive Law, he, like Shakespeare, laid the basis from which future conservatives would resist the reformer's radical transformations of society. Liberty, Yes, both men would affirm, but liberty within the context of authority.

## ENDNOTES

1. *The Human Condition*, Arendt, Hannah, University of Chicago Press (Chicago), 1958, pp. 79-247.
2. Pico Della Mirandola, Giovanni, "The Dignity of Man" in *The Portable Renaissance Reader*, ed. Ross, James, The Viking Press (New York), 1953, p. 474.
3. Erasmus, Desiderius, *The Enchiridion*, trans. Himelick, Raymond, Indiana University Press (Bloomington), 1963, pp. 38-40.
4. *Loc. cit.*
5. More, Thomas, *Utopia*, Harland Davidson (Arlington Heights, Ill), 1985, p. 5.
6. Pocock, J. G. A, *The Machiavellian Moment*, Princeton University Press (Princeton, N.J.), 1975, p. 37.
7. Hooker, Richard, *Of the Laws of Ecclesiastical Polity*, J. M. Dent and Sons (London), 1907, p. 77.
8. Luther, Martin, "On Christian Liberty," in *Discourse on Free Will*, trans., Ernst F. Winter, New York, Continuum, 1988.
9. *Ibid.*
10. Hooker, Richard, *Loc Cit.*

# Seventeenth Century:
# Thomas Hobbes and Emergent Modernity

I t is a formidable undertaking to follow Rufus Fears, Ralph McInerny, and George Martin in the Goodrich Lectures on the history of liberty. Moreover, I have been entrusted the task of expounding the emergence of modern liberty in the seventeenth century, a pivotal point in the history of political philosophy. What began to emerge then was a sharply distinguishable idiom of thinking that eventually came to be known as the liberal political tradition.

I shall examine Hobbes's political philosophy. Hobbes is an incomparably powerful, if stark, proponent of modern liberty, neither the most typical nor the most comfortable. Yet I believe that Hobbes is most revealing of what we need to think about.

There are two critical issues before us in our time when we speak of liberty: One is the issue of estrangement among individuals under the auspices of the impersonal state; the other is the radical repudiation of the rule of law by many who believe that the subordination of the rule of law is the means to overcoming estrangement or alienation among human beings. This combination of thoughts results from the fact that the hallmark of virtuous achievement in the liberal tradition is self-regulation. Self-regulation is centrally understood to mean self-imposed limitations on one's passion for self-fulfillment out of prudential regard for the necessity of living one's life in the society of others. The mark of virtue thus understood is willingness to associate under the rule of law.

For Hobbes, the rule of law was central. Nothing else could become possible without it, and it was this *sine qua non* that he considered the principal creative achievement of the covenant to erect a sovereign power which could actualize a legal order. In his view, law-abidingness is in itself a high moral accomplishment, dependent on the continuous willing by individuals to regulate their natural passions in favor of civil association.

In the more severe rejections of this view, such as those of Nietzsche or Marx, the rule of law is seen as a complex social institution that masks the domination of the strong over the weak, the intimidation of the strong by the collective power of the weak, or, speaking dialectically, both of these at once. Both Nietzscheans and Marxists would characterize their revolt as opposition to the indecisive middle world of ordinary politics. If there is to be a radical transformation rescuing us from this bourgeois mediocrity, it must entail the abandonment of the formality and civility of the rule-of-law polity. Philosophical grandeur has been lent these ideas through an existential vocabulary asserting that law-abidingness is merely acquiescence in the dailiness of life, a preference for the routine and inauthentic. The quest for authenticity has led, in turn, to a disparagement of the idea of liberty we have inherited from the seventeenth century. The notion of negative liberty, or freedom from restraint, without specification of a necessary end or good for man, is hard pressed to defend itself in light of the necessary indeterminacy that liberty in this sense seems to require.

Yet, one may wonder, why should the blessings of liberty not speak for themselves in the experience of the Western democracies today? What can explain the intellectual fascination with these radicalisms in our time, assuming we do not simply take their own diagnoses at face value?

In order to make some headway on these questions, I shall reprise a recent book, remarkable primarily for its poetic evocation of individual liberty as a burden in the modern state: Michael Ignatieff's *The Needs of Strangers* (1984). Mr Ignatieff exemplifies the proponent of liberalism who lives the anxieties of the twentieth century. He is fearful of abandoning the liberal political order, but he longs for an experience of community which the liberal political order seems incapable of supplying. In his experience of living surrounded by the "respectable poor" in central London, he discovers:

> a parable of moral relations between strangers in the welfare state. They have needs, and because they live within a welfare state, these needs confer entitle- ments—rights—to the resources of people like me...a silent relation between us. As we stand together in line at the post office, while they cash their pension cheques, some tiny portion of my income is trans- ferred into their pockets through the numberless capillaries of the state. The mediated quality of our relationship seems necessary to both of us. They are dependent on the state, not upon me, and we are both glad of it. Yet I am also aware of how this mediation walls us off from each other. We are responsible for each other, but we are not responsible to each other.[1]

Ignatieff goes on to say that this responsibility extends to basic necessities of survival but not to "love, respect, solidarity with others."[2] In order for a society to be decent and humane, he asserts, we need a "shared language of the good" which we currently do not possess. This expression of good seems to mean to Ignatieff the expression of mutual cooperation in a relation- ship not governed by merely transitory desires requiring transac- tions of calculated self-interest: "we are more," Ignatieff says,

than rights-bearing creatures, and there is more to

respect in a person than his rights. The administrative good conscience of our time seems to consist in respecting individuals' rights while demeaning them as persons. In the best of our prisons and psychiatric hospitals...the cuffs and clubs are kept in the guard house.... Yet every waking hour, inmates may feel the silent contempt of authority in a glance, gesture or procedure."[3]

These remarks remind us of a pattern of criticism, based on the same ambivalence toward modern liberal society, that may be traced back to its classic formulation in Rousseau's *Discourse on the Origins of Inequality*. There Rousseau attacked the politeness and civility of manners of modern European society. He took them as a disguise for the deep-seated indifference of modern individuals toward each other, even while, in their acquisitiveness, they draw themselves into ever tighter bonds of economic interdependency. The bonds of economic interest had replaced the bonds of self-sacrificing patriotism.

Since fraternity, love, belonging, dignity, and respect "cannot be specified as rights...we ought to specify them as needs and seek, with the blunt institutional procedures at our disposal, to make their satisfaction a routine human practice."[4] Yet on the other hand, Ignatieff forces himself to recall that politics is dangerous: "to mobilize a majority for change you must raise expectations and create needs which leap beyond the confines of existing reality. To create needs is to create discontent, and to invite disillusionment. It is to play with lives and hopes."[5]

What we would need, then, is a grasp on the good to legitimate this perilous political endeavor. This is necessary if only because what Ignatieff longs for cannot, he thinks, maintain the absolute priority of liberty:

In the end, a theory of human needs has to be premised

on some set of choices about what human beings need in order to be human: not what they need to be happy or free, since these are subsidiary goals, but what they need in order to realize the full extent of their potential.[6]

I take Ignatieff to be saying that modern liberty demands interdependency without dependency and this he sees as a form of estrangement or a substitution of formalities for intimacy. It is the liberal choice of liberty over solidarity.[7] But this choice requires that the political order remain "largely silent" on the "need for metaphysical "consolation and explanation" regarding the "purposes of our existence."[8] Thus we are caught between estrangement and utopia, "the dream of redemption of human tragedy through politics."[9]

Modern man hovers indecisively between understanding himself as free and understanding himself as estranged. He knows arguments on all sides of this dilemma and so remains resolutely irresolute. Indeed, Ignatieff is a perfect example of modern irresolution. He illustrates the pronounced modern habit of equating such irresolution with liberty: so long as nothing is decided, freedom abounds. I believe this goes a long way towards explaining why modern liberals are resistant to, but feel guilty or ashamed, about radical utopianism in politics.

To the extent this is true, the contemporary commitment to liberty is the acceptance of a lesser evil, a negative commitment to negative liberty—not a heartfelt affirmation. Liberty is defended for lack of something better.

But as in the declining days of the Roman Republic, the lesser evil of liberal individualism is made palatable only to the extent that we may enjoy the tranquility of untrammelled pursuit of private desires. The escape from civic duty is the release from the ordeal of consciousness, or from direct confrontation with the question of the purpose of human existence, and the duty to defend and promote what is positively good.

It is difficult to avoid the conclusion that the liberal tradition as formulated in the seventeenth century is in a state of dilapidation today. Some argue that the seeds of decline were sown in the beginning, and that the end of an episode in civilizational movement is inevitably unfolding. This is not how the great political thinkers of the seventeenth century understood themselves or their situation. Thus, let me turn to Hobbes in some detail.

In doing this, I shall be presenting a Hobbes somewhat unfamiliar to those who are used to the allegation of Hobbes's absolutism or authoritarianism and the hedonism of his political theory. In fact, for Hobbes the rule of law was central. Numerous passages in his major works proclaim this. This is revealed also when we recognize that for Hobbes the crucial point of human experience was the tension between the natural man and the civil man, and the difficulty of resolving this tension. What Hobbes saw was that these were differing images through which a man could understand himself. Moreover, both of these are plausible images, eligible to fit with human experience. Hobbes did not think one without the other adequately characterized the human condition.

It is clear to everyone that the modern understanding emphasizes the individual and subjective freedom. But the freedom of the individual is complicated by the fact that it has continually been interpreted in two different ways which are in tension with each other.

Let us recall that Plato understood justice as good form which may be present among the members of the city whether they understand it or not. A well-formed character may be inculcated upon an intellectually passive recipient. Hobbes, and most modern political philosophers, have begun from the premise of the natural freedom of every human being: the individual must understand what he is to accept, and accept it only if he understands it. His freedom is completed only in obedience which is freely given and his subscription to duty is the display of a freedom that is moral. It is this willing self-regulation, or moral freedom, that suggests a link between the ancient emphasis on duty and the loftiest form of the modern aspiration to self-fulfillment. Clearly this notion of freedom that is moral cannot be defined merely as the satisfaction of material desires. And it is hard to see how the modern idea of the rule of law could ever have enjoyed profound development, or actually have been achieved, if natural freedom had been understood only in terms of material satisfaction. In the modern preoccupation with rights, it tends to be forgotten that there is a modern conception of moral duty. It is this latter that receives Hobbes's attention and it is essential to his theory of man's capacity to undergo a creative self-transformation into a rule-of-law polity which Hobbes called a commonwealth.

With us also, of course, there is the freedom of desire, the liberty that obtains, as Hobbes put it, where the law is silent, often referred to as economic freedom, whose logic is elaborated in the science of economics. It is unfortunate that this conception of freedom has tended to dominate much of modern thought at the expense of the other conception. The result has been to mislead the critics of liberalism into thinking that its principal achievement has been economic growth rather than the rule of law, and that property rights are the special interest of a few rather than a necessary feature of the dispersion of power. What may be worse is the capacity of the liberal tradition to mislead itself on these matters.

In fact, the modern political order has never been able to synthesize economic freedom and moral freedom, and it would appear to be antithetical to the genius of the modern political order to choose between them. The modern political order remains, therefore, in continual tension between the call of conscience which understands freedom as liberation from desire, and patronizing spontaneous desire as the essence of self-discovery. Moral freedom realizes itself in acknowledging rules as authentic stipulations of the conditions to be observed in our conduct. Acknowledging the rules proclaims us as worthy of respect and instills a sense of mutual confidence overcoming and replacing the natural diffidence Hobbes specified as a central feature of the natural condition of mankind. From the perspective of moral freedom, then, rules are not only not impediments to freedom; they are indispensable conditions for us to display our capacity for self-regulation, to show we are not merely natural beings driven by impersonal and automatic forces and processes.

From the point of view of economic freedom, authority and rules are a convenience, useful to protect our private adventures, and we judge them with respect to the advancement of our self-chosen definitions of satisfaction. Moral freedom discovers intrinsic worth in subscription to rules, economic freedom judges rules in terms of advantage and disadvantage. Economic freedom scruples less to look beyond the rules because they are devices of convenience.

Now it is clear that the modern tradition distinguishes itself primarily by the promotion of economic freedom to a respectable status. In short, the liberal tradition necessarily creates the tension between moral freedom and economic freedom, and it does so willingly. The liberal tradition assumes that the passions in man can be channeled in an orderly fashion into interests which may be pursued rationally and not chaotically, that there is reason in the passions and not just above and beyond them. This is symbolized in the great metaphor of the "invisible hand." In Hobbes this is summarized in the twenty laws of nature, or maxims of rational conduct, which, as Hobbes tells it, must be apparent on reflection to any person of ordinary ability. In any case, if the ordinary person does not see them, he has but to read the *Leviathan* to find them out.

Every human being is henceforth the repository of *both* civil duty and individual desire. The possibility of moral self-overcoming is constituted on the foundation of passionate, desiring existence. Every human being is simultaneously a desiring being and a moral agent, caught between the satisfaction of duty and satisfaction of desire. The genius of Hobbes's political theory lies in his insistence that every human being can creatively reconcile these in a stable character, that both moral freedom and economic freedom are forms of *self-realization*. In order to see this, let us briefly again consider ancient political philosophy:

In Plato's *Republic*, the best city is ordered by maintaining the separate existences of the guardians and the producers. There is an absolute distinction between the rulers as such and the ruled as such. Alternatively, Aristotle's *Politics* speaks of the statesman as one who learns to combine his ability with the insights essential to ruling in terms of the way of life of his city. In either case, the ruler opens his soul to an order that carries him beyond himself in order to become a lawgiver or a policy maker. For both Plato and Aristotle, the economic or producing man is restricted to making objects, providing the means of subsistence. These are ways of life that, because they inhere in different kinds of people, can be held together in a unified city only by the artistic devices of the founder or the prudential practices of rulers who seek to avert each element of the city from carrying its own outlook to an independent, logical conclusion. Failing these arrangements, the philosophic souls will refuse to rule and will not be asked to rule. Economic souls will be moved by momentary caprice. As Socrates says, the mortal possessions will dominate the divine possessions, and the cycle of corruption will relentlessly unfold.

But political life is neither the life of speculative insight or philosophy, nor is it the life of productivity. Political life is an unresolved in-between, a world of clashing opinions, pulled by a golden string towards the divine beyond politics, and by an iron rod towards the beasts. The political is the revelation of the

human tragedy in which one can imagine release but cannot have it. But the tradition from Hobbes onward turns to redeeming what is rejected in the *Republic*: the theory of the social contract. The redemption consists in showing that reason is immanent in human passions and not merely imposed upon them. It became necessary to show that the highest human achievement is self-regulation and not conformity to an independent order knowable only through speculative ascent or indirectly through the inculcation of an unreflective habit. Aristotle certainly adumbrated such a morally virtuous man in the *Nicomachean Ethics*, but it remains for the modern theorists of liberty to see this possibility in every human being.

In this respect, the moderns were catalyzed by Christianity. It was argued that rationality is immanent in the creation of a rational creator, one who wished his creature, man, to continue and to complete, through human endeavor, the intention of the creation itself. For the tradition explaining nature's economy, running from Hobbes and Locke to Adam Smith and beyond, the logic of the passions or the theory of moral sentiments, and delineating the virtuous self were taken to be tasks amounting to the maturation of man in assuming full responsibility for completing the divine intention.

In this respect, it was never a logical necessity for Enlightenment to deny the divine ground of order, even though the exploration of that order was increasingly transposed into a vocabulary of impersonal operations generated by the rise of modern science. But even the power of science itself was associated with the capacity of man to assume a cooperative role in the divine activity. The extremity of this self-understanding revealed itself in Hegel's claim to have discovered how to make accessible to human understanding the essential meaning of providence through an account of history as the immanent culmination of God's intention through human action.

Human dignity become a project to be achieved, urged on by

developing
evolving ORDER

the noble task of completing the order of creation itself. Man is that undetermined element that is entrusted with the responsibility of perfecting himself. Thus our dignity and virtue can no longer be seen as conformity to or imitation of a pre-existing pattern. Rather, human beings must imagine order and then bring it into being. We must submit ourselves to a pattern we have created, and which we find worthy. This is not so much a light from nature as a creative interpretation of nature's possibilities. Whatever this achievement may turn out finally to be, it will come about only through a process of repeated trial and error. We are put in charge of ourselves as beings who legislate for themselves within the limits of nature's economy and the lessons of historical experience.

Each self becomes an experimental offering to the universally shared task of self-understanding. There is a hope and an expectation but no prospect of immediate fulfillment. It is a condition neither individualist nor collectivist, but a dynamic field of action polarized by individual and collectivity, in which the human spirit wills to maintain without end the polarity. The self is the specific focus of this polar tension bound to other selves by an acquired mode of discourse which may be called the great human conversation.

From this modern perspective, Plato does not seem to have a notion of self, or, if he does, it is not the organizing feature of political order. For Plato it is transcendence of self that is the harbinger of rational order. Transcendence of self is not identical to self-regulation.

Hobbes calls law the word of him who has the right to command. The right to command is constituted through consent. But the natural person who transforms himself into a subject under authority is, in consenting, providing himself the opportunity to subscribe to order. The premises of this transformation are two: First, the man who turns himself into subject shows he cannot do without laws and that he knows this; second, he shows that he can understand the character of law—that it is general and impersonal for example—so that he can distinguish between what is obligatory and what is not. The self generates its own limitation in consenting to law-making authority, but makes the opposition fruitful and positive in acknowledging the rational necessity of such limitation.

This all is to be done, according to Hobbes, not in terms of an extrinsic end or goal to which the law is subordinated, but for the sake of having law or self-regulation itself. The choice of the law is not founded on a hoped-for promotion of private desires, although it may be true that law is a necessary force for that order without which private desires cannot safely be pursued. Thus, in common understanding, there may be a variety of motives that encourage law-abidingness. Hobbes is content to live with the fact that a mixture of motives between moral freedom and economic freedom is the usual case. He did not seek a Kantian transformation in terms of moral freedom alone, nor a Marxian transformation in terms of which the dichotomous motives of the material and spiritual spheres would somehow simply be superseded. Also, now the ruler and the ruled belong to the same class of humanity. They differ only with respect to office. Obedience to authority is not servitude but a demonstration of the cooperative capacity through commonly shared reason to order the polity—to establish fixity in the midst of contingency. The constituted authority is the device through which our own aspirations to order may be concretely actualized.

The law must be posited because it cannot come into being in any other way. It is the fundamental contingency of human existence that drives us to posit something as necessary for us. By authorizing someone to posit law we are able to reconcile desire with conscience which is impossible in the state of nature. The question is not of the superiority of reason to desire, but rather of the cooperative union of reason with desire. Law proceeds from human willing, then, but what will prevent law from mere arbitrariness?

First, the character of law is knowable to all alike; no one has any natural authority or special insight that others do not have. Second, it is reasonable to expect that rulers will act consistently with their own commands. Even if sovereignty is absolute, it is not the function of sovereignty to override its own ordinations, just as the absolute power of God is not employed for the purpose of spreading chaos in the order of the universe. Third, as Hobbes conceived law, its functions were quite limited and the subjects of law must be expected to apply the law in their peculiar circumstances. Hobbes was no great admirer of standing armies. Quite to the contrary, he believed that his commonwealth would preclude the need of them. The genius of Hobbes's idea of political order is not the discovery of a device to remove contingency from the human condition, but the teaching of a form of self-understanding that will make the contingent manageable. Hobbes proclaimed his intention to show not "what is law here, and there; but what is law; as Plato, Aristotle, Cicero and divers others have done... "[10] Hobbes wants to elucidate the ideal character of law. Hobbes also distinguished "authority" which is a right to act from "dominion" which is a right to possess. The sovereign may act *vis-à-vis* his subjects but he does not own them. And in a little noticed passage Hobbes advances a remarkable theological demonstration of the necessity of this authority. Speaking of the fall of Adam and Eve, Hobbes says,

> Whereupon having both eaten, they did indeed take upon them God's office, which is judicature of good and evil; but acquired no new ability to distinguish between them aright.

The moral is that mankind may rebel against divine authority, but mankind cannot live on earth without order, and they cannot have order without authority. To rebel against divine authority, therefore, forces man to invent surrogate authority. But if we were then to rebel against that authority too, an authority we have constituted by our own agreement in recognition of an insurmountable need, we act absurdly and repeat the original fall from grace all over again:

> Whereby it is clearly, though allegorically signified, that the commands of them that have the right to command, are not by their subjects to be censured, nor disputed.[11]

Hobbes, of course, wants laws that are good and not merely just in the sense of being promulgated by duly constituted authority. But whether or not we are fortunate enough to get good laws, we cannot live without some order of justice. It is the curse of Adam that this is so, and I believe this indicates the Augustinianism that is latent in Hobbes's whole way of thinking. We are free to choose a way of life, but we are not free to know that it is simply the right way. Moreover, the sustenance of a way of life is in the fact that we will it to be, for the foundation in paradise has been lost and we have been allowed to go on our own. This is the promise, but also the ordeal, of freedom.

Thus, laws laid down by a duly authorized sovereign cannot be merely rational. Reason can comprehend the human predicament, but reason does not know how to reconcile the necessity of justice to good in an indisputable way. Thus, law must proceed from will as much as from reason.

That this is so need not be taken as a discouraging sign, however. Whereas Plato theorized the relation of reason and desire as a matter of arranging, in objective hierarchy, different classes of men, in the modern state reason and desire come together in the self-determining operation of the individual subject. Hobbes never forgot nor abandoned this insight. There is nothing more real to him than the individual.

Hobbes's vision of commonwealth was based on full awareness of the tenuous bonds of all civil associations wherein the natural man lurks behind the self-imposed civil personality. He was fully cognizant of the dependency of political authority on consent.

It is true, as everyone knows, that Hobbes gave prominence to the motive of fear in men removing themselves from the state of nature. But Hobbes also knew that if the only basis for civil association was fear, then the life of a man in the society of others would be reduced to incessant calculations about when one would have to observe law and when one could break it.

This latter is not Hobbes's view, but rather the view of Glaucon and Adeimantus in Book II of Plato's *Republic*. They assert that what men call justice is a mere compromise for the fearful between doing as they please without penalty and having to suffer at the hands of others without hope of revenge.

I think it is exactly this view which Hobbes hoped to remove through his account of the dignifying self-transformation that individuals undertake when they covenant with each other to create a commonwealth. The covenant becomes the symbol of the power of the self to transform itself into a civic being without losing its natural identity. Fear is unquestionably a spur, but it is reason that imagines the stability to be created in the midst of contingency. This is a lofty achievement for a being which, though given freedom and equipped with reason, is nonetheless lacking in the divine wisdom necessary to unify the "good" with the "just."

The authority of sovereignty is absolute but not natural. The right to give law is absolute in the sense that it is not limited by the idiosyncratic motives of the different individuals that induced them as individuals to covenant with each other at the outset. The covenant is not conditional upon the sovereign making this or that particular law or the law that I would like to have, but only upon the sovereign giving what is law. The independence of the sovereign results from the fact that the covenanters all know the logical requirements of the covenant. Motives are personal and individual but the reasoning of covenant is universal. Thus the conscious self becomes self-conscious or, in Hobbes's own terms, learns to "read in himself, not this or that particular man; but mankind."[12]

In short, economic or desiring motives are combined with the idea of self-regulation or moral freedom in order for the covenant to succeed. The association thus covenanted may both stand above the private aims of individuals and yet leave the private aims intact. The latter need not be suppressed, but nor are they the only considerations that can attract a human being. The covenant proclaims that the self-interested beings can also be self-limiting beings.

The rule of law cannot be properly comprehended, nor the real foundation of commonwealth revealed, until the individual includes in his sense of fulfillment the possibility of moral duty. Of course, it is true that there is a tendency to think in terms of desire rather than duty. That tendency must remain present, for it is this tendency than the will to overcome it that makes possible the moral individual. The price of this moral achievement is the continual risk of falling away from it. We are responsible agents and the commonwealth rests on no surer foundation than the possibility that we can act responsibly.

It is true that Hobbes, like most theorists of modern political order, emphasizes "peace" and "prosperity" as the common enjoyments of the commonwealth. But these desiderata have no specific and fixed meanings. They are not the "products" produced by adherence to law and authority. There are no unarguable definitions of these or any other goods. They are goods in the abstract. Political life is an endless debate over the connection between actual states of affairs and these abstract desirabilities. The real moral achievement, for Hobbes, is adherence to the rule of law among a set of people who disagree forever on the final definition of goods or the good. The most admirable man for

Hobbes, though not likely to be found in large numbers, is the one who is so gallant as to need no other reason than the preservation of his self-respect and sense of honor to keep his promises.

To conclude, I must return to the issues with which I began: the sense of estrangement and the repudiation of the rule of law. To some who think on these things it seems necessary to choose: either the rule of law plus estrangement or else communal intimacy and abandonment of the rule of law. For many, the momentous nature of such a decision is paralyzing and they seek a compromise in a vaguely unsatisfying makeshift.

In part, the dissatisfaction emanates from the residual memory of the ancient and medieval strictures on material desires, on acquisitiveness, and the admonition to self-sacrifice. In part, as Hobbes himself said, learning to read mankind in oneself is harder to learn than any language or science. What is so hard to learn is that no one possesses any natural authority, and yet no one can pick and choose his obligations even though he must choose to be obligated. When Hobbes said this was hard to learn I think he meant it was hard to live in full and continuous commitment to the validity of these principles. Individual responsibility to reconcile duty and desire is a constant endeavor. While we are alive it cannot come to an end. Some commentators have insisted that with the emergence of the modern concept of liberty we lowered our aspirations. From the perspective of the proponents of modern liberty, however, we have taken on an awesome commitment.

## ENDNOTES

1. Ignatieff, 9-10.
2. *Ibid.*, 15.
3. *Ibid.*, 13.
4. *Ibid.*, 14, p. 3.
5. *Ibid.*, 12, p. 3.
6. *Ibid.*, 15, p. 3.

7. *Ibid.*, 18, p. 4.
8. *Ibid.*, 19, p. 4.
9. *Ibid.*, 19, p. 4.
10. *Leviathan*, Ch. 26, p. 172.
11. *Ibid.*, Ch. 20, p. 135; Ch. 26, p. 173.
12. *Ibid.*, Intro., p. 6.

# Eighteenth Century:
# Montesquieu and America

## William B. Allen

How we regard the birth of liberty in North America greatly influences our appreciation of its value today. Scholarship has long and rightly portrayed its origins in traditions antedating the American Revolution. They derive it from the English Common Law, and see in the American founding a confirmation of that tradition of English law and custom. The colonists are regarded as having gradually acquired the arts of independent self-government from the historic practices of English indulgence. In that light, they have seen the Revolution as a break from English administration of the colonies, rather than as a decisive advance in theory and principles of self-government. Accordingly, they have systematically discounted the influences of thinkers—English, Scottish, and continental—in originating the Revolution. Rather, they insist, Whiggish activists borrowed the rhetoric of their English cousins to defend their unparalleled exertions on behalf of independence, but with little idea whatsoever of a way of life other than that for which colonial experience had prepared them.

There is considerable truth in this account, inasmuch as the Americans treasured most highly the rights and liberties of Englishmen. They began to defend and articulate their rights to life, liberty, and estates from the earliest date. The 1646 case of Robert Childs, *et al.* testifies powerfully to this history, and not alone. We would be neglectful, however, if we failed to note that these early challenges were generally directed toward colonial exercises of power—as was the rhetoric of Patrick Henry in the Parson's fee case of the late 1750s. In short, it was in the context of seeking out limitations on the colonial exercise of power that Americans so frequently and habitually invoked their ancient rights under the British constitution. This process reached its peak in the use made of the work *English Liberties*, by Henry Care. It was no accident, to be sure, that Care was probably the most radical of post-settlement Whigs. Yet he did not go far enough for the Americans. In the case of men like Sam Adams, his virulent anti-popery survived far better than his scholarly reliance on English law.

Accordingly, contemporary scholarship is wrong in its central claim—namely, that prior to the Revolution Americans did not meaningfully divide over questions of rights and liberties. They are also wrong to minimize the influence of modern political philosophy in the direction that debate ultimately took. Not only was it the case that the British Constitution ceased to offer adequate authority from the moment the imperial power itself came into question (the evidence for which may be gleaned from the Massachusetts General Court's instructions to its British agent, Jasper Mauduit, in 1762, which instructions elevated John Locke above immemorial usage).[1] It is more dramatically the case that Americans well before, in small groups to be sure, began to search for a more express articulation of the foundations of liberty. In the late 1740s a small group in Massachusetts, Sam Adams at its center, had already opened the quest—prior to the outbreak of the Seven Years' War and well before the questioning of imperial power. They published a short-lived but frankly political journal, taking North America and Americans, not just Massachusetts, as the natural arena and objects of their efforts.

One member of this group, Daniel Fowle, provides the most dramatic evidence of the direction in which their thoughts turned. Fowle's work from 1754-1756 remains extant, though it

Fowle

has apparently been only rarely consulted. It is perhaps the first comprehensive discussion of the principles of government, in the tradition of the literature of the Revolution, written and published by an American. Fowle's *A Total Eclipse of Liberty* bridges the old and new worlds; aimed at exposing abuses of power in Massachusetts, it celebrates the English constitution and English liberties. At the same time, however, Fowle explicitly introduces reason and the "poor dim light of nature" as the standards of political judgment.[2] It is therefore no accident that his short essay contains all the essential forms and objectives of Revolutionary rhetoric, including the robust version of the consent of the governed and an express assertion of the right of revolution.

Where did Fowle derive the principles of his analysis? Primarily from the philosophical traditions of the west, including the eighteenth-century enlightenment and continental thought. Inasmuch as my particular concern is to discuss the status of liberty in the eighteenth century—and that primarily of Montesquieu—this last point is the one to which I will draw ultimate attention. Before I take up that direct discussion, however, I wish to set forth with some clarity the significance of Fowle's essay and its exact content (which, I believe, is no longer familiar to any scholar apart from my wife and myself).

I derive the significance of Fowle's work indirectly. Scholars like Spurlin and Lutz have conducted exhaustive surveys of Revolutionary and colonial thought for indications of intellectual antecedents. Spurlin considered Montesquieu alone, while Lutz surveyed the whole range of moral and philosophical literature. They agree on the enormous significance of Montesquieu, but largely confine his influence to a point when the direction of the Revolution had already been set. Lutz's more recent and more accurate work demonstrates Montesquieu's great importance but expressly maintains that the *Spirit of the Laws* served as a reference source in a context where, confronted with an accomplished Revolution and needing to establish a government, the founders were searching for guidance. In short, Montesquieu did not inspire the Revolution; he only provided much needed practical advice after it had occurred. Spurlin and Lutz agree: Montesquieu appeared in America only after 1760 and then mainly in the 1780s. This judgment was certainly a reasonable one from all direct and indirect evidence. In terms of direct evidence, we cannot find advertisements for Montesquieu's works prior to the 1760s and have few, if any, records of its being offered for sale. Further, few persons have ever uncovered citations prior to that period. In terms of indirect evidence, America was not exactly on the intellectual main line. While Montesquieu took Europe and England by storm, it is not unrealistic to think that a work published effectively in 1749 and translated into English in 1750 might take a few years to penetrate the less developed corners of the world. In fact, however, Daniel Fowle's essay reproduced extensive citations from the book in 1754. How early he saw it—and he refers to the book, not to someone else's citation—we are as yet unable to judge. Clearly, however, he saw it early. Further, he published an important part of it to his countrymen. The cause of liberty had a boost from the continent long before the King and parliament had become liberty's enemies. That is the significance of Fowle's work.

As to the content of *A Total Eclipse of Liberty*,[3] I am now required to tell Fowle's story. A printer-publisher in Boston, he was summoned before the Lower House of Assembly on 24 October, 1754 to answer questions concerning a publication entitled "Monster of Monsters." The House considered the anonymous piece a libel on itself and wished to find and punish those responsible. Fowle denied that he either authored or printed the piece. He admitted that he had handled it, receiving some ten copies which he offered for sale. He was vague about his knowledge of the source, indicating only that the pamphlets had been delivered to him by some youth, presumably employed by the printer. There was some indication that Fowle's brother, Zechariah, and a Royal Tyler were involved, but he did not say so squarely. In the end the House remanded him to the common jail, pending further word from the Speaker. There was no finding of guilt and no formal presentation of charges. But Fowle was jailed, and there began his work, *A Total Eclipse of Liberty*. He succeeded in writing only a few pages before pen and paper were removed from him. He spent forty-eight hours confined in the stone jail, and another three days in the jailer's quarter, during which time his distraught wife lost her health and miscarried. Fowle complained bitterly of this *"unheard of attack upon the Liberty of an Englishman*, than which scarcely anything is dearer, if he has but the spirit of a Man...." In his own words, the experience seemed thus:

> I had no bed to lodge on, but a pillow and one blanket. I walked about, and when tired sat down, and heard the Clock strike every Time from 12 till eight. There is but one Window, and that without anything to keep off the Weather, as there is only several Iron Bars, no Winder-shut, which the *Murderer was favour'd with*. The Place *stunk prodigiously*, which oblig'd me to tye my Handkerchief over my Mouth and Nose, for fear of being *suffocated*: worse than the *Smell of Brimstone*. I heard no Noise for some considerable Time; *All Nature seem'd to be dead*; the first stiring of any Thing I could hear, was the Noise of Rats, which seem'd to be of a prodigious size....[4]

After forty-eight hours of this Fowle was removed to the jailer's quarters, where an order was received commanding that he be released privately. Upon this news he responded, "I now desire that the same Authority that put me in, would by virtue of that same Power take me out, and not thrust me out privily."

On October 28th Fowle remained a prisoner, whereupon, in his account, he inserted a lengthy extract from "that approved piece," Montesquieu's *Spirit of the Laws*. He used those passages which recur throughout the founding era, culminating in *Federalist* number 47 in 1788. As he transcribed them, evidently from the translation of Thomas Nugent but corrected here and there against the French original, they read thus:

> The [political] Liberty of the Subject is a Tranquility of Mind, arising from the Opinion each Person hath of his safety. In order to have this Liberty, it is requisite the Government be so constituted as *one man* need not be *afraid of another*....
>
> When the Legislative and Executive Powers are *united in the same Person*, or in the same *Body of Magistrates*, there can be no *Liberty*; because Apprehensions may arise least the same Monarch or Senate should enact *tyrannical Laws*, to execute them in a tyrannical Manner.
>
> Again, There is no Liberty, if the *Power of Judging* be not *separated* from the Legislative, the Life and Liberty of the Subject would be exposed to *arbitrary Controul*; for the *Judge* would be the *Legislature*. Were it joined to the *Executive Power*, the Judge might behave with all the Violence of an Oppressor [violence and oppression].
>
> There would be *an End of every Thing*, were the same Man, or the *same Body*, whether of the Nobles or of the People, to exercise these three Powers, that of *enacting Laws*, that of *executing the Publick Resolutions*, and that of *judging the Crimes* or Differences of Individuals [trying the causes of individuals].[5]

Placed in the context of Fowle's ordeal, we should have less difficulty to hear the apocalyptic and revolutionary nature of Montesquieu's teaching. Where liberty (he had said "political liberty," but Fowle altered it) is not assured, man must fear man; without the separation of powers, laws will be tyrannically framed and executed; without separation of powers, judges act with all the violence of an oppressor (he corrected Nugent's "violence and oppression"); and everything would collapse if the different powers were exercised by the same man or men.

In fact, in colonial America as in Montesquieu's France, it was commonplace to find the powers of government promiscuously mixed. The case of Robert Keayne in Massachusetts, at a hundred years removed, but not very different in form from Fowle's case, testifies to this. Accordingly, these radical claims about the danger to liberty constitute as much an indictment in the one case, America, as in the other case, France. Moreover, even as Fowle celebrates English liberty, he has learned from this Frenchman of radical defects in that liberty. Hence, he is at the start of that train of reflections which produced the American Revolution and introduced a new, non-customary standard for the defense of Liberty. What is of great interest in this story is the fact that Montesquieu was also the last Enlightenment thinker on the continent who could have left such a legacy. In the very year Fowle wrote, Montesquieu completed the definitive version of his classical work and then died. In that same year, Jean Jacques Rousseau published his *Discourse on the Origins of Inequality Among Men*, which opened the modern assault on nature as a moral standard and natural rights as a source of political principles.

True, for Rousseau man was good in nature—if to be good it suffices to be peaceful and stupid. But that is the point: man in nature is not the man we know. The man we know, Rousseau held, is wicked. What changed him? "only the changes occurring in his structure, the progresses he had made and the knowledge

free but everywhere in chain.

which he has acquired."[6] Thus, in the "Second Discourse," in footnote "I," Rousseau repeats the critique he had offered in the "First Discourse on Science and the Arts":

> It was not without difficulty that we succeeded in making ourselves so unhappy. When one considers, on the one hand, all the prodigious labors of men, so many profound sciences, so many invented arts, so much strength applied, abysses filled in, mountains levelled, rocks crushed, rivers made navigable, land cleared, lakes dug out, swamps dried up, enormous buildings erected on land, the sea covered with vessels and sailors, and when, on the other hand, one investigates with but little meditation the true advantages which have resulted from all this for the happiness of humankind, one can only be struck by the astonishing disproportion which exists between these things and deplore man's blindness... Admire human society as much as one may, it will be no less true that it necessarily inclines men to despise one another in proportion as their interests intersect....[7]

This art alone, this capacity for progress, for self-perfection, is the sole distinguishing characteristic of man for Rousseau. And it is a sufficiently ambiguous distinction that there is room to wonder where man begins and orangutan ends—or whether African cannot mate with orangutan. It is on this ground that Rousseau entertained the idea of a progressive development of humanity. The very uncertainty of humanity's identity renders a reliance on nature as a guide impossible. There could not be a more complete contrast with Daniel Fowle, who assumed not only that he could recognize men, but

That all Men are so *Just*, that not any one *individual*

would do any Thing he imagin'd injurious to his Neighbor, but that they were only liable to some Mistakes about their own and others' Rights....[8]

The contrast was produced by the Enlightenment's inclination to follow in the paths of Galileo and Descartes, in the paths of natural science.

We can discern the threat to liberty in this approach by considering its effect on Thomas Jefferson's thought in the context of America, where Jefferson tried to mate natural science and freedom. He, more than any other founder, was profoundly influenced by the European Enlightenment, and the result was some confusion in his own mind as to the force of American principles in the context of natural history. The confusion was sufficiently great that he almost repudiated the truths of the Declaration of Independence.

Jefferson's position, stated most forcefully in the *Notes on the State of Virginia*, has long been misunderstood and abused by scholars, who have accused him of being simply a racist. The controversy centers in an exchange Jefferson had with Benjamin Banneker. The case: Banneker's impassioned appeal of August 19, 1791 was that Jefferson (as Secretary of State as well as author of the Declaration) exert himself to remove the baseless prejudice of an inherent inferiority of black people. For the purpose Banneker condescended to make himself an exhibit. While he did not appeal to the instance of his producing an almanac, the formal occasion of his letter was to transmit that philosophical effort to a kindred soul. Thus, the implication was unavoidable that Banneker considered this a case made; his mathematical and astronomical abilities were the acquisitions of his race. He appealed to Jefferson, therefore, to join in procuring for black people "their promotion from any state of degradation to which the unjustifyable cruelty and barbarism of men may have reduced them." Banneker attributed the entire prejudice concerning the blacks' lack of "mental endowment" to the enforced brutishness of slavery.[9]

Jefferson responded by immediately recognizing the almanac as the "proofs you exhibit, that nature has given to our black brethren, talents equal to the other colors of men," although Banneker had treated the transmission as incidental and even apologized for including the messages in the one letter. Moreover, Jefferson saw the exhibit as aimed at the prejudice of color, with the distinction that Jefferson derived it not only from slavery but from the "degraded condition of their existence, both in Africa and America."[10] Jefferson, therefore, rejected Banneker's claim that the whole cause of black imbecility was American despotism. Much like Rousseau, he had *public*, if speculative, doubts about the place of the black man in the chain of being.

This story actually begins with Jefferson's *Notes*, in which he pondered whether black men were not inferior to whites. Scholars have assailed first the passages in the *Notes* and then Jefferson's response to Banneker (as well as later correspondence) as evidence of his indelible prejudice. They overlook in the *Notes* his prayer that matters stand other than they seemed.[11] The later charges center on the fact that Jefferson allegedly wrote in a private letter to Joel Barlow (some say Benjamin Rush, mistakenly) and questioned whether "Banneker had done the almanac or that any black man could have."[12] The implication has been that Jefferson spoke differently to his "white equal" than to Banneker, as well as differently in public and private. Obviously, the *Notes* are every bit as public as the Declaration was, and at the least Jefferson is exculpated from the charge of hypocrisy. We are concerned to know whether he is equally exculpated from the charge of confusion.

Jefferson returned to these questions in a letter to Joel Barlow on October 8, 1809. He wrote concerning a Frenchman who had assumed the mission to prove black capacities, having taken up

Rousseau's challenge. I quote at length:

> He wrote to me also on the doubts I had expressed five
> or six and twenty years ago in the Notes on Virginia,
> as to the grade of understanding of the negroes, and he
> sent me his book on the literature of the negroes. His
> credulity has made him gather up every story he could
> find of men of color, (without distinguishing whether
> black, or of what degree of mixture,) however slight
> the mention, or light the authority on which they
> quoted. The whole do not amount, in point of evi-
> dence, to what we know ourselves of Banneker. We
> know he had trigonometry enough to make almanacs,
> but not without the suspicion of aid from Ellicot, who
> was his neighbor and friend [and employer, in laying
> out Washington, D.C.], and never missed an oppor-
> tunity of puffing him. I have a long letter from
> Banneker, which shows him to have had a mind of
> very common stature indeed.[13]

Here, of course, Jefferson accepts Banneker's authorship, while
retaining the suspicion that he was aided in the work. More
importantly, he takes what little he finds in Banneker's mind as
evidence sufficient as to "the grade of understanding of the
negroes." What grade was that: "a mind of very common stature
indeed." The term of reference for this "common stature," of
course, has to be the intellectual attainments of white folk, since
the questions grow out of the suspicion that the black mind was
inferior to the common.

Some scholars have imagined this phrase to imply defect,
inferiority. They read the word "common" to mean base or vulgar
(certainly a possible meaning), and there differ from me, who
recalls the euclidean term "common notion" as the critical

linchpin in constructing the intellectual edifice of geometry. That is, what Jefferson sought in every black mind was not evidence of genius but of ordinary intelligence, intelligence sufficient to warrant confidence that the axioms of nature would command the souls of ordinary black folk as they do those of ordinary white folk. That must be the level of intelligence of the common intellect, else the "consent of the governed" will lose all intelligibility. Here, then, is where confusion enters, for this is the light in which *Notes on the State of Virginia*, querying whether freed blacks could become citizens, developed Jefferson's doubts as forcefully and publicly as those doubts are ever developed anywhere. I give the relevant text:

> In general, their existence appears to participate more of sensation than reflection.... An Animal whose body is at rest, and who does not reflect, must be disposed to sleep of course. Comparing them by their faculties of memory, reason, and imagination, it appears to me, that in memory they are equal to the whites; in reason much inferior, as I think one could scarcely be found capable of tracing and comprehending the investigations of Euclid...
>
> * * * * *
>
> ...not withstanding these and other discouraging circumstances among the Romans, their slaves were often their rarest artists. They excelled too in science, insomuch as to be usually employed as tutors to their master's children...not their condition then, but nature, has produced the distinction. —Whether further observation will or will not verify the conjecture, that nature has been less bountiful to them in the endowments of the head....

* * * * *

To justify a general conclusion, requires many observations, even where the subject may be submitted to
the anatomical knife.... How much more then where
it is a faculty, not a substance, we are examining; where
it eludes the research of all the senses; ...let me add too,
as a circumstance of great tenderness, where our
conclusion would degrade a whole race of men from
their rank in the scale of beings which the Creator may
perhaps have given them.... I advance it therefore as a
suspicion only, that the blacks...are inferior to the
whites in the endowment both of body and mind.[14]

In light of these passages everything should become clear.
Jefferson's disagreement with Banneker over the source of black
degradation derived from Jefferson's own confidence in the
sufficiency of natural history to answer that question. Only
natural history could provide such an answer as would remove
the truth beyond mere political taste or sentiment. It would have
been foolish to embrace the equality of blacks and whites, if to
do so were to entail the denial of the natural rights on which the
laws of free men were based. Such a result would have had to
follow, if the political union of blacks and whites had to be forced
against the evidences of natural history. If the souls of black folk
could not be commanded by the axioms of nature, their political
union with whites could not be based on that mutual consent
which derives from recognition that all men are created equal—
that is, black men could not recognize the equality of all men or
the superiority of life in accord with natural right. It was not
Banneker's appeal to the Declaration which could persuade
Jefferson. It was rather the demonstration that Banneker possessed "a mind of very common stature indeed." This was for
Jefferson not merely a disposition of the heart, for he regarded

the agreement of natural history with natural right as the necessary foundation of that elevation of mind and body to which he aspired on behalf of all men.

Jefferson's proclivity for natural science betrayed him in this case into seeking a proof for the axiom that all men are created equal, which is not only impossible but oxymoronic. His problem emerges from his entertaining the question of humanity as a matter of natural science. As Euclid's common notions reveal, through the centrality of the term "equal" in the five axioms, the self-evidence and truth of axioms revolves around a principle of identity. That is, the native operation of the intellect is the distinction of same and other—the recognition of the principle of equality.

What that means in this case is that to recognize that all men are created equal, and to recognize all men as men, are one and the same. The one cannot be accomplished without the other. To push the question, Are blacks men? Are Indians men? Are Chinese men? Are Saxons men? Are Persians men? is already to deny the radical insight of the Declaration. Jefferson, speculating Rousseau-like on orangutans and near-men, threatened to overturn the liberating foundation of the American polity. Since in Rousseau human equality meant nothing, inasmuch as a changing and deviating nature constantly undermined the meaning of humanity itself, such speculation was vacuous. But for Jefferson, to whom humanity was founded in an immutable identity, such speculation was dangerous in the extreme, however natural in the context. To his credit, however, he protested to Barlow that "nothing was or is farther from my intentions, than to enlist myself as the champion of a fixed opinion, where I have only expressed doubt."[15]

The path cleared by Rousseau led at the century's end not only to Jefferson's confusion but to Kant and Hegel and ultimately to Nietzsche. In the course of time reason, revelation, and nature came to be supplanted by history as the principal moral cause to which most thinkers turned. Even in the French Revolution, where Montesquieu's work was remembered, the spirit of Rousseau ultimately prevailed. It realized itself in Hegel's identification of the Napoleonic consummation of that revolution as wisdom's dawning. Thus, the eighteenth century, and the Enlightenment, closed on a dismal note of anticipated slavery, fully realized in the form of the modern totalitarianisms since. It did not bring liberty; it brought tyranny.

American liberty alone preserves historic evidence of the path not taken by Europe. Through it we are enabled to recover the true direction of Montesquieu's thought. We can ask what there was in his thought which enabled him to stop short of Rousseau's plunge. How was he enabled to preserve nature and natural rights in the face of what seemed Europe's philosophical fate? I have provided one answer to that question in a previous essay for the Académie Montesquieu on "Montesquieu and Natural Law."[16] Here I will content myself to describe the impact of Montesquieu through the eyes and experience of Daniel Fowle (and, by implication, Sam Adams).

While Fowle's experience may seem particular, he approached it throughout, more than John Peter Zenger did, as having general significance. He made this clear at the outset, when he apologized for the moderate tone of his work by his fear that "it should be accounted a libel" and some reader

> be thrown into a stinking stone Gaol, though never so innocent, and suffer in the same Manner as if he was the real Author: without Law, and in direct opposition even to the poor dim Light of Nature, if I am not very much mistaken.[17]

Fowle's approach brings the light of nature to the support of law. Following the citation from Montesquieu, a lengthy citation from Henry Care was entered, in which Fowle fastened on those

"Rights that from age to age have been deliver'd down to us from our Renown'd Forefathers...." Needless to insist, it would be a miracle if the "poor dim light of nature" concurred in every bequest from the past. Still, the singular freedoms enumerated by Care all eventuated in "this Truth, that when Liberty is once gone, even *Life itself grows insipid,* and loses all its Relish."[18]

*A Total Eclipse* divides into four parts, after the "Preface." The last part is an appendix, entitled "The Original of Civil Government, the Rights of the People, etc." In the final section Fowle recurred to the ultimate foundation of government, the right of consent, rather than to immemorial usage. He took as his authoritative model, Roman liberty, and the subjection of the "chief ruler" to the will of the people. This democratic sentiment flew in the face of British tradition, which entertained a notion of an original contract only as a point of departure and to which no return was conceivable. Under English principles, as Blackstone was later to codify, the people's original authority, once alienated, was alienated for good.

Fowle's intention to present a design of good government which could be defended "against the Invaders of our Liberties and Privileges" required him to go beyond English tradition. It required him to argue for enforceable limits on all delegated authority. In the course of his argument he adduced all of the principles which were later to coalesce in the ideas expressed in the Declaration of Independence. I quote at length:

> this observed, 'No Governors are the natural Parents or Progenitors of their People,—Nor has God by any Revelation nominated Magistrates, shewed the Nature, or Extent of their Power, or given a Plan of Civil Polity for Mankind.' 'Tis also allow'd 'to constitute a State or Civil Polity in a regular Manner, these three deeds are necessary: First, a *Contract* of each *one* for *all,* that they should unite in one Society to be gov-

erned by one Counsel. And next a *Decree* or *Ordinance* of the People concerning the Plan of Government; and the Nomination of the Governors. And lastly, another *Covenant* or *Contract* between these governors and the People, binding the Rulers to a faithful Administration of their Trust, and the People to Obedience."[19]

*[handwritten note: State aumd / How it came How it will / continue]*

Fowle's plan envisions two contracts, an original and an operational or ongoing contract, identifying the people as the true sovereign. He did not overthrow the divine right of kings; he added to it a superior divine right of the people. He plainly conceived a written constitution as the organic and mediating tie between rulers and communities. And he sought some form of election of rulers by the whole society, albeit unspecified.

These provisions of political philosophy—derived from the proposition that no man is the natural ruler (or parent) of any other—Fowle derived from a standard of right, as opposed to English inheritance. On this right, he argued, if there is no such thing, "there could be no Oppression or Injustice, for Oppression or Injustice is when that which is another's Right is detained or taken from him against his Consent."[20]

*[handwritten marginal note: if No rights there's no injustice]*

It must come as no surprise, therefore, that in Boston in 1754 he also preached a right of revolution, without which a rule of right, or higher law, remains inefficacious. Representatives have "no more than a *delegated* Power from the Fountain (anticipating George Washington and the *Federalist*, among others), chose for the Defense and Protection of the People." They hold their power conditionally, not only "from" but "by" the people.

> So that it's natural, nay a Duty, when the common Rights of this Community is trampled upon, or only the Liberty of *one* is attempted against, and that made a *Precedent* of, then they are perfidious to their Trust,

and that Moment forfeit all the Power committed to
them; the Alarm then ought to be given, but with
*Prudence* and *Moderation*....[21]

One would think this Lockean in its form, but for Fowle's faith
in the efficacy of revolution. Locke, too, conceived that the
original contract constituted an irretrievable surrender of rights—
not in right, to be sure, but for all practical purposes. Fowle,
however, considered a patient, suffering people as "herds of
miserable abject Slaves or Beasts of Burden, rather than civil
Polities of rational Creatures." To him, "the point in hand is very
short." Either representatives—kings included—are limited in
their power or they are not. He concluded that "there is no
middle State betwixt *Slavery* and *Freedom*."[22]

At the heart of Fowle's view of the origins of civil government,
then, is a view of representation which itself reposes on a
principle of right conceived as deriving from the nature of
things—human equality. That is precisely the point which
Fowle drew from his reading of the *Spirit of the Laws*. What
seems to have prevented Montesquieu's plunge into the European abyss was a view of government as conditional, not total,
itself deriving from a view of the individual man, of human
equality as the fundamental datum.

In the very middle of the Enlightenment, whose direction was
to apply an ever increasing power over nature to man himself,
Montesquieu held a different course. While modern political
philosophy in general adopted the idea that human polity was
purely arbitrary and conventional, Montesquieu considered it
necessary in the course of nature. On the basis of this distinction
one would think that Hobbes, for instance, would emphasize
choice or consent over determination, while Montesquieu would
emphasize some form of determinism. And so he has often been
misinterpreted, by those departing from his discussions of the

force of climate and *moeurs* in determining the conditions for human laws.

In fact, however, Hobbes produced the greater determinism, precisely because, there being no non-arbitrary standard on which to found human society, superior force alone prevailed and set in motion a course of events as determined as a stone's flight. Montesquieu, on the other hand, albeit realist enough to concede the power of superior might, found in the necessities of nature ample ground for choice. Particularly, arguing that man could not live but by choosing, while nevertheless inclining to choose the natural course, there was a moral force which prevailed in determining people's constitutional courses.

The signal fact about the eighteenth century was that there was no liberty to speak of throughout the monarchies of Europe. The eighteenth century opened on a note established by Louis XIV in France, absolute monarchy: *"l'état, c'est moi."* While the victories of Marlborough secured the settlement of liberties in England, they did not contribute materially to any political improvement in Europe. Montesquieu turned to the English constitution precisely because it alone boasted a constitution which promised liberty. Indeed, all eighteenth-century reflection turned to England, in order to appreciate such niceties as the trial by a jury of one's peers.

Eighteenth-century political philosophy—Enlightenment thought—turned largely to the world of science and the idea of relieving man's estate through mastery over nature. Its implicit reliance on a democratization of science, and hence society, went unnoticed, until Rousseau forced it upon the attention of the world. Montesquieu redirected it by raising the question of political alternatives in a way which had not received as close attention since Aristotle. He indicated that European monarchies, "the monarchies that we know," did not have liberty for their direct object. He did so, however, in a context in which he had clarified liberty as an object for man. That is, he derived from nature, even natural necessities (to speak in mores) a standard by which to assess the politics of his era. While other Enlightenment thinkers (Voltaire included) had regarded nature primarily as an object of material reflections, Montesquieu charted a different course. That course was not followed in the balance of the eighteenth century. Rousseau, though writing almost exclusively in the realm of political philosophy, does so to the effect of denying the existence of a human nature (man is infinitely pliable), rejecting reason as a source of political principles (the general will is not a rational will), and giving birth to the school of historical determinism (the first man to chain off a plot of ground and get away with it changed forever the condition of man).

The fact that Montesquieu made liberty over virtue the fundamental organizing principle of political life altered completely the modern conception of politics. As virtue required a comprehensive, all-powerful state, so liberty called into being the idea of a state limited by the superior prerogatives of citizens. That contrast might alone explain the difficulty Europe experienced in taking Montesquieu's teaching to heart.

Montesquieu did not go unheeded in North America, however. Although his understanding of the English constitution was under assault in England at the end of the eighteenth-century, on the North American continent it had inspired a new English constitution—one in which the roles of the people and their parliament had been reversed. The people became for the first time in history the exclusive guardians of their constitution, conformable to the vision of Daniel Fowle. The new theory of representation had become the concrete form of the idea of liberty in the modern world. Montesquieu was its creator and, for that reason alone, eighteenth century Europe the source. In North America it became what Daniel Fowle wished, that liberty for which everyone had "as high Esteem...as the ancient *Romans* had, that they made it one of their Goddesses... "[24]

## ENDNOTES

1. The General Court wrote to Mauduit June 12, 1762: "The natural Rights of the Colonists, we humbly conceive to be the same with those of all other British Subjects, and indeed of all Mankind. The principal of these Rights is to be 'Free from any superior Power on Earth, and not to be under the Will or Legislative Authority of Man, but to have only the Law of Nature for his Rule.'" Massachusetts Archives, xxii, 247.

2. Daniel Fowle, *A Total Eclipse of Liberty* (Boston: 1755).

3. And the subsequent *Appendix to a Total Eclipse of Liberty* (Boston: 1756), which concludes, "there is no middle State betwixt Slavery and Freedom."

4. Fowle, *A Total Eclipse...*

5. *Ibid.*

6. Jean Jacques Rousseau, *Discours sur l'origine de l'inégalité parmi les hommes* (Paris: Editions Garnier Freres, 1962), fn. i, p. 100.

7. *Ibid.*

8. Fowle, *A Total Eclipse...*

9. Benjamin Banneker, *Copy of a Letter from...*, *to the Secretary of State, with his Answer* (Philadelphia: Daniel Lawrence, 1792), 15 pp.

10. Thomas Jefferson, to Benjamin Banneker, August 30, 1791, *Writings of Thomas Jefferson*, Andrew A. Lipscomb, ed. (Washington, D.C.: Thomas Jefferson Memorial Association, 1904).

11. Thomas Jefferson, *Notes on the State of Virginia* (New York: Harper Torchbooks, 1964), "Query XVIII," pp. 155-156.

12. Thomas Jefferson, to Joel Barlow, *Writings*.

13. Thomas Jefferson, to Joel Barlow, October 8, 1809, vol. XII, p. 322.

14. Jefferson, *Notes*, "Query XIV," p. 138.

15. Thomas Jefferson to Joel Barlow, October 8, 1809.

16. "L'Éthique de Montesquieu: Principe de la fondation de la démocratie américaine," *Actes* 2, 95-128 (1986), Académie Montesquieu (Bordeaux).

17. Fowle, *op. cit.*, p. 4.

18. *Ibid.*

19. Fowle, *An Appendix to the Total Eclipse of Liberty* (Boston: 1756), pp. 20-25.

20. *Ibid.*

21. *Ibid.*

22. *Ibid.*

23. Charles de Montesquieu, *De l'esprit des lois*, Bk. XI, Ch. 7.

24. *Total Eclipse...*

# Eighteenth Century:
# American Contributions

## GEORGE W. CAREY

T he most striking difference between the modern view or
conception of liberty and that which prevailed during our
founding era is, I believe, the diffuseness of the former and the
coherence of the latter. This is to say, it is possible to piece
together a relatively coherent picture of what our Founders
meant by liberty, what they believed its sources to be, and where
they differed concerning its limits. In fact, John Phillip Reid has
done so in his work, *The Conception of Liberty in the Age of the
American Revolution*.[1] As he shows, there was a common universe of discourse at this critical juncture in our history that
enables us to reconstruct their understanding of the various
dimensions of liberty. On the other hand, any similar comprehension of liberty and its various manifestations seems virtually
impossible today. Whereas the substance and source of the
"rights" that the colonists asserted can be specified with some
precision, today we have an ever expanding plethora of new, ill-
defined "rights" whose foundations, in many cases, rest only
upon sincerity, expediency, or political ideology. The distinction
between liberty and license, which was almost universally acknowledged at the birth of our republic—and which endured as
a well recognized and meaningful distinction until relatively
recent decades—has now all but vanished; a fact readily attested
to by the escalating vulgarity in our movies, television, art, plays,
and popular music. What is more, as this distinction recedes, a

persistent counterculture busily seeks novel ways to outrage the sensibilities of the ordinary American.

I begin with these general observations, which I believe few would contest, only to highlight the differences between the "then" (the formative years of the republic) and "now" (present-day America) concerning the sources, meaning, and content of liberty. Clearly, there has been a sea change that prompts critical questions: Has this change resulted from an "organic" development, that is, a development or differentiation of theories, concepts, or ideas integral to the Founders' understanding of liberty? Can, in other words, our modern views of liberty be traced back, in one fashion or another, to those of our founding era? Do they arise, perhaps, from tensions inherent in the Founders' comprehension of liberty? Or is it that we must seek an explanation for the change elsewhere, in theories that arise outside of, and may even be alien to, the American tradition? And if so, what are these outside influences?

What follows necessarily deals in a limited fashion with certain facets of these questions; namely, those that seem to reveal the fundamental differences between the "then" and the "now" concerning liberty, as well as some of the principal reasons why the modern conception of liberty differs so markedly from that of the founding period.[2] The best starting point for this purpose would seem to be a survey of the relatively compact conception of liberty that prevailed during the founding period, since it will yield a benchmark against which the degree and direction of change in its meaning and nature.

*"Then"*

The essence or core of liberty during the founding period was felt to be the absence of arbitrary and capricious government. Such is evident in Montesquieu's formulation of the conditions

that characterized liberty that were generally accepted throughout the formative years. First, as he put it, individuals have a
"right of doing whatever the laws permit."[3] It follows from this
that if the laws are highly mutable, if they are changed in a fashion
so that the individual does not know from one day to the next
what they do or do not permit, then the individual's liberty is
violated. Certainly, if the laws can be applied retroactively, the
individual's liberty is in constant jeopardy. Hence, the prohibition on *ex post facto* was regarded as indispensable for liberty.
Second, largely for the foregoing reasons, a measure or index of
liberty for Montesquieu was the "tranquility of mind" enjoyed by
an individual with respect to "his safety;"[4] that is, to put this in
slightly different terms, the inner security that flows from the
absence of arbitrary and capricious rule—or, put positively, the
uniform, equal, and predictable application of the laws—which
allows for action within the confines of the law without fear of
punishment.

Liberty so conceived, while conveying its essential meaning,
requires ancillary rights, guarantees, or conditions that extend
well beyond protection against *ex post facto* laws in order to guard
against the possibilities of arbitrary rule. Nor, at another level, are
the defining conditions sufficient without serious qualification:
as several commentators of the era noted, tyrants may well govern
by law.

Now with regard to the additional elements required for the
realization of liberty there also seemed to be general agreement.
Turning first to the matter of rights or guarantees necessary for
liberty, the colonists were as one in protesting what they took to
be the abrogation of their rights as Englishmen by the mother
country. The reason for this is obvious: they considered these
rights as the best possible guarantees against an arbitrary and
capricious government. Indeed, the colonists sought from the
very outset to insure that they would enjoy these rights. The
Virginia Charter of 1606 provided that the colony, its inhabit-

ants and their descendants "shall have and enjoy all Liberties, Franchises and Immunities within this our Realm of England or any other of our said Dominions."[5] Similar statements are to be found in all of the subsequent charters, which attests to the high regard, frequently bordering on reverential awe, accorded these traditional rights, liberties, and immunities.

These guarantees, as I have intimated, were well known and relatively specific. They had emerged from the ground up, so to speak, from the English tradition through the *Magna Carta*, the common law, the Petition of Right, the Bill of Rights and found their way into the colonial charters. Later, they were incorporated into the state constitutions and added on to the Philadelphia Constitution to form the core of our present bill of rights. The linkage is clear and undeniable. For instance, the famous Chapter 39 of the 1215 version of the *Magna Carta*— "No freeman shall be arrested, or detained in prison, or deprived of his freehold, or outlawed, or banished, or in any way molested; and we will not set forth against him, nor send against him, unless by the lawful judgment of his peers and [or] by the law of the land"[6]—found its way into the colonial charters and state constitutions. The equivalent of this chapter is the first article of the Massachusetts Body of Liberties (1641), later to be incorporated verbatim into the 1776 Connecticut Declaration of Rights:

> No mans life shall be taken away, no mans honour or
> good name shall be stayned, no mans person shall be
> arested, restrayned, banished, dismembered, nor any
> wayes punished, no man shall be deprived of his wife
> or children, no mans goods or estaite shall be taken
> away from him, nor any way indammaged under the
> colour of law, or Countenance of Authoritie, unlesse
> it be by vertue or equitie of some expresse law of the
> Country waranting the same, established by a generall
> Court and sufficiently published, or in case of the

defect of a law in any parteculer case by the word of
god.[7]

More frequently, the phrases "judgment of his peers" and "by law
of the land" of Chapter 39 were joined by specific procedural
common law guarantees that related to judicial and executive
processes. Section 8 of the 1776 Virginia Declaration of Rights
is typical:

> That in all capital or criminal prosecutions a man hath
> a right to demand the cause and nature of his accusa-
> tion, to be confronted with the accusers and witnesses,
> to call for evidence in his favour, and to a speedy trial
> by an impartial jury of his vicinage, without whose
> unanimous consent he cannot be found guilty, nor can
> he be compelled to give evidence against himself; that
> no man be deprived of his liberty except by the law of
> the land, or the judgment of his peers.[8]

All of the major procedural and substantive rights—save those
relating to speech and religion—in the first eight amendments
of our Bill of Rights can be found, in one form or another, in the
various Declaration of Rights (Pennsylvania, Declaration of
Independence, Maryland, North Carolina, and Connecticut) or
the state constitutions adopted shortly after the Declaration of
Independence. The enumerations of rights in these documents
are very similar, as we might expect, because they are all drawn
from the common law. Maryland's Declaration of Rights is
typical. It contains specific prohibitions against *ex post facto* laws;
cruel and unusual punishment; double jeopardy; self-incrimination; quartering of troops "in any house" without the consent of
the owner; excessive bail; bills of attainder; and unwarranted
searches and seizures. Chapter 39 of the Magna Carta is repro-

duced verbatim in article 21, while the wording of article 19 differs only slightly from that found in section 8 of the Virginia Declaration in providing a number of significant procedural rights.[9] The Pennsylvania Declaration even declares that "the people have a right to bear arms for the defence of themselves and the state." Here, too, unlike the other Declarations and even state constitutions, there is specific mention of "a right to freedom of speech."[10]

In sum, to go no further, from the first settlements through the revolutionary period and well beyond there existed a consensus concerning "rights" and their purpose. Most of them clearly were designed to secure liberty; that is, to check arbitrary government by prohibiting a capricious and partial administration of the law. Besides these rights or protections, the realization of the conditions of liberty, as intimated above, also required a common understanding concerning the nature of its substance. The rights and protections surveyed above, to be sure, constitute indispensable elements of liberty in safeguarding against arbitrary government and in securing the rule of law. But the observation of an anonymous pamphleteer during the pre-revolutionary period, "To do what the laws of Turkey permit, certainly is *not* liberty," points to the need for understanding broader dimensions of liberty, apart from simply the rule of law or the absence of arbitrary government.[11] This is to say, that the question of what the laws should permit and forbid arises because, given the framework within which liberty was discussed during the formative period, this "zone" between the permissible and forbidden was seen to determine the range or limits of liberty.

The literature of this period does not provide us with any hard and fast boundary lines for determining the zone of liberty, save with respect to the rights and protections necessary for the rule of law. Nor should we be surprised at this, given the fact that fixing these limits has been and continues to be a matter of intense debate. Nevertheless, and significantly, we do find a high degree of uniformity in the approach to this matter; a uniformity that reveals fundamental agreement on the dangers to liberty and civil order. In fact, the approach also signifies the existence of a common moral universe that clearly suggests a broad consensus on salient issues concerning the limits of liberty.

As Reid points out, there were differences during the formative years concerning the precise source of liberty: some stressed its divine origins, others thought that it resulted from a contract, still others that it was a birthright that had been won by preceding generations. Whatever its source, liberty was generally pictured as a condition between the extremes of licentiousness and slavery, conceived of as a servile compliance with the arbitrary commands of oppressive rulers. This in-between state and the need for limits was presented most vividly by those employing a state of nature/social contract approach. In this account, men enjoyed *natural* liberty in the state of nature. But, and here most followed Locke's lead, this state of nature was marked by insecurity, inconveniences, and injustices because of men's licentious behavior. As Samuel West wrote, "perfect freedom consists in obeying the dictates of right reason, and submitting to natural law," but when "man goes beyond or contrary to the law of nature and reason, he becomes the slave of base passions and vile lusts; he introduces confusion and disorder into society." West concluded from this that "where licentiousness begins, liberty ends."[12] Men, therefore, relinquished part of their *natural* liberty when they contracted to form a government. In return, they were promised the benefit of *civil* liberty—liberty under law—which, as many writers such as James Wilson contended, was even greater than the *natural* liberty of the state of nature.[13]

In these terms, then, *civil* liberty could not be so expansive that it would lead to the licentiousness of the state of nature; nor could it be so restrictive as to lead to slavery and oppression by government. Moreover, the guiding principle that should govern the extent of *civil* liberty was generally put in terms of the common welfare or public good. Civil "liberty," wrote Simeon Howard, "will be different in different communities. In every state, the members will, probably, give up so much of their natural liberty, as they think will be most for the good of the whole." In this vein, he continues, "different states will judge differently upon this point, some will give up more, some less, though still with the same view, the public good. And every society have doubtless a right to act according to their own judgment and discretion in this matter, this being only an exercise of that natural liberty in which all are bound."[14]

Two aspects of the thought of this era closely related to the foregoing may be briefly surveyed to provide a fuller picture of the backdrop against which to measure the degree and direction of change in our conception of liberty. First, our relationship to Great Britain prior to the revolution was depicted in terms of master to slave; that is, that the American people were subject to the arbitrary will of the Parliament. "A Son of Liberty" [Silas Downer] was among the first to express concern in 1768. "Of late," he wrote,

> a new system of politics hath been adopted in Great Britain, and the *common people* there claim a sovereignty over us although they be only fellow subjects. The more I consider the nature and tendency of this claim, the more I tremble for the liberties of my country. For although it hath been unanswerably proved that they have no more power over us than we have over them, yet relying on the power logic of guns and cutlery ware, they cease not to make laws injurious to us; and whenever we expostulate with them for so doing, all the return is a discharge of threats and menaces.... It is now an established principle in Great

> Britain, [he contended] that we are subject to the
> *people* of that country.... They expressly call us their
> subjects. The language of every paultry scribbler, even
> of those who pretend friendship for us in some things,
> is after this lordly stile, *our colonies—our western do-*
> *minions—our plantations—our islands—our subjects in*
> *America—our authority—our government*—with many
> more of the like imperious expressions.

Eventually, as this argument took hold, the definition of political
liberty was modified to read "the right every man in the state has,
to do whatever is not prohibited by laws, TO WHICH HE
HAS GIVEN HIS CONSENT."[15]

Second, the Founders were not unaware of the roles that virtue
would play in determining the limits of liberty and, ultimately,
the character of the regime. The framework discussed above
provides the context for understanding the more important roles
of virtue. To begin with, as Jeremiah Atwater put it, "the more
virtuous a people are, the less need is there of the restrains of civil
government, to promote order."[16] In other words, what seemed
"evident" to Atwater is that the zone of civil liberty, the permissible realm of conduct free from the fetters of law, would be
wider, the more virtuous the people. Beyond this, of course, if the
people, as in a republican regime, are to set the limits of civil
liberty to promote the common good, then they must be prepared to set aside personal, private, and selfish interests. "The
real importance of virtue to the welfare of society," as one
observer of the founding period put it, "consists in...[the]
uniform direction of the public will to that which is good....Virtue
of necessity aims at the public good; invariably seeks the common welfare and gives no pain, where it is not necessary for the
promotion of that welfare."[17] "But when,"—as Timothy Stone
cautioned, repeating a common refrain—"party spirit, local

views, and interested motives" cause a people "to loose slight of the great end of government the public good, and give themselves up, to the baneful influence of parasitical demagogues, they may well expect to reap the bitter fruits of their own folly." These bitter fruits, he continues, are loss of liberty and submission "to the avarice and ambition of designing and wicked men."[18]

Finally, in this regard, it was generally recognized that the virtue needed for the widest latitude of civil liberty would not come naturally. Virtue, some suggested, could be enhanced and reinforced through the proper institutions of government, but most seemed to believe that the primary sources were to be found in the family, education, and religion. Atwater presents a brief, but relatively comprehensive, view of how virtue is sluiced into the society. "If man is here formed a good citizen, it is not because he needs no restraint," he writes,

> but because, from his youth, he has been taught to restrain those passions, which it is the principal business of law and government to restrain. This restraint is begun in the family. Children are early inured to family government, and are taught habits of subordination and respect. In the school, the same system is continued, while the seeds of knowledge and virtue are sown in the youthful mind. Higher seminaries of learning also, accord with the same system, as do the instructions of the bible and the desk. Man, from the cradle to the grave, is constantly learning new lessons of moral instruction, and is trained to virtue and order by perpetual and salutary restraints. To all which may be added the restraint of public opinion, which, in a country where Christianity is believed, compels even profligates to be outwardly virtuous.[19]

Others, such as Samuel Kendal, regarded firm religious foundations as indispensable for order and liberty. Restraints of law, he
argued, will not suffice to secure civil liberty "if they are not
supposed to proceed from some superior power." "Belief in the
being and providence of God, and that he hath given to men a
perfect law, the transgression of which is an offense against him,"
he continued, will furnish motives to virtue suggested by no
other consideration."[20]

### *"Now"*

As indicated at the outset, there appears to be little cohesiveness
or coherence to the contemporary understanding of liberty. Such
disarray creates obvious problems. In the first place, the absence
of integrating principles or concepts renders organized and
systematic treatment of our contemporary understanding of
liberty extremely difficult, if not impossible. Beyond this, there
is the matter of where we should look for authentic expressions
concerning the meaning and scope of liberty in hopes, at least,
of finding widely shared views about its character and purpose.

Given these and similar difficulties, a methodological note is
in order. In what follows, I attempt to provide an integrating
framework built around the principles and values normally
associated with the "open society," a concept popularized some
years ago by Karl Popper.[21] Popper, as he wrote in the first
American edition of his *Open Society* in 1950, was sure that the
United States, more so than any other nation in the world,
epitomized the principles of his open society. What has transpired since that time could only serve to reinforce this belief.

To the matter of where I look for a "fit"—that is, to see
whether the open society framework helps to explain or give
meaning to our current conceptions of liberty—I turn to the
opinions of the Supreme Court on the meaning and scope of
"liberty," particularly with regard to the first amendment free-

doms of speech and press. In doing this, I am assuming that the Court is articulating at least an "official" consensus, as well as presenting a legitimate and acceptable version of the limits and role of liberty. Certainly, it can be said that the Court's formulation is that which is taught and, to some degree, extolled in the Academy and media. I will also deal very briefly with another, though similar, way of looking at liberty that has gained some adherents principally in the academy.

To begin with the realm of common knowledge, one of the more striking differences, and one already alluded to, between the earlier understanding of liberty and our modern usages is the virtual disappearance of the distinction between liberty and license. Plato's description of the disordered soul of the "democratic" man seems appropriate to our present circumstances:

> he will set all his pleasures on a footing of equality, denying to none its equal rights and maintenance, and allowing each in turn, as it presents itself, to succeed, as if by the chance of the lot, to the government of his soul until it is satisfied. When he is told that some pleasures should be sought and valued as arising from desires of a higher order, others chastised and enslaved because the desires are base, he will shut the gate of the citadel against the messengers of truth, shaking his head and declaring that one appetite is as good as another and all must have their equal rights.[22]

This relativism finds its modern expression in the corollary "one man's vulgarity is another's lyric," a view that manifests a breakdown of shared community standards and values. This breakdown—which, of course, precludes drawing any distinction between license and liberty—also signifies a fundamental change in the modern understanding of the nature of liberty from that which prevailed in the formative period. Clearly the linkage drawn between liberty and the common good is all but lost in the modern conception: if the distinction between liberty and license cannot be drawn, there is no foundation for achieving any consensus on what constitutes the common good.

This point can be dramatically illustrated by comparing our modern notion of freedom of the press with that at the time of the founding. The early view, by all evidences, is found in Blackstone's *Commentaries*, wherein he acknowledges the need for liberty of the press in a "free state." But he defines this liberty in terms of "no previous restraint" on publication, not as "freedom from censure for criminal matter when published." From the modern vantage point, of course, Blackstone's position seems most illiberal because subsequent punishment is viewed as restraint, as no doubt it was intended to be in some cases. But from Blackstone's point of view, holding one to account for "writing" judged to be "pernicious" after a "fair and impartial trial" served the cause of liberty because it was "necessary for the preservation of peace and good order, of government and religion, the only solid foundations of civil liberty."[23] By way of contrast, the modern view is highly restrictive regarding what is "pernicious," particularly when it comes to "peace and good order." What is more, in modern discourse, a stress is frequently placed on the need for "toleration" so that individuals will accept with equanimity that which they find offensive. Moreover, as this example suggests, notions of liberty advanced today usually lack any teleological dimension that extends to anything beyond the conditions necessary for the modern version of liberty. Liberty of the press or freedom of speech, for instance, are often looked upon as if they were the highest ends of society.

The foregoing points to a significant shift in thinking, and deals with one very important dimension of the modern view of liberty that is probably best understood by reference to the animating principles of the "open society" with its strong emphasis on toleration, diversity, individual rights, and freedom, and its antipathy toward custom, habit, tradition, taboos, and the like that serve to restrain or inhibit individual expression or behavior. To show precisely how the principles of the open society came to predominate in our modern conception of liberty is, perhaps, impossible, largely because it is so difficult to measure the impact and progress of ideas or how they permeate the social fabric. Yet, our constitutional history, the ways in which the Court shifted its grounds on interpretation, particularly with respect to the First Amendment freedoms of speech and press, offers a rough picture of our not-so-gradual evolution toward these principles. In one sense, as I have already suggested, the evolution seems complete: our public discourse about liberty, its meaning and limits, is conducted in terms largely derived from the principles and goals of the open society.

In tracing this evolution, it is well to remember that the salient provisions of our bill of rights are derived from the English tradition, principally the common law. In the bill of rights we find mention of rights—phrased, significantly, not as "individual" rights, but in each case as the "right of the people"—with respect to peaceable assembly, security against unreasonable searches and seizures, and possession of arms. The word "liberty" is to be found only in the "due process" clause of the fifth amendment. Now the meaning of liberty in this specific context was well understood at the time of founding in light of the English tradition, as well as from colonial and state practices. In the reign of Edward III, the 39th chapter of the Magna Carta (quoted above) was revised to read: "No man...shall be put to death, without being brought to answer by due process of law" (that is, "due process of law" replaced "law of the land" found in the original formulation). At the time the Fifth Amendment was drafted, Blackstone's understanding of the word "liberty" as used in the "due process" clause was commonly accepted: it was, he believed, an extremely important "personal liberty" which he defined as the "power of locomotion, of changing situation, or moving one's person to whatever place one's inclination may direct, without imprisonment or restraint, unless by due course of law."[24]

There is no reason to believe that the "liberty" of the due process clause of the Fourteenth Amendment was understood in any different light. But, despite the fact that a majority of the Court had consistently held to this originalist position for over fifty years, interpretations to the effect that this liberty embodied the basic civil liberties contained in the Bill of Rights began to gain favor in the later part of the nineteenth century. Finally, as students of our constitutional history are well aware, the Court, in one brief sentence of *Gitlow v. New York* (1925), adopted the view that the "liberty" of the Fourteenth Amendment embraced the free speech provision of the first amendment, thus opening the way for this liberty to become the receptacle for all the civil liberties contained in the bill of rights.

Two aspects of this particular decision are worthy of note. First, that the court would use a case involving freedom of speech as the occasion for reversing its course is unusual in light of our history. On the basis of the historical record, the status of free speech as a fundamental right that deserved protection is far weaker than that of most of the provisions of the bill of rights— e.g., trial by jury, protection against self-incrimination, double jeopardy, unreasonable search and seizure, indictment by grand jury—if, that is, we look to the rights set forth in the state constitutions that were in effect at the time the Constitution was ratified. Indeed, we find that free speech was not protected by any of the state constitutions in effect at the time of the adoption of the Constitution. Clearly on the basis of its subsequent behavior, the Court did not intend to send the message that by including speech, a right with a "weak" claim, its intent was henceforth to include all rights with superior claims. Rather, an entirely plausible answer for the Court's behavior is that free speech had already come, through a variety of avenues, to hold a position of primacy among the values associated with liberty. This view is indirectly reinforced by the fact that the court did not take the opportunities to change its course with regard to the Fourteenth Amendment by incorporating clearly fundamental rights, those more closely associated with the common sense understanding of "due process" than free speech.

Second, the *Gitlow* decision was only the first in a two-step process. Those most energetically pushing for an expansion of the traditional understanding of the "liberty" of the Fourteenth Amendment wanted freedom of speech freed from the restraint of the common law. Certainly the effect of expansion would be relatively minor if the Court's role was simply to be that of determining whether the states had properly applied the common law tests to speech. As the record will attest, after Gitlow there was constant pressure to abandon the restrictive "bad tendency" test of the common law in favor of Holmes's more lenient "clear and present danger" test whose origins can be traced directly to John Stuart Mill's *On Liberty*. Once this was accomplished in the late 1930s, the states and localities henceforth were obliged to meet the national standard—a standard which has embraced, so to speak, the lowest common denominator or the least restrictive approach to controlling the substance or content of speech or press. Additionally, once this test was in place, it was but a short step to the proposition that the only legitimate reason for restraint is to prevent harm or definite risk of harm to oneself or others, another standard taken from Mill's classic work.

I need not detail here how the right of free speech evolved in a manner fully consistent with the ends of the open society. Suffice to say, freedom of speech has been interpreted to mean freedom of expression in order to embrace the full range of liberties that characterize a fully open society. And, it is in the area of freedom of expression that we encounter the most significant breakdown of the older distinction between license and liberty.

This is not to suggest that the evolution toward the open society is now complete. True enough, as mentioned above, our view of liberty has been conditioned by the theory underlying the open society so that, among other things, we exalt individual rights, deviant lifestyles, and readily accept the "do your own thing" mentality. But the full realization of the open society requires liberties and rights that go beyond those that can be found in our Bill of Rights, simply because its provisions grew out of a different tradition of liberty. To some extent, it would appear, this need for new rights explains why, in very recent decades, so much controversy has come to surround the proper role of the Supreme Court in interpreting the Constitution. Those who advance the position that the Court ought not to be bound down to original intent—that it should be free to interpret the Constitution in a fashion consistent with changing times and morality, or that it should look to the "spirit," not the letter of the Constitution—seem to be aware of the need to move beyond specified constitutional rights to establish the liberties needed for a fully open society.

Protecting individual rights, expanding the areas of permissible individual expression and behavior, to some degree, involve restricting government or curbing majorities that seek to curtail liberty through the ordinary lawmaking processes. But there is another side to our modern thinking about liberty, one that is not concerned with protection from arbitrary government or majorities, but rather with using the compulsory powers of government to maximize or promote liberty. To a great degree, this conception of liberty supplements that which is integral to the open society since it is concerned with the distribution and enjoyment of liberties that have become part of the open society. For instance, it has been argued that the "right" to an abortion, to be meaningful, means that the government is obliged to pay for the abortions of women who cannot afford the costs. More commonly, however, this view is concerned with political, economic, and cultural factors that lead to an unequal distribution of liberty.

The concerns about liberty from this aggregate perspective are multifaceted and take various forms so that detailed examination of them is not possible here. We should note, however, that virtually all are concerned with unequal distribution of wealth as a prime cause of diminished aggregate liberty. In part, wealth is seen as a means to control or influence others, particularly in the political and economic spheres, thereby rendering the poor subservient to the wants or views of the rich. Wealth is also seen as making the "race" in the competitive society "unfair"; the children of wealthier families, for obvious reasons, are seen as having a head start over those of the poor, a state of affairs that perpetuates inequalities over generations. Moreover, virtually all such theories assume that there is a point at which liberty is maximized in the aggregate through appropriate governmental programs and policies designed to achieve greater equality. In this regard, "equality of opportunity" is the phrase most commonly used to describe what the appropriate mixture of liberty and equality ought to be.

It should be remarked in passing that those of the founding era were not oblivious to the ill effects of wealth, politically and otherwise. Phillips Payson, for one, wrote to this very issue: "The exorbitant wealth of individuals has a most baneful influence on public virtue, and therefore should be carefully guarded against." But, he observed, "It is...acknowledged to be a difficult matter to secure a state from evils and mischiefs from this quarter; because, as the world goes, and is likely to go, wealth and riches will have their commanding influence." Because men are disposed to pursue their self-interest over the collective good, he continued, "A wicked rich man...soon corrupts a whole neighborhood, and a few of them will poison the morals of a whole community." "This sovereign power of interest," he contended, "seems to have been much the source of modern politics abroad, and has given birth to such maxims of policy as these, *viz.*, that...'every man has his price,' that 'the longest purse, and not the longest sword, will finally be victorious.'" How, then, were the "baneful" influences to be counteracted? Through, he wrote, "the general diffusion of knowledge" which "is the best preservative against them, and the likeliest method to beget and increase that public virtue, which...will prove...an impregnable bulwark to the state."[25] Still others suggested restricting the suffrage to those who could resist the bribes of the rich or, like Perez Fobes, prayed *"give us not riches—nor poverty."*[26] There was no counterpart, however, to the modern notion of achieving "equality of opportunity" through government.

### *"Then" and "Now": Some Observations*

Certain facets of the early formulations of liberty are particularly pertinent to any assessment of the status of our contemporary liberty. One of the more important of these concerns the relationship between consent, liberty, and the common good that grew and hardened during the pre-revolutionary period and today's emphasis on liberty in terms of new and refined individual and group rights, many of which have been "derived" from the Constitution through imaginative interpretation. Certainly a problem we face today is that, in many instances, the common good is clearly subordinated in the exercise of individual or group liberty; a subordination that is sanctioned by the open society theory on various grounds. One such view would seem to be that liberty is the highest value. (I say "seem" because this view, to my knowledge, has not been articulated even though certain organizations and not a few judges have written of liberty, particularly freedom of speech, as if it were the highest value.) Another is the "slippery slope" argument: any limitation on liberty or rights will open the way for further limitations that will ultimately lead to the loss of all liberty. Still another, of course, is that the common good and the inviolability of individual rights come down to pretty much the same thing; the long-term interests of the community are served by treating individual and group rights as sacrosanct, whatever the short-term costs may be.

Leaving to one side the justification for this subordination, the fact is that these new rights are relatively immune to modification, limitations, or regulation by the political agencies of government because of their constitutional status. The acknowledged rights are, consequently, fixed or inflexible; incapable of being changed or modified in light of the common good, save through constitutional amendment. And this is precisely the status that proponents of the open society would like them to enjoy.

Looking back to the founding era, there are strong evidences that a different view prevailed. By and large the common law rights were amenable to change or alteration by the state legislatures. The literature of the period indicates that complete awareness that license, the abuse of liberty, could result in lasting harm for the individual and community. On the other hand, it is true that a legacy of this period is a Bill of Rights which exempts certain areas and concerns from control by the majority through ordinary political processes. But at the time this addition of rights was not regarded as a very serious matter. The basic constitutional design which provided for deliberative self-government, Madison argued, would not be endangered. Yet, the "rights" part of our tradition has been seized upon and glorified, albeit in a distorted and intellectually dishonest manner.[27] Over the decades it has come to predominate in the form of individual rights so that today we are apt to forget not only the common good, but also the Framers' understanding of the proper relationship between liberty and self-government; a relationship based on the belief that self-government is the most precious right a people can possess and, for that reason alone, a free people will not enslave or oppress itself.

Finally, by way of illustrating a basic difference between "then" and "now," we may note that, consonant with their views on license and liberty, our forefathers accepted the proposition that spoken and written words have consequences, harmful or beneficial. Today, by way of contrast, when the right of free expression in all its forms is considered paramount, the first line of defense for the excesses and vulgarities that result, ironically, is denying that the exercise of this right has effects. The relationship between what is shown on television and in the movies and how people who watch them think and behave, so we are told, cannot be proved. What is more, unless their effect be physical violence or demonstrable harm, there is no warrant in the modern conception of liberty for any regulation.

The framers, this is to say, accepted the commonsensical view of man and his place in the world about him. This molded their views on liberty, the more so as they stressed man's imperfections and susceptibilities. The moderns, on the other hand, seem far less concerned with man's propensities and inner character and more inclined to view him as an individual apart from society. The older liberty stressed restraints in the name of virtue and decency; the newer, freedom from restraints and inhibitions, to prevent only physical harm or the threat thereof.

## Endnotes

1. John Phillip Reid, *The Concept of Liberty in the Age of the American Revolution* (Chicago: University of Chicago Press, 1988).
2. Obviously, the answer to these and like questions involves a great deal of conjecture. To show a linkage or the impact of thought in the manner suggested above, no matter how plausible it may appear, is always—to some degree at least—a matter of speculation. Likewise, the range of materials relevant to these relationships is enormous, so that "weighing" it, sifting the significant from the not so significant, would necessarily involve a high degree of subjectivity. Moreover, and leaving these and related methodological concerns to one side, accumulating the relevant knowledge for anything approaching a definitive answer to these concerns would be an enormous undertaking.

3. *The Spirit of the Laws*, trans. Anne M. Cohler (New York: Cambridge University Press, 1989), Ch. 11, Sect. 3.

4. *Ibid.*, Sect. 6.

5. *Foundations of Colonial America*, ed. W. Keith Kavenagh, 6 vols. (New York: Chelsea House, 1983), III, p. 1702.

6. McKechnie's translation, "Source" materials in Roscoe Pound, *The Development of Constitutional Guarantees of Liberty* (New Haven: Yale University Press, 1957), p. 123.

7. *The Roots of the Bill of Rights*, ed. Bernard Schwartz, 5 vols. (New York: Chelsea House, 1987), I, p. 72.

8. *Roots*, II, p. 235.

9. *Roots*, II, p. 281, p. 282.

10. *Roots*, II, p. 266.

11. *American Political Writing during the Founding Era*, eds. Charles S. Hyneman and Donald S. Lutz, 2 vols. (Indianapolis: Liberty Press, 1983), I, p. 29.

12. *American Political Writing*, I, p. 415.

13. *American Political Writing*, II, p. 1269.

14. *American Political Writing*, I, p. 188.

15. *American Political Writing*, I, pp. 101-102.

16. *American Political Writing*, II, p. 1177.

17. Zephaniah Swift Moore, *American Political Writing*, II, p. 1212.

18. *American Political Writing*, II, p. 846.

19. *American Political Writing*, II, p. 1177.

20. *American Political Writing*, II, p. 1245.

21. I am referring here to his work, *The Open Society and Its Enemies*, which first appeared in 1944 and has subsequently appeared in revised editions over the years.

22. *The Republic of Plato*, trans. Francis MacDonald Cornford (London: Oxford University Press, 1982), IV, Bk. 6 pp. 31, 286.

23. William Blackstone, *Commentaries*, 4:150-53; reproduced in *The Founders' Constitution*, eds. Philip B. Kurland and Ralph Lerner, 5 vols. (Chicago: University of Chicago Press, 1987), V, p. 119.

24. On this point see George W. Carey, *In Defense of the Constitution* (Indianapolis: Liberty Press, 1994), chapter 6.

25. *American Political Writing*, I, pp. 528-29.

26. *American Political Writing*, II, p. 1002.

27. Two excellent articles on this point are: Ralph Rossum, "The Federalist's Understanding of the Bill of Rights" in *Securing the Revolution: The Federalist Papers and the American Founding*, ed. Charles Kesler (New York: The Free Press, 1989) and Richard E. Morgan, "Self-Government and the Wantonness of Rights," *Public Interest Law Review* (1991).

# Eighteenth Century: The Counter Enlightenment

LEONARD P. LIGGIO

The mercantilism of Louis XIV and Colbert was developed in an attempt to capture revenues for the crown in a period of declining economic conditions stemming from the previously high levels of taxation to finance the Thirty Years War. Louis XIV's own wars, for which mercantilism was the preparation, caused widespread economic and social dislocation, misery, and crisis. Mercantilism was the economic system of the militarily aggressive state. Mercantilism's purpose was to assure the state of financial and economic resources for the conduct of war. As a result, a large religious opposition to mercantilism or state intervention in the economy grew. This essay will cover a number of the leading intellectuals who contributed to the concept of liberty and liberal thought in France of the eighteenth century.

Archbishop Francois Fenelon (1651-1715) drew on the humanist traditions of the Catholic Reformation to challenge the growth of state power. This Catholic tradition exalted human reason and minimized the role of original sin among ordinary men, and saw the consequences of original sin more in the opportunity of multiple evils in the decisions of politicians. The Spanish Jesuit, Louis de Molina, was one of the large number of Catholic thinkers emphasizing the optimistic view of human nature when not associated with state power.[1]

Fenelon's mentor, Abbe Claude Fleury (1640-1723) shared

in this attack on mercantilism and war, based on their positive view of ordinary human nature. The mercantilists saw conflict and immoral aggrandizement as part of original sin, and mercantilism as the necessary means to achieve success in a state of permanent war. Fenelon and Fleury opposed assumptions that showed contempt for man's reason as the premise for human depravity, and supported the notion of a consumer revolution, where the free choices of morally good and rational men revealed the positive aspects of God's plan. The market society, they held, was a morally approved, natural society, in contrast to immoral, and state imposed, economic regulation and taxation.

An important part of this view of Fenelon and Fleury was the their positive attitude toward science, which they felt could provide solutions to man's problems, and technology, which could improve the conditions of men. Fleury and Fenelon emphasized that the mercantilist attempt to subsidize particular industries in order to maintain employment, actually was destructive of this end, since it was based on taxes and restrictions on the mass of the population whose purchasing power and freedom of choice were destroyed. Their views were to provide a foundation for many reformers at the beginning of the eighteenth century.[2]

The disaster of wars and mercantilism under Louis XIV led to attempts to solve the financial problems associated with central banking and inflation in John Law's "Mississippi Bubble." The Mississippi Bubble's collapse resulted in Bishop Andre Hercule de Fleury (1653-1743) becoming Prime Minister and Cardinal (1726-1743). Viewing war as the cause for economic and social crises, Cardinal Fleury, along with Sir Robert Walpole, his counterpart in England, pursued a policy of detente. England was the greatest beneficiary of this period of detente, because Walpole was better able to keep England out of military conflict than was Fleury. Consequently, Walpole reduced military costs, reduced taxes, and through "salutary neglect" permitted the enforcement of mercantilist regulations to lapse. Lower military spending and taxes permitted a vast increase in savings and the rapid growth of consumer demand. In addition, new technology satisfied increasing consumer demand.

In France there were much greater mercantilist structures to be dealt with than in England, and this fact accounts for, in large measure, why there were better opportunities for the development of industrialism in England than in France. This was the era of Whig hegemony in England that so impressed both Voltaire and Montesquieu. During Fleury's premiership, Anglomania was wide spread in French intellectual circles. It was fed in large measure by Voltaire's introduction into France of Locke's political thought and Newton's scientific thought; as well as by Montesquieu's praise of the constitutional and legal system of England. Montesquieu, in his *L'Espirit de Lois*, maintained that the English system of minimal government and lack of centralized bureaucracy provided the necessary foundation for liberty, and made popular the idea of the value of checks and balances and separation of powers as the marks of enlightened government.[3]

By the middle of the eighteenth century, the renewal of hostilities between England and France brought increased taxes; halted the reform of mercantilism; and induced the introduction of more modern economic thinking among the French. Leading in this respect was the Irish-French financier Richard Cantillon, who was a leading critic of John Law's inflationary schemes, and who is viewed by F. A. Hayek as the major forerunner of the monetary theory of the "Austrian School."

Hayek praised Cantillon's *Essai sur la nature du commerce en general*, in his introduction to the 1931 German translation of this work, noting Cantillon's impact on the Physiocrats.[4] Cantillon's most important influence was on J.C.M. Vincent de Gournay (1712-59) who Schumpeter considers to be one of the greatest teachers of all time. Gournay's work is based on Cantillon's ideas, and Gournay is considered by many to have originated modern economics. Gournay's work influenced not only Turgot, but also Adam Smith. Turgot's *Reflexions sur la formation et la distribution des richnesses* was published in 1766 with an introduction by Du Pont de Nemours, and was later anonymously translated (attributed to Adam Smith) into English.

Anne-Robert-Jacques Turgot's early work contributed significantly to historical scholarship in arguing that history is discovery process that could provide data that would enable men to avoid errors in the future. Turgot's conception of human rights was intimately related to his economic theories which contained a subjective theory of value, and inaugurated the a theory of markets.[5] Joseph Schumpeter says of Turgot the following:

> If we are to compare Turgot's scientific personality with those of Becarria and A. Smith, significant similarities strike us first; all three were polyhistoric in learning and range of vision; all three stood outside the arena of business and political pursuits; all three displayed a single-minded devotion to duty in hand. Turgot was undoubtedly the most brilliant of the three....[6]

Further Schumpeter writes:

> It is not too much to say that analytical economics took a century to get where it could have got in twenty years after the publication of Turgot's treatise had its content been properly understood and absorbed by an alert profession. As it was, even J.B. Say—the most important link between Turgot and Walras—did not know how to exploit it fully.[7]

The second half of the eighteenth century was filled with

important debates and writings, one aspect of which was the growth of Anglophobia in France. Ideas about English constitutionalism and English political thought, that had been so favored in the earlier part of the century, fell into disrepute. Criticism of matters English came from both liberal and conservative sources. This criticism intensified in light of the American Revolution and increased even more in the era of the French Revolution and the Napoleonic era. One facet of this anglophobia was reflected in the writings of the Physiocrats, another in the writings of followers of Rousseau including Abbe Mably, Baron d'Holbach, Denis Diderot, and Jean-Paul Marat. The focus of the debate tended to be on the understanding to be given to the English constitutional system—particularly the matter of separation of powers and the checks and balances system.

The later philosophes began to think in terms of the legislature as the expression of the "General Will," and, therefore, sought a governmental structure that would operate without a system of checks and balances, since such an arrangement, it was argued, was medieval. There was also present in these debates a strong utilitarian current, which argued for "efficient government" that would express in its legislative activity the "General Will." Such arguments became a virulent source for the creation of the modern bureaucratic state which would replace the older and more balanced institutions formed under the influence of medieval thinking.

The emergence of the modern bureaucratic state constituted a watershed in the era of political thought. The French Jacobin notions of the state were paralleled in many ways by the thinking undergirding the continental Enlightened Despotisms. These two elements created a conservative and a radical justification for the bureaucratic state an offspring of which, were certain socialist currents of thought emerging in the nineteenth century. In all of these developments classical liberalism remained a staunch defender of the traditional political philosophy of western civilization which was expressed in both American and English thought.[8]

A major source of debate in France arose with the formation of the new states in the former British colonies in America and the adoption of both the Articles of Confederation and the Federal Constitution. The divisions among the French philosophes about these American constitutions was very diverse. Some of the advocates of greater governmental control and less economic freedom, based their position on the argument that morality was undermined by material goods and the commercial spirit. In that light they viewed the American State Constitutions as a means to check commercial development and consumer demand. Others, including Turgot, saw the American State Constitutions in this light as well, and criticized them for that reason. Finally, some thinkers saw these American constitutions as barriers to the introduction of government controls or the attempts to construct a moral economy. America was seen as the highest example of economic growth that occurred on the basis of Whig "salutary neglect," and the American revolution was held to be a defense of that free economy insulated from new forms of taxation and restriction. Thus, these American constitutions were viewed from this perspective, as defenses of a free society from runaway enthusiasms for government regulation and taxation.

Adams and Jefferson, and their ideas, became a part of the social circle of Liberal intellectuals in Paris which:

> was dominated on the one hand by that most ardent liberal, the Duc de la Rochefoucald, and his remarkable mother the Duchesse d'Anville, by their most intimate friend the Marquis de Condorcet, and a little later, by Lafayette. The distinguished Abbes Morellet, Arnauld, Chalut, de Mably, Barthelmy, and the Papal Nuncio, Comte Dugnani, with whom Jefferson kept

up relations until the Cardinal's death in 1820, were what might be called the theorizers of this group in contrast to the men of action.[9]

In her introduction to her translation of *The Autobiography of Du Pont de Nemours*, Elizabeth Fox-Genovese notes:

> An emergent individualism—the sense of the self—did not appear as something new in the eighteenth century. Classical, Christian, and Renaissance individualism, to name but the most obvious forms, had all testified to awareness of the excellence or responsibilities of the self. There is something rash, even condescending, in assuming that all peoples in all times and places have not taken account of the perceptions and stimuli experienced in the individual body and mind. The recent and widespread tendency among scholars to point to the modern personality as qualitatively different in some way from its predecessors easily leads into such related and offensive propositions as that until the fairly recent past parents did not love their children. At its mindless worst, it suggests that premodern personalities did not attain the autonomy and maturity of modern personalities. Such attitudes easily explain the reactions of other scholars who insist upon the individualism of, say, the Middle Ages.[10]

Fox-Genovese characterizes Pierre Samuel du Pont de Nemours (1739-1817) as one of the "growing number of political economists and sociological historians in England, Scotland, and France, especially those now known collectively as the Scottish Historical School."[11] Du Pont had become an associate of Francois Quesney, and Victor de Riqueti, the Marquis de

Mirabeau. Thus, du Pont occupied a prominent position among the physiocrats.

Quesney was an intellectual authority for du Pont, and Quesnay looked to du Pont to continue the physiocratic school. However, du Pont became part of another school of economics founded by Vincent de Gournay. The major expositor of this facet of economic thought was Anne-Robert Jacques Turgot. Du Pont with others, including Marie Jean Antoine Nicolas Caritat, the Marquis de Condorcet, became Turgot's closest aides.

Du Pont contributed to the discussion of the nature of property, and as in many matters of philosophy, premised much of his argument on Locke's view regarding the nature of property. Locke himself, was aware of the interest and debate related to his thought that occurred in France in the late seventeenth century and which had generated considerable interest in analyzing the nature of money and property.

Interest was defended by P. Chaduc,[12] and LeCorreur. The latter, however, based most of his argument on that of the fifteenth century theologian and archbishop St. Antonio of Florence, the sixteenth century theologians Molina, Cardinal Cajetan, and Sylvius.[13] John Dormer, S.J. defended interest when it was attacked by de Tetre.[14]

Locke's *Second Treatise on Civil Government* was published in French in Amsterdam soon after its first publication, but did not see another French edition until 1795. However, Locke's thought, and English ideas generally, had been praised and discussed by a number of French writers in the eighteenth century, starting with Voltaire and Montesquieu. Voltaire travelled to England in May, 1726, where he was introduced into society by Viscount Bolingbroke, who had been allowed to return from exile by Sir Robert Walpole. Voltaire had met previously with Bolingbroke in Paris, where they had mutually enjoyed Locke. Here Voltaire began his lifelong admiration for "England: A Nation of Philosophers" as he called them, and Bolingbroke provided Voltaire with an understanding of what accounted for England's stability and prosperity, particularly under Walpole.

In 1733 Voltaire published his *Lettres philosophiques* which he dedicated to England as a country under the "rule of law." Peter Gay calls Voltaire's description:

> a positive vision of a civilization that assimilates, protects, and profits from a variety of citizens. A sound civilization, Voltaire tells his readers in one vivid image, is unity in multiplicity; since its virtues and vices constantly act upon each other, the strength of one institution is the strength of all. The rule of law, commercial prosperity, religious toleration, the flourishing of arts and sciences, civil liberties—all are necessary, all sustain each other.[15]

Voltaire's Anglomania was reinforced by that of Montesquieu. Montesquieu began an European tour in 1726 and spent eighteen months of this tour in England. He was already famous among English readers for his *Persian Letters*,[16] which some consider to be the first critique of the political conditions in France. Twenty years after his visit to England, Montesquieu published his *L'Esprit des Lois*,[17] generally considered the greatest book of the eighteenth century. Although the influence of English thinkers at this time, including Smith and Hume was great, Montesquieu's writings competed favorably with them. Montesquieu was greatly influenced by the English system of toleration; the moderating effects of its commercial civilization; and the separation of powers and balance of powers that were reflected in English political order.[18]

The main concept of property rights in eighteenth-century France were focused in the writings of the Physiocrats whose views may be summarized as follows:

There are certain physical laws governing social phenomena which, if obeyed, will infallibly secure the welfare of society as a whole. From the economic point of view these laws may be reduced to self-interest. Not only is it man's interest not to interfere with this natural law, but it is also his duty. Thus duty and self-interest could never collide.[19]

Consequently, the Physiocrats viewed the role of the state as that of protecting life, liberty, and property. The distribution of wealth would be best governed by each pursuing his own self-interest without the use of the state to attempt to equalize or redistribute the outcomes of such pursuits. Social problems would be the result of inequalities brought about by unequal taxation, not the unequal distribution of wealth.[20]

The major critique in the Constituent Assembly (1789-1791) came from Honore-Gabriel de Riqueti, Comte de Mirabeau, whose views differed substantially from the Lockean ideas of the absolute right of property held by the majority of the assembly.[21]

In addition to their position on the rights of property and the value of self-interest, Quesnay, Turgot, and Du Pont believed that their work indicated the real possibilities of a science of man; that social science was about to be developed in ways that would parallel the developments in the physical sciences. The Physiocrat, Pierre Le Mercier de la Riviere, felt that such a development would characterize the next stage in man's development; that human ignorance would be replaced by a knowledge of the natural social order among men, that would remove the inappropriate historical attempts to impose a social order by force.[22]

Abbe Etienne Bonnot de Condillac (1715-1780) is, perhaps, the least well-known philosophe among English speaking scholars. Condillac was acquainted with Jean Jacques Rousseau who had served as a tutor in Condillac's uncle's home. Condillac pressed support of Locke's theory of knowledge against the work of Descartes, Leibniz, Spinoza, and Malebranche. Condillac's critique of the theory of innate ideas significantly influenced nineteenth century English philosophers, particularly James Mill, John Stuart Mill, and Herbert Spencer. Condillac refined Locke's "historical, plain method" to a more precise form of analysis with a stress upon language. Along with Turgot and Lavoisier he believed that language was the key to development of true knowledge. As Keith Baker notes:

> The idea that a successful science is primarily a well-made language became the watchword of the Ideologues—in this, as in many other things, the true heirs of the Enlightenment—who regarded *ideology*, the philosophy of signs, as the only means of reducing, the moral and political sciences to positive truths as certain as those of the physical sciences.[23]

Keith Baker reports that Condillac detested Condorcet. Ironically, Condillac died from a fever attributed to hot chocolate served to him by Condorcet. After his death, Condorcet published an article asserting that Condillac, unlike Locke, was not an original thinker. Further, he charged that Condillac had neglected those economic writers who preceded him.[24]

Baker quotes from Condorcet regarding his opinion of Condillac:

> We do not make these observations in order to diminish the glory of M. de Condillac. He knew better than anyone that no man discovers a complete science single-handed. The motto *prolem sine matre creatam* will never be adopted by a philosopher who has made true discoveries.[25]

Condorcet's use of this line of Ovid was an implied attack on Montesquieu since the line had been placed at the head of the *L'Esprit des Lois*. The future Ideologue, Dominique-Joseph Garat, replied to Condorcet in the *Journal de Paris*, praising Condillac as the "rival and perhaps the conqueror of Locke," and also advanced a defense of Montesquieu. Condorcet told Turgot he would not bother to respond. However, he did write a draft essay in response. Baker reports Condorcet's conclusion regarding the debate over Condillac:

> In a great number of questions in philosophy, morals, and politics, this analysis of ideas is identical with the method of discovering truth because the truths involved are so simple that they need only to be stated to be accepted. But one should not therefore conclude in general, Condorcet insisted, that the method of making a discovery and the analysis of ideas in the abstract sciences are one and the same thing....
>
> Like the physical sciences, then, the moral and political sciences must be reduced by the method of analysis to positive truths based on "general facts and rigorous reasoning." So convinced was he that positive scientific truth was grounded upon the twin foundations of observations and analysis, that Condorcet suggested in a fragmentary plan for the history of the sciences that they advance by the dialectical movement, oscillating between periods dominated successfully by the spirit of observation necessary to elicit facts and to detail them accurately and by the systematic spirit necessary to classify these facts and to perceive their relations and consequences. There arrives a stage in the development of every science where it demands so much of the energy of the scientist to work through the detailed facts accumulated by observation that the

discovery of general principles requires superhuman intelligence. At such a stage, Condorcet maintained, the scientist must await a revolution in method that will make it possible to reduce the inchoate mass of detail to general truths.[26]

Attitudes toward Condillac's importance vary. For example, Stanley Jevons considered Condillac to be "original and profound," and writes:

> The true doctrine may be more or less clearly traced through the writings of a succession of great French economists, from Condillac, Baudeau, and Le Trosne, through J.B. Say, Destutt de Tracy, Storch, and others, down to Bastiat and Courcelle-Seneuil. The conclusion to which I am ever more clearly coming is that the only hope of attaining a true system of economics is to fling aside, once and forever, the lazy and preposterous assumptions of the Ricardian school.[27]

Schumpeter, on the other hand, felt that Condillac derived his economic ideas from Turgot, and paled in comparison with that most brilliant economist of the eighteenth century.[28]

Baker, in concluding his estimate of Condillac's importance, states:

> His achievement was to combine, digest, and put into systematic form, views often found scattered elsewhere in the philosophical and scientific thought of the period. Yet if Condillac by his very typicality may be regarded as the 'philosopher to the Philosophes':

his direct influence upon them remains problematic. If Condorcet is representative in this respect, we must beware of the assumption that the philosophes automatically or uncritically found their philosophical themes in Condillac's writing.[29]

Condillac's influence remained strong through the period of the French Republic and into the Bourbon Restoration, and was continued by Destutt de Tracy and the Ideologues. The last publication of his collected works was in 1822. After that the Lockean ideas of Condillac and the Ideologues, were replaced by the idealistic philosophy of writers such as Victor Cousin whose ideas were based on German influences.

Peter Gay, in his works on the Enlightenment,[30] and Georges Gusdorf,[31] see the Enlightenment as marking the beginning of the social sciences. Also, the Scottish Enlightenment, represented by such writers as Hume, Smith, and Ferguson played a central role in this development. On the other hand, Michael Foucault insists that the social sciences were not possible in the eighteenth century, and were possible only after the important redeployment of epistemology accomplished by Destutt de Tracy in his *Ideologie.*[32] Focault's insistence that the clarity of thinking achieved by de Tracy's approach as the necessary precondition of social science, however, is extreme. Destutt de Tracy did indeed make a monumental contribution to the social sciences in general by his writings on will and political economy. But, whatever his contribution to clearer thinking may have been, de Tracy's contribution must be considered as only a continuation of the eighteenth century, of which he was very much a part.

Keith Michael Baker's *Condorcet* is the single most important contribution to understanding the intellectual history of this period.[33] Baker's work offers the key to the understanding of the Enlightenment, the French Revolution, and most important,

the development of French Classical Liberalism in the nineteenth century.

Condorcet drew upon the English thinkers, especially Newton and Locke, for his general ideas. But, it was from Hume that
he seemed to take the most in his approach to science. The
parallels in Condorcet with Hume's *A Treatise of Nature* are
strong, especially in reference to the chapter "Of Knowledge and
Probability." Blaise Pascal and Jacob Bernoulli had contributed
greatly to the theory of probability, and of the latter, Condorcet
said:

> [He] seemed to recognize more clearly than anyone
> the full potential of the applications of this calculus,
> and the manner in which it could be extended to
> almost all questions subject to reasoning.

Baker argues that Condorcet's definition of the social field
parallel to a mathematical model was based on the fact that
political questions for administrative reasons were "already associated with a quantitative approach to social phenomena."[35] Not
the least of these reasons was the close connection between
political questions and the quantitative problems associated with
tax-collection.

For Condorcet, as for Turgot, the fundamental issue of the
moral sciences were deeper than the utilitarian issues of self-
interest. The moral sciences provided a guide to the rights of
man, which Condorcet dealt with in an essay written in 1786, in
which he maintained that there are four fundamental rights. The
first of these rights were liberty and security. Equally important,
however, was the right to property. Baker observes:

> Of all the natural rights, Condorcet argued in the *Vie
> de M. Turgot*, property, the free disposition of what

one legitimately possesses, is the most fundamental. It follows that *laissez faire, laissez-passer* must be the first law of civil society. Everywhere they are untrammeled, particular interests tend naturally to the common good. Everywhere they are hindered, agriculture, industry, and commerce must be set free. 'For what right can society have over these objects? Instituted to preserve man's exercise of his natural rights, obliged to watch over the common good of all, it is required by justice and the public interest equally to limit legislation to protecting the freest exercise of the individual's right to property, to establishing no obstacles and destroying those that exist, to preventing fraud and violence from contravening the laws.' The science of citizenship, as Condorcet learned it from Turgot, clearly implied the liberal economic program for which Condorcet campaigned so vociferously throughout his public career.[36]

The third natural right was the right to the rule of and equality before the law; and the fourth was the right to participate, directly or indirectly, in the formation of laws. Baker feels that the logical step from Condorcet's discussion of rights was to "The Calculus of Consent,"[37] the term for which, he further observes, he is indebted to Gordon Tullock and James Buchanan whose "methodological individualism" Baker says Condorcet would have appreciated.[38]

The Physiocrats, when defined to include Turgot and Condorcet, made a major contribution to the concepts which led to the *Declaration of the Rights of Man.*[39]

Condorcet's ideas were clearly influenced by Turgot, but also by Locke, Hume, Smith, and Ferguson.[40] Condorcet was very active in the pamphlet war that preceded the French Revolution and argued that property is not respected when taxes are levied arbitrarily. He also favored multiple votes by tax payers—weighted in proportion to the amount of taxes paid—and would allow small taxpayers to combine their proportions into one vote. These ideas Condorcet had adopted from Turgot's stated belief that taxpayers should be considered the same as stockholders and that, therefore, their voting should be proportional to the amount of stock they held, or the amount of taxes they paid.

During the early years of the French Revolution, Condorcet was very active in the debates on the new constitution, the protection of individual rights, and education. With the end of the constitutional monarchy Condorcet, who had been a Girondin representative for Paris in the Legislative Assembly, was elected by his native department to a seat in the Convention. On October 11, 1792 Condorcet, along with Thomas Paine, was elected to the nine-member Committee on the Constitution, and became its leading member, as well as the principal author of the 1793 proposed Constitution. Much of the constitutional work was devoted to the mechanics of rational decision-making and voting. Reflecting Turgot's influence again, Condorcet urged a radical decentralization of administration, and a dispersal of power, that would make it nearly passive. According to Baker, Condorcet believed:

> It was essential, and for the same reasons, to restrict government to a minimum. 'The action of governments is too complicated; they act too much, on too many matters. This complication, this useless action, necessarily results in an obscure, indirect influence which arouses suspicion.... The people that wishes to be free and peaceful must have laws and institutions that reduce the action of government to the least possible quantity.' Anarchists who had recognized this principle intuitively were right in their goals,

Condorcet insisted, but wrong in their methods. This 'virtual nullity' of government would be achieved not by disorder, conflicts of power, or its parcelling out among incoherent little units but by a 'profoundly conceived system of laws: that would transform politics entirely by replacing coercion with the gentle yoke of reason.'[41]

Condorcet's constitutional plan was furiously opposed by the Jacobins in the name of Rousseauist principles of a republic of virtue. On May 13, 1793 Condorcet proposed that the Convention submit a constitution to the people or resign for new elections. On June 2, Condorcet and others were expelled from the Convention and the Terror began. He wrote in protest to these measures, and was subsequently ordered arrested by the Convention and his papers sealed and his library confiscated. He went into hiding. After his arrest, Condorcet was imprisoned, and found dead on March 29, 1794—a victim of either a heart attack or poison.

Antoine Louis Claude Destutt de Tracy was the founder of *Ideologie*, was a descendant of early fourteenth Scottish Archers who served in the Dauphin's Regiment. De Tracy was a disciple of Voltaire's. In fact de Tracy when he was sixteen made a pilgrimage to Voltaire's home in order to receive a philosophical benediction from him. De Tracy studied mathematics and geography at the University of Strasbourg, but seemed to benefit most from the courses of the Protestant, rationalist historian Christopher Koch, in that these had a lasting impact on de Tracy's approach to social evolution.

De Tracy's formal education was mixed with the informal education he received at his ancestral home of his grandparents who exposed him to Jansenist thought and that of the Physiocrats. With the calling of the Estates-General, de Tracy became associated with the liberal nobles in Paris in the Committee of the Thirty. With his election to the Second Estate, de Tracy supported most of the reform measures that were presented. After reading Burke's critique of the French Revolution, de Tracy denounced Burke in the National Assembly.[42] De Tracy felt that France's problems were due to the wars of Louis XIV and Louis XV. He did not think that England's oligarchy, with its rotten boroughs and impressment of seamen, was a model France should follow. Rather, he believed, that the new constitution would create a federation of republics under an hereditary monarchy that would be more preferable.

De Tracy was also a member of the *Societe de 1789*, which included, in addition to LaFayette, De Pont de Nemours, Condorcet and others, as well as several future Ideologues— Garat, Volney, Cabnis, and Roederer.[43] De Tracy was also closely associated with the Feuillants, the liberal monarchist party, which was opposed to the Jacobins, and actively sought voting rights for the colored and blacks in Santo Domingo who were property owners. Later de Tracy was appointed a brigadier general under Lafayette's command on the German front. After leaving service, de Tracy settled in Auteuil where Condorcet also lived. Both Condorcet and de Tracy, who had been influenced by the writings of Condillac, looked for progress in the humane, moral, and political sciences.

With the onset of Terror, Condorcet went into hiding; de Tracy was arrested for "incivisme." De Tracy, expecting execution at any time, wrote on July 29, that "if heaven leaves me some time to live and study" he would write on "thought-knowledge-truth-virtue-happiness-loving, and on liberty-equality-philanthropy." In early October, following the overthrow of Robespierre, de Tracy was released from prison. Because of his experience with imprisonment it is understandable that de Tracy totally disdained politicians, and refused to engage any further in politics. In a letter to his friend and disciple, Stendahl, de Tracy wrote:

Why are men always more concerned about the means of seizing power than about learning...what they should want to do when they become powerful? It is a failing apparently inherent in our species. It did us much harm during the French Revolution, or rather it was what made it fail. And this is what long ago made Swift say, in his mordant style, that men love to climb up ladders like apes...and when they are on top, they don't know how to do anything but show their behinds.[44]

During the terror the universities were closed, the French academies abolished, and many leading scientists were executed. Indeed, the terror had been a declaration of war against the Enlightenment, and de Tracy viewed it as an attack on civilization itself.

In the spring of 1795, the Convention printed three thousand copies of Condorcet's *Esquisse d'un tableau historique de progres de l'espirit humain*, which was co-edited by Pierre Claude Francois Daunou, who wielded great influence during the period of the Directory, although he came into conflict later with Napoleon. Daunou's writings were prodigious and his *Essai sur les garanties indivduelles*, was a great statement of the value of constitutional protection of individual rights, and which became as influential in South America as de Tracy's *Commentary on Montesquieu* had been in North America. Daunou was also the author of a twenty volume work *Cours d'etudes historiques* as well as the author of *Discours sur l'etat des lettres en France au XIIIe siecle*. After the restoration Daunou was made editor of *Journal des Savants*, and a professor of history in the College de France, where his lectures were attended by de Tracy.[45]

Through Daunou's efforts, the Convention in 1795, created the *Institut National* which offered classes in literature, science, and the moral and political sciences. De Tracy was associated with the faculty of moral and political sciences in the *Institut*. Other faculties were staffed with such persons as Christopher Koch, Daunou, Sieyes, Du Pont de Nemours, and Talleyrand. Daunou became the president of the *Institut*, which he said was a living encyclopedia. De Tracy and his associates had learned from their experiences in the terror that human nature required a complete analysis and explanation, if the foundations of self-government were to be devised, and these men, like Jefferson, considered education—both in the narrow formal sense and in the broader informal sense—as crucial for the success of self-government.

De Tracy also was a major critic of the philosophic system which was to challenge that of Locke and Condillac-Kantianism. De Tracy, along with J. B. Say, the editor of the *Decade Philosophique*, criticized the philosophy of Kant and Descartes. According to Emmet Kennedy:

> Attention to these innate traits of 'deep structure': has been revived by modern linguistic theory, Chomsky argues, after centuries of neglect by empiricists and behaviorists. Few eighteenth-century linguists probed as deeply into this elemental structure as Tracy, yet strangely Tracy was the century's most adamant critic of Cartesian or Kantian theories of innate ideas or forms. Tracy's combination of a strong conviction in the possibility of general grammar with empirical, sensationalist psychology marked a phase very charac-teristic of eighteenth century 'ideology' which Chomsky overlooks.[46]

De Tracy was influenced by Hobbes' concept of self-interest, but disagreed with Hobbes contention that war was man's natural state, "for if it had been, he would never have escaped primitive bellicosity."[47] For de Tracy:

The origins of society could be explained ideologically: or grammatically: men enter into society as they learn to communicate and negotiate their conflicting rights. Like Hobbes, Tracy believed the ensuing agreements which constitute society were the result of conventions, but Tracy stressed the *natural* standard for all conventions. Conventional property could not exist without faculties. In entering society, man neither abandons a part of his rights nor sacrifices his liberty, as all contract theories had presupposed. Rights for Tracy were 'always limitless': and were only modified by the way they were realized.[48]

Through his son-in-law, George Washington Lafayette, and the latter's father, the Marquis de Lafayette, as well as Du Pont de Nemours and J.B. Say, de Tracy was introduced to Thomas Jefferson, a member of the *Institut National* and, since 1797, president of the American Philosophical Society. In 1806 Jefferson wrote de Tracy to thank him for copies of his books and to announce de Tracy's election into the American Philosophical Society. In 1809, complementing Jefferson on retiring as President, de Tracy asked Jefferson to translate and to publish his *A Commentary and Review of Montesquieu's Spirit of Laws*.[49] In response, Jefferson wrote to de Tracy and informed him that the *Commentary* was a most precious gift to mankind. Jefferson did translate a part of the *Commentary*, but sent the rest of it to William Duane, editor of the *Aurora* to finish.

De Tracy's *Commentary* represented a change from his earlier explicit admiration for Montesquieu, largely because he had become influenced by Condorcet's critique of Montesquieu. Both Madison and Montesquieu had agreed that representative government could exist in large territories only by federation. De Tracy argued a non-Girondin line that maintained that representative government could exist in large states without federalism because of military threats to the nation's existence. For de Tracy, war was the enemy of mankind, and he repeated Montesquieu's arguments that discredited all justifications for war. De Tracy advocated a European federation as the solution to war. He agreed with Montesquieu that republics should not have colonies and he advocated the granting of equality to all territories and the inclusion of Louisiana as a state in the U.S. federation.

De Tracy differed from Montesquieu in part because more than over one-half of a century separated them. Montesquieu's great work had been published at the high point of English and French economic development under Sir Robert Walpole and Cardinal Fleury, whose policies had lowered taxes, and created consumer demand to which the Industrial Revolution had been the response. France, however, deviated from this direction in the second half of the eighteenth century. Wars had caused higher taxes and created national debt, and France was reluctant to undertake any economic reforms despite the analyses of Turgot and Hume. The French Revolution was the result. What Montesquieu had seen as unchangeable facts in England— medieval institutions protecting the individual from the emerging central state, and commerce serving to eliminate social and economic problems—had not taken place in France. Condorcet and de Tracy, therefore, differed from Montesquieu on the matter of active reform, since they had seen that evolution had not operated to eliminate government intervention and domination.

De Tracy made several points central to the Liberal analysis in nineteenth-century France. For example, he argued that the political ruling class would continue to incorporate the most capable of the rising middle class, and that the poor would be able to become wealthy and powerful if they were not prohibited from doing so by the operation of governmental power.[50]

Many of de Tracy's ideas had been expressed in his *Quels sont les moyens de fonder la moral chez un peuple?* which he wrote for the *Institut National's* competition of 1798. In the essay, de Tracy expressed a "quasi-Hobbesian conception of human nature where individual wills conflict with other wills, striving to be free in their movements, but continually meeting opposition."[51]

De Tracy critiqued the Jacobins as follows:

> By reducing taxes the government could furnish the working class with the financial means and leisure for their children to profit from school, without which a "legion of school masters" and learned societies would be useless. Reliance upon a few moral lessons, a few civic *fetes*, was to ignore the crucial role of more basic institutions, "to neglect the artillery of an army to occupy itself with its music."[51]

The contrast between de Tracy's views in this 1798 essay and the later *Commentary*...can be found in his views about general education, and his opposition to state education. The themes of general education, and the exclusion of the state from education, were well received by de Tracy's readership of the *Commentary*. Kennedy notes the complete reversal of de Tracy's earlier position, and in this later exposition he condemned, in effect, all forms of government involvement in society, including, but not limited to education; and held that government "leave nature to act."[53] Further, he urged the free exchange of opinions and a complete freedom of thought and expression.[54]

In his *Commentary*..., de Tracy rejected the geographical and climatic determinism advanced by Montesquieu, in favor of a sort of economic determinism. He felt that commerce should have the central role in modern society, and maintained that mercantilist theories about the balance of trade were illusory.

Also, influenced by Malthus, de Tracy rejected the view that population growth was an indicator and a part of prosperity. He wrote:

> To deprive [man] of his life is a crime authorized by many legislators, against whom the theologians of these countries have not protested. On the other hand to take measures in advance, to prevent animated beings from being born, when they could only have been unhappy and rendered their species so, is an act of prudence which some theologians have considered a crime.[55]

Further, de Tracy emphasized the mutual benefit that results from every exchange, and contrasted it with the deleterious affects of taxation which he viewed as an attack on private property and purely negative in its applications. He urged that so-called public works would be better performed by private enterprise; and he feared the government's control over the issuance of money.

By November, 1811 de Tracy had completed the fourth volume of his *Ideologie*, and sent a copy to Thomas Jefferson, who translated the work and arranged for its publication in Georgetown in 1817.[56] Jefferson expected this book to become the textbook in economics that would be used in American colleges, and it was, indeed, adopted by many colleges and made a major contribution to academic economics in America. However, the work which finally become pre-eminent in the teaching of political economy was J.B. Say's *Treatise on Political Economy*.[57] Say's and de Tracy's works both were very influential in the field of academic economics in America until the late nineteenth century. French political economy had many attributes that made it superior to English Utilitarianism and Ricardian-Millian economics, and America benefitted greatly from the choice of the French views on this topic.

De Tracy had a basic understanding of the role of utility in determining prices; and the role of the capitalist and entrepreneur. He viewed government as a parasitical activity whose use of expenditures was non-productive, useless, and destructive.[58] De Tracy advocated the unity of the sciences and, like Descartes and Leibniz, saw mathematics or calculus as the means to unify the chaotic accumulation of knowledge. His rejection of the social mathematics of Condorcet and Condillac which urged the notion that social mathematics would provide a solution to man's problems, was explicit. De Tracy believed that much of man's activity was not quantifiable, and that mathematics and statistics alone could not provide a social panacea.[59]

After the Bourbon restoration in 1814, de Tracy was able to expand substantially his contacts, and during the years of the restoration and until 1848, de Tracy's ideas had continuing impact on the intellectual life of France, especially up to the time of de Tracy's death in 1836.

However, the influence of Jean Baptiste Say was more lasting. After the Bourbon restoration Say was able to teach and write extensively. Although there were substantial similarities of the views of Say with those of de Tracy, the latter's were more philosophical and more clearly reflected the ideas and influence of the eighteenth century Enlightenment *philosophes*. Say's economic and political views placed him in the mainstream of eighteenth century economists such as Turgot and Smith. Also, Say had substantial influence in American intellectual life, partly because his work had undergone fourteen English editions.[60]

Although Benjamin Constant emerged in the same intellectual context as de Tracy, he was not a child of the Enlightenment *philosophes*. Being Swiss and having studied in Edinburgh, his political philosophy was formed in total reaction against the Jacobin Terror. Constant was an Anglophile and rejected the

Enlightenment's emphasis on system-building. During the period of the Directory, Constant was strongly influenced by William Godwin's *Enquiry into Political Justice.*[61]

Hayek re-discovered Constant while writing *The Constitution of Liberty*, and found Constant very congenial to his way of thinking. Constant himself was strongly influenced by Montesquieu and contributed to the restoration of Montesquieu's influence on nineteenth-century French liberalism. Guy Dodge has noted that Constant's political philosophy has been neglected in the twentieth century due to the "sustained attacks on it (liberalism) by the exponents of conservatism, and Marxists, Freudians, existentialists, and the New Left...."[62] Although Constant has received some recent attention in American scholarship, these have been insufficient given the impact Constant had on French thinkers as well as on Hegel and Lord Acton.

Constant saw the necessity of avoiding "two false propositions": "religion is the natural ally of despotism," [and] "the absence of the religious sentiments favorable to liberty." Germaine de Stael, a companion of Constant, provides the following commentary:

> The secret had been found of exhibiting the friends of liberty as the enemies of religion; there are two pretexts for the singular injustice which would exclude from this earth the noblest of sentiments, alliance with Heaven. The first is the Revolution as it was effected in the name of philosophy; an inference has thence been drawn, that to love liberty it is necessary to be an atheist. Assuredly, it is because the French did not unite religion to liberty that their revolution deviated so often from its primitive direction.[63]

Constant rejected theories of egoism, since he felt that only religion could establish the moral foundation that would support the idea of liberty and provide a resistance to oppression. He writes, when:

> Christians appeared, they placed their point of support beyond egoism. Liberty is nourished by sacrifices. Liberty wishes always for its citizens, sometimes for heroes. Religious convictions give men strength to become martyrs.[64]

Constant was influenced equally by Condorcet and Burke. In 1822 Constant expressed his opposition to the utilitarian thinking of Bentham in an economic work regarding the economic writings of one of the economists of the Neapolitan school.[65]

Constant distinguished between ancient military society and modern commercial society, and subjected the latter to extensive analysis. Ancient liberty of active participation in collective society, required the sacrifice of the enjoyment of the peace given by individual liberty. This liberty of the ancients, Constant held, was anachronistic. Thus the thought of Rousseau and Mably, for example, based on this anachronistic view, led to the shedding of blood, and the Napoleonic wars which were propelled by this same vision.

Leo Strauss maintains that moderns:

> ...lack the public spirit of the patriotism of the ancients. They are more concerned with their private affairs than with the fatherland. They lack the greatness of soul of the ancients. They are bourgeois rather than citizens.[66]

Strauss should have emphasized that the modern commercial societies are Christian. The "liberty" of the ancients is possible only under paganism. It requires paganism to have worship of the fatherland and the spurning of private virtues. Christianity is the necessary condition for the liberty of moderns, for the modern commercial society, the opposite of the ancient military society which is rooted in state worship. Constant associated the exclusion of the public realm and the supremacy of the private realm in commercial societies to the absolute recognition of private property due to Christianity. Constant's theme can be found in Acton's "The History of Freedom in Christianity."[67] Edouard Laboulaye, the editor of Constant's political writings, notes: "To proclaim that God has rights is to tear asunder the unity of despotism. There is a germ of revolution which separates the ancient from the modern world."[68]

Ralph Raico has correctly identified the central concern of Constant—to rebut the political ideas of Jean Jacques Rousseau regarding sovereignty and the general will. He writes:

> Accepting the idea that social life necessarily brings with it the total alienation of one's rights, Rousseau was thus the modern originator of the notion that freedom in a social context is identifiable with a condition of equal submission to the interest of the community and equal participation in the exercise of political power. Constant believed that the championship of unlimited popular sovereignty by Rousseau and others represented much less of a break with the historical political pattern than might at first appear to be the case.[69]

In an addition to the *Cours de politique constitutionelle ou collection de ouvrages publies le gouvernment representatif,* published in 1815, Constant reinforces his critique of Rousseau:

The precaution recommended to be followed is all the more indispensable for the fact that party leaders, however pure their intentions, are always reluctant to limit sovereignty. They regard themselves as its heirs-presumptive and are concerned to preserve it for future use even while it is in the hands of their enemies. They distrust this or that kind of government, this or that class of governors; but if they are allowed to entrust it to agents of their choice they will try to extend it to its maximum....

Unlimited popular sovereignty creates...a degree of power in human society too great by definition, which is an evil no matter in whose hands it is placed. Whether it is entrusted to a single man, to several, or to all, it will be found equally an evil.... There are weights too heavy for human hands. The error of those who, out of genuine love of liberty, have given popular sovereignty unlimited power derives from the way in which their political ideas have been formed. They have seen in history a small number of men, or even a single one, in possession of immense power which did a great deal of harm; but their anger was directed against the possessors of the power and not the power itself. Instead of destroying it they thought only of displacing it. It was a scourge which they considered a conquest.

The consent of the majority by no means suffices in all cases to make its acts legitimate; there are some acts that nothing can make legitimate. When any authority commits acts of this sort it matters little whether it is called an individual or a nation; it might be the entire nation with the exception of the citizen whom it oppresses, and the act would still not be legitimate. Rousseau did not recognize this truth, and this error has turned his *Social Contract*, so often invoked on behalf of liberty, into the most terrible aid to all kinds of despotism.... Once granted that the general will can do everything, the representatives of that general will are the more to be feared the more they declare themselves to be merely the docile instruments of this so-called will, and the more they have at their disposal the force or the form that suits them. These people, by virtue of the unlimited extent of social authority, legalize that which no tyrant would dare to do in his own name.[70]

According to Raico, Constant represents the complete break with the Enlightenment and French Revolution which becomes the character of nineteenth century liberalism. The ideas of Constant provide a probable and possible intellectual bulwark against the type of dominating state associated with the French Terror. Raico notes further that Constant was a severe critic of the desire for uniformity and pseudo-mathematical symmetry, that formed the foundation for much of the actions of the Terror, and this was particularly the case with notions of regionalism:

The interests and memories which are born of local customs contain a germ of resistance which authority suffers only with regret, and which it hastens to eradicate. With individuals it has its way more easily, it rolls, its enormous weight over them effortlessly, as over sand.[71]

Constant was a leading force in nineteenth-century liberalism's rejection of utilitarianism; he did not find the greatest happiness principle to be a foundation for a free society. Rather such a foundation was to be found in the principle of self perfection:

[I]s it true that happiness—of whatever sort it might be—is the unique end of man? In that case, our road would be quite narrow, and our destination not a very lofty one. There is not one of us, who, if he wished to descend, to restrict his moral faculties, to degrade his desires, to abjure activity, glory and all generous and profound emotions, could not make himself a brute and a happy one...it is not for happiness alone, it is for self perfectioning that destiny calls us.[72]

Raico calls our attention to Constant's prediction of the evils of legislation. Legislators' errors have consequences for all of society, and not a single individual as with individual decisions; legislators feel the burden of errors in legislation less than the ordinary citizen does; the information feedback to legislators of the affects of their actions is longer than that among citizens; it is difficult for legislators to admit of errors because of the affect on their prestige; and:

legislation has the defect of all collective decisions: it is a 'forced give-and-take between prejudice and truth, between interests and principles,' while decisions taken by individuals have the chance of being, in this sense, purer.[73]

As F. A. Hayek emphasized, Classical Liberalism achieved a peak with the writings of Benjamin Constant. Later writers may have equaled him, but none surpassed him in depth and subtlety. Constant's liberalism speaks to and for the modern man.

French classical liberalism's foundation was Western Christianity's intellectual tradition. The Christian philosophical tradition rooted in Stoicism received an organizational structure with the reintroduction of Aristotelianism in the thirteenth century from the Islamic scholarship in Spain. According to Lord Acton, Thomas Aquinas was the first Whig. The pamphlet literature of the Gregorian Reform and the Conciliar Movement expressed the tradition in the middle ages.

But the political centralization which accompanied the Renaissance and the Reformation challenged the medieval tradition of liberty. Tocqueville saw modern centralization as the opposite of "the individualistic system of the Middle Ages."[74] In response the sixteenth century University of Paris produced not only Basque reformers, Ignatius Loyola and Francis Xavier, but also the Iberian Scholastics, Dominican and Jesuit, de Vitoria, Suarez, Mariana, Molina, de Lugo, etc.—the School of Salamanca. These Scholastics were the sources of debates in French legal and political thought, as they were for the English, such as John Locke.

John Locke has been called a Late Protestant Scholastic by Joseph Schumpeter. John Locke's contribution as a natural law political philosopher has been the bedrock of liberal political philosophy. Today's classical liberal moral and political philosophers express the Aristotelian/Thomist tradition. The growth of the centralized state in France was characterized by the decision not to call the Estates General between 1614 and 1789. The contrast between the movement toward political and economic liberty in England, and the increased restriction on political and economic liberty for the fiscal benefit of the centralized state in France, became a major theme in French intellectual life.

The positive example of English liberalism became a stumbling bloc for the national pride of French authors. The constitutional limit on power in England which impressed Montesquieu and Voltaire was denigrated by later authors. Indeed, in the late eighteenth century, French authors drew on Jeremy Bentham and Utilitarianism in their criticism of England's legal and constitutional systems. Bentham's works were published in French translation before they were published in English (and published in Spanish with a very wide impact on Latin American legal thinking). English Utitilitarian criticism of English liberalism was favored among French authors. Some French liberals criticized inconsistencies in English practice, for example, in imperialism.

The French Revolution was the defining event for French political writers. Liberals recognized early the slippery slope to despotism when the property of the Catholic Church was confiscated and used as the reserve for the printing press money which led to runaway inflation. The law of maximum prices and Economic Terror were indelible benchmarks of statism and negation of the principles of liberty.

The French Revolution clarified the dangers of Jean-Jacques Rousseau's writings. Rousseau would be the perfect Establishment newspaper's op-ed columnist—each day starts with amnesia. There is no consistency in thinking from day to day, only consistency in confusion of thinking. Thus, the freshness and originality which defines both Rousseau and the columnists. Before 1789 Rousseau was the gadfly with the unusual perspective. After the Terror he was recognized as the source of the violence caused by ideas of collectivism and egalitarianism. For the classical liberals, Rousseau was the premier example of the social democrat. After the French Revolution, the use of liberty by Rousseau was seen as a dangerous misuse of words; Benjamin Constant made the greatest contribution in clarifying and enhancing the idea of liberty. Constant confronted Rousseau:

> Were it the whole of the nation, save the citizen whom it oppresses, it would be none the more legitimate. Rousseau overlooked this truth, and his error made his *Social Contract*, so often invoked in favor of liberty, the most formidable support for all kinds of despotism.[75]

Constant considered that the claim that life was preferable in the rain forest than in polite society as showing the intellectual failure of the intellectuals.[76]

During the course of the nineteenth century, French liberalism continued to develop and to deepen the analysis of the impact of the state on society. The evolution of economic thought was healthy, but the development of political philosophy was strongly challenged by the consequences of successive revolutions. The Revolution of 1848 and the Second Republic led to the almost two decades of the Second Empire. The Paris Commune of 1871 was followed by the Third Republic. Fundamental principles were not encouraged by social uncertainties and the waves of fresh clients of public moneys.

## Endnotes

1. Robert R. Palmer, *Catholics and Unbelievers in Eighteenth-Century France*, Princeton, N.J.: Princeton University Press, 1939.

2. Lionel Rothkrug, *Opposition to Louis XIV: The Political and Social Origins of the French Enlightenment*, Princeton, N.J.: Princeton University Press, 1965.

3. Simone Goyard-Fabre, *Montesquieu: la Nature, les Lois, la liberte*, Paris: Presses Universitaires de France, 1993. See also: F.A. Hayek, "Richard Cantillon," *Journal of Libertarian Studies*, VII, 2 (Fall, 1985), pp. 27-47.

4. Joseph A. Schumpeter, *A History of Economic Analysis*, New York: Oxford University Press, 1954, esp. pp. 243-249, 492, 560, 625. Turgot's *Eloge de Gournay*, 1759 is the major source for understanding Gournay, and Du Pont de Nemour's *Memories sur la view et les ouvrages de M. Turgot* 1782, and Condorcet's *Vie Turgot* are major sources for the examination of the ideas of Turgot. Du Pont de Nemours also edited the *Oeuvres de Turgot* (9 vols., 1809-1811) Cf. Gustave Schelle ed., *Oeuvres de Turgot* (5 vols., Paris, Alcan, 1913-1923).

5. Schumpeter, *A History...*, p. 248.

6. *Ibid.* p. 249.

7. Frances Acomb, *Anglophobia in France, 1763-1789: An Essay in the History of Constitutionalism and Nationalism*, Durham, N.C.: Duke University Press, 1950.

8. Marie Kimball, *Jefferson: The Scene of Europe, 1784-1789*, New York: Coward-McCann, Inc., 1950. p. 82.

9. Wilmington, Delaware: Scholarly Resources, 1984. p. 6.

10. *The Autobiography....*, p. 7.

11. *Lettre d'un Theologien*, 1671.

12. *Traite de la practique des Billets entre les Negocians*, Louvain, 1682. For a fuller

examination of these contributions see: Cardinal van Roey, *De Justo Auctario ex Contractu Criditi,* Catholic University of Louvain, 1903.

13. *Usury explained; or Conscience quieted in the case of putting money out at Interest.* London, 1695 & 1699. Pseud for Le P. Jacques Thornentier, *L'Usure Expliquee et condamnee,* Paris, 1673.

14. Peter Gay, *Voltaire's Politics,* New York: Vintage Press, 1965. pp. 52-53.

15. Amsterdam, Cologne, 1721.

16. Geneva, 1748 and London, 1750.

17. Joseph Didieu, *Montesquieu et la tradition politique Anglais en France.* 1909.

18. Paschal Larkin, *Property in the Eighteenth Century, with Special Reference to England and Locke,* New York: Longmans Green & Co., 1930, p. 199.

19. Cf. Larkin, *op. cit.* pp. 200-202; Turgot, *Reflections on the Formation and Distribution of Wealth,* London: F. Spragg, 1793.

20. Larkin, *op. cit.,* pp. 217-220. Cf. I.C. Lundberg, *Turgot's Unknown Translator, The Reflexions and Adam Smith,* The Hague, Martinus Nijhoff, 1964.

21. Keith Michael Baker, *Condorcet: From a Natural Philosophy to Social Mathematics,* Chicago: University of Chicago Press, 1975.

22. *Ibid.,* p. 112.

23. *Ibid.,* p. 115.

24. *Ibid.,* p. 115.

25. *Ibid.,* pp. 117-118.

26. Stanley Jevons, *Theory of Political Economy,* 3rd ed., London, 1888. p. xlix.

27. Schumpeter, *op. cit.* pp. 124-125, 174-176, 302.

28. Baker, 116-117.

29. Peter Gay, *The Enlightenment: An Interpretation. 2 vols.,* New York, 1966-1969.

30. Georges Gusdorf, *Introduction aux sciences humaines,* Paris, 1960, and *Les sciences humaines et la pensee occidentale,* Paris, 1966, esp. vols. 4, 5, & 6. See: Murray Forsyth, *Reason and Revolution: The Political Thought of the Abbe Sieyes,* Leicester: Leicester University Press, 1987; New York: Holmes and Meier, 1987, pp. 32-33, 175-176.

31. Michael Focault, *The Order of Things: An Archaeology of the Human Sciences,* New York, 1970.

32. Baker, *op. cit.,* pp. 200-208.

33. *Ibid.,* p. 157.

34. *Ibid.,* p. 202.

35. *Ibid.,* pp. 218-219.

36. *Ibid.,* pp. 225-244.

37. *Ibid.,* p. 447.

38. See: V. Margacci, *Les origines de la Declaration des droits de l'homme de 1789,* 2d Ed. Paris, 1912.

39. Franck Alengry, *Condorcet, Guide de la Revolution francaise, theoricien de droit constitutionnel et precurseur de la science sociale,* Paris, 1903.

40. Baker, *op. cit.,* pp. 324-325. Baker is quoting Condorcet, *De la nature des pouvoirs politiques dans une nation libre.* 1792.

41. Destutt de Tracy, *Translation of a Letter from Monsieur de Tracy, Member of*

*the French National Assembly to M. Burke., in Answer to his Remarks on the French Revolution*, London, 1790.

42. See Keith Michael Baker, "Politics and Social Science in Eighteenth Century France: *The Societe de 1789*", in J.F. Bosher, ed., *French Government and Society, 1500-1850: Essays in Honor of Alfred Cobban*, London, 1973. pp. 208-230.

43. Emmet Kennedy, *Destutt de Tracy and the Origins of "Ideology": A Philosophe in the Age of Revolution*, Philadelphia: The American Philosophical Society, 1978.

44. The major study of the Ideologues is Francois Picavet, *Les Ideologues: Essai sur l'historie de idees et des theories scientifiques, philosophique, religieuses, etc., en France depuis 1789*, New York: Burt Franklin, 1971. See also: Charles Hunter Van Duzer, *Contribution of the Ideologues to French Revolutionary Thought*, Baltimore: Johns Hopkins University Press, 1935.

45. Kennedy, *op. cit.*, p. 131.

46. *Ibid.*, p. 167.

47. *Ibid.*, pp. 167-168.

48. Philadelphia, 1811.

49. Kennedy, *op. cit.*, p. 173.

50. *Ibid.*, p. 65.

51. *Ibid.*

52. *Ibid.*, pp. 174-175.

53. *Ibid.*, p. 175.

54. De Tracy, *Commentary...*, p. 251.

56. *Destutt de Tracy, A Treatise on Political Economy: to which is prefixed a supplement to a preceding work on the Understanding, or Elements of Ideology; with an Analytical Table, and an Introduction on the Faculty of the Will, Georgetown, 1817.*

55. Paris, 1803, & 1814. American editions became available in 1821.

56. Kennedy, *op. cit.*, p. 200.

57. *Ibid.*, pp. 49-50.

58. Ernest Teilhac, *Historie de la pensee economique aux Etats-Unis au 19e Siecle*, Paris, 1928. pp. 33-34. For further examination of the influence of de Tracy and Say see: Michael Foucault, *The Order of Things: An Archaeology of the Human Sciences*, London and New York,1970; Cheryl B. Welch, *Liberty and Utility: The French Ideologues and the Transformation of Liberalism*, New York: Columbia University Press, 1984; Brian Williams Head, *Ideology and Social Science: Destutt de Tracy and French Liberalism*, Dordrecht, Martinus Nijhoff Publishers, 1985.

59. Constant's uncle had translated Godwin's novels into French, and Constant himself had written on Godwin, however, his translation of Godwin, while it circulated among French intellectuals, remained unpublished, and was re-discovered only a quarter of a century ago.

60. Guy H. Dodge, *Benjamin Constant's Philosophy of Liberalism: A Study of Politics and Religion*, Chapel Hill: University of North Carolina Press, 1980. p. ix.

61. Germaine de Stael, *Considerations on the Principle Events of the French*

*Revolution*, Paris, 1817; New York, 1818. 2 vols., Vol. II, p. 335.

**62.** Benjamin Constant, *De la Religion 5 vols.*, Paris, 1824-1883. Vol. I, Preface, p. xxxix. Vol. II., p. 335.

**63.** Benjamin Constant, *Commentaire sur l'ouvrage de Filangieri 4 vols.*, Paris, 1822-1824.

**64.** Leo Strauss, *Natural Right and History*, Chicago: University of Chicago Press, 1953, p. 253.

**65.** Lord Acton, "The History of Freedom, Christianity," *Essays in the History of Liberty*, Vol. I, Indianapolis: Indiana Liberty Classics, 1985 pp. 29-53.

**66.** Edouard Laboulaye, "La liberte antique et la liberte moderne," in *L'etat et ses limites*, Paris, 1863, pp. 103-137.

**67.** Ralph Raico, "Benjamin Constant," *New Individualist Review* (Winter, 1964), Vol. III, pp. 3, 49. Liberty Press Edition, 1981. p. 503.

**68.** From Benjamin Constant, *Cours de politique constitutionelle ou collection de ouvrages publies le gouvernment representatif.* Ed. with Introduction by Edouard de Laboulaye, 2 vols. Paris, 1861. Quoted in Walter Simon, ed., *French Liberalism*, 1789-1848, New York: Wiley, 1972. pp. 64-66.

**69.** Raico, *op. cit.* p. 53; Constant, *Cours de Politique Constitutionell*, Paris: Guillsumin, 1872, Vol II. pp. 170-171.

70. Raico, *op cit.* p. 47.

**71.** *Ibid.* p. 48.

**72.** Alexis de Tocqueville, *Journeys to England and Ireland*, tr. George Lawrence and K. P. Mayer, J.P. Mayer (ed), New Haven: Yale University Press, 1958, p. 77.

**73.** Benjamin Constant, *Principles of Politics*, in *Political Writings*, Biancamaria Fontana, (ed), (tr), Cambridge: Cambridge University Press, 1988, p. 177. Cf. *Ibid*, pp. 105-109.

**74.** Benjamin Constant, "De M. Dunoyer et de quelques-uns de ses ouvrages," in *De la Perfectabilite de L'Espice humain*, Pierre Deguise, Lausanne, Droz, 1967, pp. 66-95. See: Dodge, *op. cit.*, pp. 141-142; and Pierre Balinski, *An Intellectual History of Liberalism*, Rebecca Balinski (tr), Princeton: Princeton University Press, 1994, pp. 84-92.

# The Nineteenth Century:
# American Challenges

JEFFREY D. WALLIN

H istorical events rarely have the courtesy to confine themselves to convenient periods, and those affecting liberty in
nineteenth-century America are no exception. Such incidents
tend to have their origins prior to the period and their results well
beyond it. To say something about the most significant aspect of
the period, the great battle over chattel slavery, for example, one
must begin with its origins in constitutional liberty during the
eighteenth century.

Of course, there is much that could be said about liberty in this
period that will not be said here. A hundred years is rather a long
time. To deal fairly with, say, the beginning of the women's
movement, or the emergence of labor unions, just to mention
two important aspects of the age, would be to attempt more than
a short address can deliver. Here I will deal with only two issues:
the struggle over nullification and slavery, and the emergence—
and subsequent rejection of—substantive due process, both
movements with serious long-term consequences, the one positive, the other less so, for liberty.

In the first *Federalist*[1] paper Alexander Hamilton asks whether
men are really capable of "establishing good government," by
which he means free government, "from reflection and choice,
or whether they are forever destined to depend for their political
constitutions on accident and force."

It has always seemed to me that this passage is much like the first book of Plato's *Republic*: the more one understands the whole work, the more one comes to see that the whole is prefigured in the beginning.

Hamilton's statement is about more than founding, although it is surely addressed above all to the question of founding. Its essence reaches beyond for the simple reason that in a free country, the deepest foundations and purposes of government are laid up in the hearts of its citizens. As each new generation comes along, it too must come to the point of sharing in the founding. This does not require every nation to entertain a revolution every generation or so, an idea the occasionally imprudent Thomas Jefferson seems to have entertained.[2] It is just that the love of liberty, and the self-restraint that lies at the heart of a people's ability to rule itself, must become internalized in each generation. For a people neither jealous of its liberties, nor capable of accepting the responsibilities that are their logical concomitant, may be said to be the lawful prey of every unruly and powerful enemy it may have to face, either externally or internally.

As Harry V. Jaffa[3] has pointed out, the essential problem of liberty may be grasped by reflecting on a story told by the English poet, Chaucer.[4] It seems there was a band of thieves, which, after plundering a few poor unfortunates, fled to the forest. But when their escape had been made good, they found that, though they had remembered to bring their loot, they had forgotten to provide themselves with food. So it was decided that one of them would venture back to the nearest village for food, while the other two guarded the booty. When the foraging thief returned with the food, his companions, who had decided that there was no good reason to share the loot three ways when sharing it between themselves would be so much more pleasant, killed him, and then ate the food he had brought. But, says Chaucer, they did not live to profit from their perfidy, because the food they had stolen from their former colleague had been poisoned. For he also had reflected on how much better it would be not to have to share equally.

The moral of this story is that even in a band of robbers, there must be justice if the robbers are to survive. And justice here means self-restraint, or, to put it in contemporary terms, it means respecting the equal rights of others if you wish your own rights to be respected.

It is important to be clear about this principle, because only principles can instruct. The great naval strategist, Alfred T. Mahan, remarked some seventy-five years ago that "[t]here is such a thing as seeing another come to grief, yes even to destruction, without being one whit wiser yourself, because you do not understand how it happened; and you do not understand...because you do not see the principle he has violated."[5] As it is with men, so is it with nations. It is only by understanding the principles of the American founding that the practical and theoretical crises of the nineteenth-century can be understood.

In the American context, Chaucer's story means that liberty and justice depend upon, as Publius puts it in the *Federalist*, the "genius of the people." This genius, or spirit of the people, is a jealous regard for their own liberty and, what is so easy to forget, a decent regard for the liberties and rights of others. And it is this spirit that Publius thinks is the *most* important safeguard of liberty, once sufficient constitutional barriers to the abuse of power have been built into the system. The dangers to liberty in nineteenth- century America were related either to attacks upon constitutional barriers, or even more substantively, to attempts at changing the "genius" of the people itself.

And what is this genius, spirit, or decency of the people to rest upon? The answer given by the Declaration of Independence is that it is to rest upon the conviction that the rights to be enjoyed are in deep and lasting accord with the rights of nature and of nature's God. They are to rest upon the conviction that liberty is a moral imperative, replete with duties and obligations as well as rights and pleasures. This is because the best citizens obey the law, not so much out of naked, paralyzing fear, as out of a sense of justice and law-bred habit.

According to the Declaration, the natural equality of all men *qua* men leads to the political principle that no man may justly rule another without his consent. All forms of government in which one or some men rule others without their consent and for the sake of the interests of the rulers only are unjust, for they violate the fundamental dictate of nature, that all men are created equal, and that therefore no man has the right to rule another without his consent. Although such equality is difficult to demonstrate, its opposite is not. On what ground can creatures who share the same nature or genius be said to have a natural right to rule others of their own kind for their—the rulers'—own private interest?

This equality requires that in the original act of forming a government, *every* individual must give his or her consent. Those who do not do so form no part of the compact or the people it creates. As between them and those who have agreed to associate, they may be said to be still in the "state of nature" with regard to one another, where no right but the right of self-preservation obtains.

But notice that this is not only the first occasion on which unanimity is required: it is the *only* occasion on which it is, or even *can* be required. Clearly, on no decision beyond this primitive agreement to associate, can there be unanimity. As Madison put it in *Federalist* 10, "As long as the reason of man continues fallible, and he is at liberty to exercise it, different opinions will be formed." Immediately after the original, unanimous decision, it becomes clear that in all subsequent decisions, a part must always act for the whole. However, nothing is said here about the part being allowed to act on behalf of the whole for *its own*, that is the *part's* interest only. The unanimous decision to form a body politic could only be made if *everyone* made that decision in order to preserve the rights and liberties that are theirs by nature (although so insecurely maintained in that state as to require the institution of governments to protect them). Surely no one would decide to give up the right he has in the state of nature, which is the "executive" power that all men have in that state, if he thought it were for any reason other than to benefit himself.

So the part must act because the whole cannot. Yet the part must act *for* the whole. And there is a corresponding duty to this right. *All* must abide by the decision of the part just as if it were the decision of the whole. Without this corresponding duty, there could be no government capable of acting at all. The purpose of the United States Constitution is to establish a system in which, because of the safeguards surrounding the exercise of power, and above all because that power is exercised by shifting parts or majorities, it would prove possible to establish and maintain a strong, energetic, safe government, so as to better secure the liberties of all.

Now how does all this pertain to the nineteenth century? The answer is that a founding based on the principle of equality generates two potentially dangerous possibilities. Men being what they are, it is easy to foresee the temptation for a "part" that happens to be in power at any given moment, to act, not in the interest of the whole, but in its own interest (although, of course, if it were prudent such a "part" would *say* that it was acting in the interest of the whole).

And there is a corresponding and opposite temptation: the temptation of the part that has lost out on any particular question it feels strongly about to refuse to abide by the decision of the duly constituted and legally constrained part, which in a democratic republic such as ours, means the majority.

With this background it should be easier to understand why the question that dominated the first half of the nineteenth century was the question of union. This was not merely a legal problem, it was a political and moral one. Unless the legally constituted majority could in fact rule on such regime-important questions, there would be little hope that Hamilton's question in *Federalist* 1 could be answered in the affirmative.

The problem of union first arises in the struggle over the Alien and Sedition Acts at the end of the eighteenth century, and in the aborted plan for a secession of northeastern states over the War of 1812. In both cases the minority part (the southern states in the first instance and the northern ones in the second) felt that the majority had engaged in a course of action that would seriously reduce either the liberties or the powers of the minor party.

But the primary importance of these events is that the latter case reminds us that the problem of secession is not a peculiarly southern one, while the former reminds us that the "answers" to the Alien and Sedition Acts, which is to say the Virginia and Kentucky Resolutions, penned respectively by James Madison and Thomas Jefferson, provided, according to the South of the 1830s, the theoretical justification of the doctrine of nullification.

It must be admitted that much of the talk of this period about interposition, nullification, secession, and the like, smacks of mere dry legalism. After all, people don't abide by laws they don't like simply because they made a promise to do so sometime in the distant past. In healthy regimes the law is upheld because people are devoted to it. As Lincoln said best, but as Madison and Jefferson surely would have agreed, in a free nation, there must be something like a political religion[6]: there must be a steady conviction that the laws, even though emanating from the people, are in some respect sacrosanct, in some respect beyond mere interest and advantage. Otherwise, it is hard to see what it is that could restrain the powerful passions that threaten government by consent.

Perhaps it is well to remind ourselves here that the American regime is one that has always seen itself as something special, a *Novus Ordo Seclorum*. Whatever the differences between men of different sections of the new nation might have been, they were agreed that the new republic would, by its very establishment and success, forever destroy the notion that good government must be based on a combination of mythology and superstition on the one hand, and the lash and sword on the other.

The promise, the hope, and the conviction in the eighteenth century, was that this superstition had been penetrated (this is really what the word "enlightenment" meant), and that the equality which let men see that the emperor had no clothes, should not only lead to a demotion of the emperor class, but to an elevation of the rest of mankind. They believed that it was the special mission of this new nation to demonstrate to all the world the truth of the proposition that all men are capable of the self-restraint, moral virtue, and public-spiritedness necessary to govern themselves.

Now, what were the great dangers to this scheme—since all arrangements have their peculiar dangers?

> 1. The willingness to submit to the lawful decision of the whole can lead to an acquiescence in the loss of important rights and liberties, and a loss of public-spiritedness.
> 2. An unwillingness to submit to legal authority, covered by arguments that one is merely protecting one's rights.

It is because these dangers present mortal dangers to democratic rule that the issues of interposition, nullification, and secession became the serpent in the garden of constitutional liberty in nineteenth-century America.

Just as Eve, according to Milton, could be brought to disobey the law that safeguarded her true liberty and happiness only when she allowed herself to be convinced that it was *right* to disobey that law, so could it be said that the greatest threat to American liberties emerged when large numbers of citizens on both sides of the Mason-Dixon Line convinced themselves that the highest morality required resisting the lawful powers of the United States. This conviction added the fervor of moral self-righteousness to hard questions of interest.

When Lincoln spoke of a political religion, he meant not only to call the South to its duty to abide by the law of the land, he also meant to call the radical abolitionist of the North to order: for many in the North had convinced themselves that they had no obligations to obey laws that sanctioned slavery.

The issue of slavery had from the beginning posed a peculiar danger to the American system. After all, this was the only country founded upon a principle hostile to human servitude. The physical presence of slavery already here might, it could be argued, justify the compromise made with it at the Constitutional Convention. It is hard to criticize actions that do not admit of alternatives. Certainly the southern states would not have joined the union without protection extended for slavery, and without union there might well have been no hope at all for its eventual abolition. Nevertheless, slavery was a reproach upon the claim that America stood for the truth, nobility, and practicality of free government.

But it was not merely the appearance, or even the fact of contradiction that mattered most in this matter. Practices are often at variance with principles. What mattered most was that slavery was the only issue upon which it might prove impossible to reconcile the different legitimate interests of the country. It was the hope of all during the founding period that the constitutional decision to let slavery alone in the states where it existed while at the same time preventing its spread (as was accomplished by the first Congress when it passed the Northwest Ordinance, a bill to organize the Northwest Territory without slavery), would remove the issue from the heat of political division and contention, a hope that was combined with a belief, as Lincoln later expressed it, that slavery, though something to which no immediate solution could be found, was being put in the course of ultimate extinction.

Of course, this solution proved to be no solution at all. The continual expansion of settlers into new territories required continual decisions regarding whether the new states they created would be slave or free, with the outcome affecting the representation of the existing states in the U.S. Senate.

Let us dwell on this difficulty for a moment longer, for it was not only the most significant issue for liberty in nineteenth-century America, it was inherently, and on principle, the most significant issue of American political life.

> 1. During the Revolutionary and Constitutional periods Americans thought of their nation as the "great hope of mankind." Its highest purpose was to demonstrate the workability of political liberty not only here, but as a model for all of mankind everywhere.
>
> 2. But there was a contradiction at the very inception of this great tale: chattel slavery.

This was, however, a *practical* contradiction, not a contradiction of principle. No one, North or South, originally argued that

Negro slavery was just, in the sense that some people ought to be ruled without their consent as a matter of *right*, rather than necessity. This consensus was soon to be challenged.

Perhaps the great struggle would never have occurred if the nation could have been confined perpetually to the original states. But the presence of vast territories dictated otherwise, especially when the issue arose of what to do with the lands of the Louisiana Purchase (1803) and later, those ceded by Mexico in 1848. Northern opinion was adamantly opposed to creating more slave states, which it thought of as something very different from abiding by the original agreement not to interfere with slavery in states where it already existed. Yet, the South recognized that if all of the new territory were to come in as free states, the South would soon be out-voted in the Senate as well as the House. From the Southern point of view, slavery even in the original states might be put in danger, since the power to abolish it would have shifted to the North in the Senate as well as in the House. Hence, the South was determined not to allow these new states to enter the Union as free, anti-slave states.

It was unlikely that a new state would adopt slavery in cases where there were no slaves to protect. Consequently, the concrete struggle took place over the issue of whether slavery ought to be protected in the territories prior to their becoming states, and the related issue of the South's adamant desire for a strong national fugitive slave law. Not surprisingly, the fugitive slave law provided fuel to the increasing abolitionist sentiment in the North.

From the point of view of the moral basis of the original political compact, the crisis came when southern leaders, having been vilified and verbally bullied for years by northern abolitionists, began to argue against the founding principles themselves. Hitherto no one had doubted that freedom was good for all human beings, at least in principle. But now people like John Calhoun began to say such things as "It is a great and dangerous error to suppose that all people are equally entitled to liberty."[7]

If this statement were to be accepted, then clearly the Declaration of Independence, the linchpin of American liberties, had to be wrong. And this is precisely what leading southerners began to argue. Indeed, one of the South's leading spokesmen, George Fitzhugh,[8] argued that every good and decent advance made by civilization was based on slavery. He thereby bore out Lincoln's contention that in arguing for the positive good of Negro slavery one would soon be driven to argue for the good of slavery in and of itself, whether for blacks or for whites. As Lincoln often said, there is no good argument for enslaving blacks which cannot be used for enslaving whites. But this meant that nearly one half of the nation was coming to believe in something other than liberty as the political and moral foundations of the Union.

Any argument for a deviation from liberty in a nation founded to promote liberty is likely to be masked, even from those who profess it, by the coloration of an argument *for* liberty. And so it was in this case, with the South arguing against the principle of liberty for some people so as to better secure its own liberty. This led to the strange sight of a Confederacy formed for the sake of maintaining its political liberty on the ground of an argument against liberty. For the political theory of the South was eloquently captured in the "Cornerstone"[9] speech of the new Confederacy's vice president, Alexander Stephens, who explicitly argued that the doctrine of equality, from which the principle of government by the consent of the governed follows, was wrong, and that the old view that some men were better off ruled by others, was right.

The problem in 1860 then, was not simply the problem of slavery, but the problem of slavery in a country dedicated to freedom. The South proposed to deal with the issue by abandoning the cause of freedom (although, of course, southerners apparently desired to retain the despised and useless thing for themselves). But it would not work to be both for and against freedom. By changing its argument the South gave notice that, in its opinion, Lincoln's "House Divided" speech was in fact right, that eventually the nation would become either all slave or all free. And in pushing for a national policy on slavery in the territories, while at the same time arguing that slavery was superior to free labor—that it was indeed better for the laborer—it appeared to the men of the North that the South had decided to change the fundamental premise of the country. About this there could hardly be much in the way of compromise.

The notion that slavery is a positive good was a serious enough challenge to political and individual liberty. But there was another view, far more subtle, and therefore potentially more dangerous, afoot. For at least this can be said for both the abolitionist and the secessionist: they believed in the eternal existence of the distinction between right and wrong, and that there is a nature and nature's god, as the Declaration puts it, that infuses moral meaning into human life and choice. They disagreed over what was right and what was wrong, at least as regarded the issue of freedom and chattel slavery.

The new, perhaps more invidious notion that arose at this time came from one of the leaders of the northern wing of the Democratic party, who had the best of intentions in mind. Senator Stephen A. Douglas wanted to remove the issue of slavery from the political agenda of the nation, for he was convinced that if this could not be done, dis-union and war would be inevitable. His solution was that the national government should legislate slavery neither into or out of the territories. The people of the territories should decide these questions for themselves.[10]

Now here is a solution that has all the appeal of democratic liberty. If self-government means anything, surely it means that the people must decide the most important political questions themselves.

As to the outcome of the decision, Douglas (who was personally, like most people from Illinois, against slavery, but who hoped to lead the southern as well as the northern Democrats in the election of 1860) argued that the best position was to abandon any concern with the outcome. To do otherwise was once again to place slavery at the forefront of public agitation. Hence he proclaimed that, as far as the territories were concerned, he did not care whether slavery "were voted up or voted down."

This "don't care" attitude aroused Lincoln as much as the proslavery argument. To hold the "don't care" position was as much as to say that one didn't care about human liberty, which is to say that one didn't care about public morality. According to Lincoln, if this position—called "popular sovereignty" by Douglas—were to be adopted by the nation as a whole, the moral conviction that lay at the heart of the regime would be undermined every bit as effectively as if the view that liberty is superior to slavery and bondage were publicly repudiated.

Popular sovereignty meant that the choice between freedom and slavery is merely a matter of self-interest. If a people thinks it in their interest to institute slavery, then they could adopt it; if another people happened to think liberty were in its interest, it could adopt liberty. Hence, the doctrine of popular sovereignty held that freedom meant the freedom to choose against freedom. Here was a serpent indeed, one which allowed its adherents to defend slavery in the name of freedom, unlawfulness in the name of the law, and despotism in the name of democracy.

While Lincoln always claimed that he had no constitutional authority to interfere with slavery in the states where it already existed, he became convinced that to allow the moral basis of the country to shift to a belief in the positive good of slavery, or to the view that it didn't matter whether a free people voted to enslave others, would be to sound the true "death knell" of the union. Lincoln's clear articulation of the issue of liberty and choice answered that, in the end, not a "death knell," but a "new birth of freedom" emerged from the bloodiest war America has ever fought.

It would, perhaps, be proper here to continue this examination of liberty in the nineteenth century with a survey of the results of the Civil War, in particular by providing a detailed history of the Thirteenth, Fourteenth, and Fifteenth Amendments to the Constitution, and of the historical course of Reconstruction. But because I wish to address another significant aspect of this subject, namely the origin of the Supreme Court's now widespread assumption of legislative authority, I will only say of this topic that the problem of Reconstruction, as far as both the extension and diminution of liberty is concerned, was due to the fact that it operated by means of a nationalization of civil rights enforcement, a movement with grave implications for the concentration of power in this country, however necessary it may have been to giving effect to the liberties of freed slaves. Perhaps a permanent nationalization would not have occurred if the Southern states had re-entered the Union with a commitment to full Negro emancipation and equality of rights. But they did not.

The powers of reconstruction emanated from a combination of Amendments and Congressional acts known as Civil Rights Acts and Enforcement Acts. The first of these, the Thirteenth Amendment, submitted to the states in January, 1865, and ratified in December of that year, radically shifted the balance of the federal system by limiting the previously exclusive state power over personal liberties. Since it conferred upon the federal government the power to enforce the prohibition of slavery against private individuals as well as against the state governments, it clearly implied a diminution of the state's power to limit federal authority.

Although the Reconstruction Amendments (including the

"national citizenship" provision of the Fourteenth Amendment) were intended to be permanent, it is important to recognize that the North as well as the South wanted to retain significant state powers over the liberties of their citizens. The Civil Rights Acts can best be understood as *temporary* measures to deal with the restored Southern governments' practice of passing discriminatory laws regulating blacks. Had these practices ceased, the extension of federal power might well have proved temporary in many instances. Certainly, it is clear from the record that President Johnson's inclination (though of course, not that of the minority radical Republicans of the time) was to have the *state* courts deal with matters of freedmen's rights, and he so instructed the Freedmen's Bureau to that effect. But in 1865 and 1866 Southern states passed Black Codes which, while granting freedmen new rights, also sought to deprive them of any practical benefits of these rights. The result was the passage of the Civil Rights Act of 1866, an act which expanded federal court jurisdiction, but which was intended, as I have indicated, to be a temporary measure. Indeed, even under the Fourteenth Amendment, which nationalized civil rights, the states remained the primary regulators of personal liberty and civil rights.

While in the present age of increased centralization of government it may appear to some that any diminution of state authority is a blow against freedom, it is important to note that the purpose of the original Constitution was, at least in part, to reduce the power of the states to engage in unjust practices. The difference between 1789 and 1865 is that in the earlier period the unjust practices had to do with debts, contracts, and property rights, and in the latter period had to do with personal liberties. In both cases justice followed in the wake of national power only when it was clear that it would make itself felt in no other way.

Once one leaves the Civil War and Reconstruction era, one

enters what appears to be an entirely new age. The 1870s on through the beginning of the twentieth century saw an almost complete reorientation of American life, witnessing the transformation of a series of primarily local agrarian economies into a national economy made possible by the last stages of the industrial revolution. This change brought in its wake the beginnings of big government, civil service, national regulation of industries, labor and management disputes of a bitter but not ultimately mortal nature, and an activist Supreme Court.

Prior to this time, wealth in America, even very great wealth, tended to be limited to reasonable amounts. Now, with the increased capacity for travel and communication of the last half of the nineteenth century, it became feasible to make a great deal of money by selling inexpensive items and services to a very large number of people. Vast fortunes of a hitherto unimaginable size were created. With great wealth, of course, goes great power, particularly when the organs of government are ill constituted to maintain a proper separation between the economic and political spheres.

Without that separation, the United States entered a period of public corruption and greed so extensive as to make honest men despair of the future of a nation devoted to the protection of private property. It is no accident that this period saw the rise of two opposing, and almost equally destructive, public teachings: a wild-eyed and naïve socialism that would abolish private property, and a flinty, grasping doctrine of *laissez-faire* inflated by a large dose of pseudo-scientific Social Darwinism. The former would abolish the private in the name of the public, while the latter recognized no good but private good.

In the event, what transpired was the creation of an immensely more powerful national government with organs of regulation intended not to abolish free markets, but rather to ensure their continued vitality in opposition to those who had made it clear that they viewed the government as merely another partner in consolidating their market positions against all comers. This is not to say that the new federal attempts to regulate business were always in the public interest. They were not. But they were, at least as far as the public believed, *intended* to be in the interest both of the public and the market. As Kelly, Harbison, and Belz[11] have pointed out, for instance, a weak exercise of governmental power often failed even minimally to protect the public interest, as was the case when Congress failed to provide a territorial government prior to authorizing the building of the Union Pacific Railroad. Instead, it allowed the railroad to enter the territories, with the U.S. Army more or less on loan, as it were, to the corporation for its own private purposes.

The alternative to a strengthened central government and at least some governmental regulation of industry was probably not to refrain from reigning in the "robber barons" as they later became known, but rather to restrict private enterprise in a far more drastic manner. This is not, however, to argue that the long-term consequences of such regulation were anything less than a diminution of the free and robust spirit of enterprise that earlier days had known.

If there is one thing the disputes concerning liberty in the nineteenth century have in common, it is that they are all, in one way or another, tied to private property. The particular question that led to the Civil War was, can a man take his property into the territories and receive the same protections for it as he did in his home state, if that property is another human being? During Reconstruction, much of what was at issue was whether ex-slaves would be allowed to use their labor to compete on a fair basis with white labor, and whether they would be allowed to keep and spend the fruits of their labor in the same way as white men. In the last period of the century the question was whether the rights of private property could be regulated or modified without unduly injuring or restricting these rights.

Regarding this last question (which continues the second topic mentioned at the beginning of this paper), one of the most interesting players on the national scene was the Supreme Court, which understood its duty in this period (1890-1937) to be one of upholding the rights of property against all comers. In doing so it went far beyond the original constitutional protections of property to elevate its protection to the single most powerful right in the Constitution.

The Court accomplished this by interpreting the due process clauses of contract and the Fourteenth Amendment as conferring substantive economic liberties that were inherent, according to it, in the natural law tradition for which the original Constitution stood as guarantor. Though clearly going beyond the letter of the Constitution, the Court did manage to protect the property rights that made the emergence of industrial and financial capitalism possible.

The Court, it might be noted, makes a pretty good argument for substantive due process, even though it must be admitted that it went beyond its legitimate scope as interpreter of the Constitution to do so. The political theory of the Constitution is clearly friendly to natural rights protections of private property, because such protection is fundamental to the protection of individual rights and liberties. On this understanding, the doctrine of natural rights limited government had been incorporated into the constitutional structure through the doctrine of vested rights (usually through the contract clause) as early as the eighteenth century.

What was new in the nineteenth century was the notion that due process not only referred to procedures to protect individuals against arbitrary takings and penalties, but that this doctrine could be extended to protect property owners from any legislative action at all concerning their property. It held, as did the doctrine of vested rights, that there are certain things the government is simply prevented from doing, even if the Constitution does not explicitly say so, and even if the government followed normal political and legal procedures in doing so.

The Court, it should be noted, originally rejected this doctrine in the *Slaughterhouse Cases* of 1873. Here the Court held that butchers excluded from a state protected monopoly on butchering could not claim that they had an inherent right to practice their trade, or that such an inherent right was protected by the due process clause of the Fourteenth Amendment. On this occasion the Court upheld the power of the states to regulate commerce as they saw fit.

Interestingly, during this period the Court, primarily (but not exclusively) through dissenting opinions, argued for strong guarantees of private property while in almost every instance upholding state laws that interfered with this liberty, as they did in the *Slaughterhouse Cases*. But the arguments that were necessary to give protection to the new economy were there, even as the Court continued to allow for increased regulation of that economy.

Changes in the decisions themselves began in the 1880s, with *In re Jacobs*, where the Court stuck down a New York law restricting the manufacture of cigars in tenement houses on the basis of the police power to regulate manufactures for the sake of public health and safety. Then, in 1894 in *Reagan v. Farmers' Loan and Trust Co.* the Court invalidated rates set by the Texas Railroad Commission as a taking without due process of law.

The Court then broadened its protection of private property with the case of *Allgeyer v. Louisiana* in 1897, where it added the doctrine of liberty of contract to that of the other elements of substantive due process limitations on taking property. This doctrine held that legislatures had no right to intervene when two parties reached an agreement, so long as the agreement was not contrary to public policy. As the Court said, the due process clause of the Fourteenth Amendment protected one's right to his "faculties; to be free to use them in all lawful ways; to live and work where he will; to earn his livelihood by and lawful calling; to pursue any livelihood or avocation, and for that purpose to enter into all contracts which may be proper, necessary, and essential to his carrying out to a successful conclusion the proposes above mentioned."

The difficulty with this line of reasoning for those who favor liberty *and* a Court restricted to original interpretation (which means deciding whether a legislative power is in keeping with the original intent of the constitutional provision), is that the Fourteenth Amendment clearly was not intended to be a vehicle for reaching this result. However laudable it might be in the eyes of some, it is not good constitutional law, since it required the Court to decide not only whether there was constitutional *authority* for the law, but also required the Court to inquire as to the *wisdom* of the law. That way judicial supremacy lies, whether or not one likes the specific outcome of a particular decision.

In this respect it may be said of the nineteenth century that, just as the effort of the slave states to protect what they considered to be their own most vital liberties led to a vindication of the one liberty that they sought to deny, so did both progressivism and the Court's attempt to protect conservative property rights lay the groundwork for the activist Court of this century.

Perhaps if there is a moral to all this it is that the people must, to be sure, guard their liberties with a jealous eye, perhaps never more so than now in this century of administrative centralization. But it must also be said that they must always be on guard against the temptation to twist the original meaning of their agreement to fit the exigencies and desires of the moment.

It may be as true to say today, as it was when Edmund Burke said it in 1791, that "Men are qualified for civil liberty in exact proportion to their own disposition to put moral chains on their own appetites...."[12]

## ENDNOTES

1. Jacob E. Cooke, ed., *The Federalist* (Middletown, CN: Wesleyan University Press, 1961), p. 1.

2. Thomas Jefferson to James Madison, January 30, 1787, in Merrill D. Peterson, ed., *The Portable Thomas Jefferson* (New York: The Viking Press, 1975).

3. As anyone familiar with his work on the political and moral causes of the Civil War will notice, I am heavily indebted to Jaffa's books and articles on the subject for much of what is said in this account. See especially, Harry V. Jaffa, *Crisis of the House Divided: An Interpretation of the Issues in the Lincoln-Douglas Debates* (1959; reprinted., Seattle, Wash.: University of Washington Press, 1973), and Harry V. Jaffa, *The Conditions of Freedom: Essays in Political Philosophy* (Baltimore, MD: The Johns Hopkins University Press, 1975).

4. "The Pardoner's Tale," in Henry N. McCracken, ed., *The College Chaucer* (New Haven: Yale University Press, 1913).

5. Alfred T. Mahan, *The Influence of Sea Power upon History* (Ingram Books, 1987).

6. See Lincoln's "The Perpetuation of Our Political Institutions," Address before the Springfield Young Men's Lyceum, 1858, in *The Political Thought of Abraham Lincoln*, ed. by Richard N. Current (Indianapolis: Bobbs Merrill, 1967).

7. John C. Calhoun, "A Disquisition on Government," in Richard K. Cralle, ed., *The Works of John C. Calhoun, 6 vols.* (New York: 1851-1867), I, pp. 55-56.

8. George Fitzhugh, "Sociology of the South," in Harvey Wish, ed., *Ante-Bellum: The Writings of George Fitzhugh and Hinton Rower Helper on Slavery* (New York: G. P. Putnam's Sons, 1960).

9. March 21, 1861, The Athenaeum, Savannah, Georgia. This was, in fact, Stephens' inaugural address as Vice-President of the Confederacy. George Fitzhugh "Sociology of the South," in Harvey Wish ed., *ibid.*

10. See Douglas' speech in Chicago, July 9, 1858 in *The Lincoln-Douglas Debates* ed. by Robert W. Johannsen (New York: Oxford University Press, 1965).

11. I am indebted to Alfred Kelly, Winfred Harbison and Herman Belz, *The American Constitution: Its Origins and Development*, 6th ed. (New York: Norton, 1983), and Christopher Wolfe, *The Rise of Modern Judicial Review: From Constitutional Interpretation to Judge-Made Law* (New York: Basic Books, Inc., 1986) for some of what follows. All of the cases cited hereafter may be found there, or in any comprehensive history of American constitutional law.

12. Edmund Burke, "A Letter to a Member of the National Assembly," in F.W. Rafferty, ed., *The Works of the Right Honorable Edmund Burke* (London: Oxford University Press, 1925), Vol. 4.

# The Twentieth Century:
# The Limits of Liberal Political Philosophy

JOHN GRAY

I n Friederich August von Hayek's work we find one of the most ambitious attempts we possess thus far to develop a comprehensive liberal political philosophy. Unlike the fashionable liberalisms which take their cues from Rawls, Hayek's is noteworthy in making plain its dependency on a particular philosophy of history and on the results of economic theory. In a way that is only comparable with the liberalism of J. S. Mill, Hayek's liberalism expresses an entire, if not always an entirely coherent world view—a fact which goes far in explaining both the strengths and the weaknesses of Hayek's thought. The system-building ambition and the cross-disciplinary synoptic perspective which animate Hayek's work make of it an extraordinary intellectual adventure, in comparison with which recent liberal theorizing is most tame and conventional. Hayek's work is, or should be, exemplary in the features it has in common with the thought of the Scottish Enlightenment—especially the connections it forges between moral philosophy and political economy, and in its general resistance to the balkanization of contemporary intellectual life by disciplinary specialization.

Unfortunately Hayek's bold and radical attempt at a systematic or architectonic comprehensive liberal philosophy fails. It fails for a variety of very different reasons: its critique of rationalism does not go deep enough, and coexists with aspects of Hayek's system of ideas which recall the positivism and scientism against which, during one period of his long intellectual life, he inveighed; it generalizes, or seeks to generalize, insights or truths, such as the superiority of the unplanned coordination of economic activity that occurs in market processes over any achievable through comprehensive central planning, across whole fields of human activity where they have no application; it strives for an eclectic synthesis of philosophical outlooks, such as those of Hume and Kant, which cannot be reconciled; and it some-times depends on theories, or general ideas, in the social studies, that—like the idea of group selection which is dominant in the later Hayek—are simply mistaken or misconceived. Because of these lacunae, Hayek's system of ideas does not hold together, but rather falls apart under any sustained critical pressure.

Though the reasons for the inability of Hayek's system of ideas are diverse, they all emanate from a single conception that is at the heart of his work, from the incoherences of which most of its central difficulties, and all those that are ultimately fatal, spring: I mean the idea of a spontaneous order in society. This is, in fact, not one single idea or theoretical framework, but an eclectic and incoherent conception, which conflates several distinct, and independently assessable, claims: the claim that market pricing allows for the utilization of knowledge that is dispersed and partly tacit in character and which can be used effectively in no other way; the claim that coordination among human activities occurs, outside the context of market ex-changes, through the emergence or evolution of conventions that permit uncoerced cooperation; the claim that voluntary exchange is, typically or normally, mutually beneficial, a posi-tive-sum game for all the parties to it; the claim that social rules may be theorized as bearers of tacit or embodied knowledge that is not available explicitly to, or articulable by, those who follow these rules; the claim that there is a sort of natural selection of rules, traditions or practices, such that those groups flourish best that adopt or follow the rules that are most functional or adaptive, and flourishing is understood in Darwinian terms of population size; and so on. These distinct ideas or theoretical claims are, in the conception of a spontaneous social order, conflated and run together, to yield a research program that is (in Imre Lakatos's expression) thoroughly degenerate. The upshot of my analysis and assessment of the idea of a spontaneous social order is that—though it will be found to contain some useful insights once it has been disaggregated—it is useless as a general conception, and should therefore be expunged from social theory. This criticism of Hayek is, of course, also a criticism of those thinkers of the Scottish Enlightenment from whose work Hayek has most borrowed. Pos itivist forebears

The central error in Hayek's attempt at a comprehensive liberal political philosophy, and thereby in the idea of a spontaneous social order that is its animating conception, is in the illicit generalization from market processes and exchanges to legal rules, political institutions, and cultural traditions. It is not merely that much of what Hayek claims to be true of market processes is so only against the background of an appropriate legal and political framework—a point I have made elsewhere,[1] and which is in conformity with the theoretical perspective of the Virginia School of Public Choice. It is that Hayek's political philosophy, like that of the Virginia School, neglects the embeddedness of market institutions in cultural traditions which, far more than any legal framework, are their social matrix, and confer upon them a legitimacy without which they are not renewable over time and across the generations. This point may be stated in another, and perhaps more radical fashion. Like all the currently dominant schools of liberal political philosophy, including the Virginia School and that of Rawls,[2] Hayek's liberalism is disabled by a species of legalist illusion which finds expression in the delusion that market institutions can be legitimated by an appropriate constitutional framework or contract whose justice has sufficient general acceptance to assure support for liberal institutions. This illusion of liberal legalism and constitutionalism, which is pervasive in recent liberal thought, neglects or suppresses the roots of allegiance to liberal regimes in particularistic cultural traditions. In particular it fails to understand, or even to perceive, that liberal polities are stable only insofar as they mirror or express national political cultures whose cultural traditions have sheltered strong civil societies. The legalist blind spot of recent liberalism, though not entirely universal,[3] is yet sufficiently pervasive to justify the error it incapsulates as specifying a limit to liberal political philosophy. If my argument is sound, then the liberal legalist quest for a set of constitutional devices—a talismanic formula or theory of justice or constitutional contract, whereby liberal institutions can be underwritten and their stability assured—should be abandoned. The course of wisdom and prudence is in relinquishing the vain search for a universal theory or doctrine of liberty— "liberalism," as it is commonly understood—in favor of the recognition of the form of life of free peoples as one form of life among many, and of allegiance to liberal states or regimes as being like allegiance to any other polity in having its sources in particularistic cultural loyalties and attachments. To admit this is to allow a very substantial amendment of received or conventional liberal political philosophy. It is also to destroy Hayek's thought as a systematic body of ideas, and its pretensions as a comprehensive liberal political philosophy.

Insofar as Hayek's work does compose a genuine system of ideas, its unifying themes are epistemological.[4] I will assess Hayek's attempt at an epistemological foundation for liberalism in the last section of this paper. The starting point of any such assessment must be in Hayek's pioneering work on the epistemic functions of market institutions. His most unequivocal achievement is his illumination of the irreplaceable role of market institutions as epistemic devices, and his demonstration of the epistemic impossibilities involved in comprehensive central planning. It is to these arguments of Hayek's that I now turn, in order to assess their place in his thought as a whole, and the role they plan in his complex, and ultimately incoherent conception of a spontaneous social order.

*I. The "calculation argument" and the epistemic functions of market institutions*

The period from 1985, in which the Soviet *glasnost* was given its public inception, and the present, in which the reformist project of *perestroika* has given way to the full-scale collapse of socialist central planning institutions in virtually every part of the world,[5] is that in which F. A. Hayek's analysis of socialist central planning[6] has been vindicated by history. His colleague, L. von Mises,[7] had argued that the suppression of market pricing entailed by comprehensive central planning imposed on the planning institutions a task of calculation that was insuperably difficult. In any complex, modern economy in which changes in preferences, in relative scarcities and in available technologies made market prices ephemeral and dynamic, the computational problems of a planning authority, in trying to capture in mathematical formulae the billions of transactions that would otherwise have occurred in markets, were insoluble. For Mises, accordingly, socialism—the comprehensive planning of economic life and the consequent suppression of private property and market pricing—was a calculational impossibility. Or, perhaps more precisely, socialist planning institutions could never hope to be successful; they would issue in calculational chaos. Hayek perceived, as Mises did not, that the epistemic problems of socialist planning authorities were not merely, or even principally, problems of calculation; they were problems of knowledge. For Hayek, market pricing was an epistemic device, a discovery procedure that made available to economic agents knowledge, dispersed throughout society, which could not be gathered together by any central planning authority. Such knowledge was often local knowledge—fleeting and circumstantial—dated by the time it was collected; it was often practical knowledge, embodied in skills and dispositions, not articulated by its possessors and users, and sometimes not articulable; it was often the knowledge acquired via entrepreneurial perception.

By its very nature, such dispersed knowledge could not be brought together in a comprehensive collation by a socialist planning authority. Such an authority would therefore lack the knowledge it needed indispensably to achieve the tasks set it by the political authorities in any reasonably cost-effective manner. It could attempt to use the prices thrown up in parallel markets, black or gray, or in historic or world markets, to achieve a semblance of rationality in its activities; but these would inevitably be accompanied by vast waste and misallocation of resources, even as measured by the targets of the planners themselves. Note, in regard to this last crucial point, that nothing in Hayek's argument turns on the suppression of consumer sovereignty under central planning institutions. His insight is not that central planning fails to generate consumer affluence, which has never been its true objective, but that it achieves even the goals of the planning bureaucracy—self-enrichment, or the development of military technology—at vast and inordinate cost, and then only patchily and partially.

Thus, the Gorbachev *perestroika* may have been initiated as a response to the realization that, though the Soviet military-industrial complex could, by techniques of market simulation, surpass the western military technology in some areas, such as aspects of aircraft and submarine development, it could not replicate western technology in the decisive areas of space-based and computer-controlled defense systems. Equally, a side-effect of Gorbachev's *glasnost* may have been the realization by the Soviet *nomenklatura* that their privileged status in the planning apparatus had gained them living standards, for all save those at the very top, comparable to those of western primary school teachers, or worse. The recognition, triggered by *glasnost*, that in international terms the *nomenklaturists* were an impoverished elite may well have been significant in demoralizing them and in stripping the Soviet regime of its remaining legitimacy even for them. The point of decisive theoretical importance is that Hayek's argument highlights the epistemological limitations and costs of central planning institutions *whatever their objectives*. The upshot predicted—entirely correctly—by Hayek's theoretical analysis of the insuperable problems of knowledge confronted by socialist central planners was economic chaos, general impoverishment, waste and malinvestment on a colossal scale.[8]

Hayek won the intellectual battles of the Thirties and Forties, in which socialist economists attempted, unavailingly, to develop models—particularly the Lange-Lerner model of "competitive socialism"—which simulated market processes by creating shadow prices; but, partly because of the account of the so-called "calculation debate" that found its way into received intellectual history through the work of Joseph Schumpeter,[9] his intellectual victory was not noticed, and his arguments were marginalized. In consequence, virtually the entirety of Western opinion, as expressed in the economics textbooks of Samuelson and others, in topical journalism and in intelligence analyses and reports, propagated the view that the Soviet economies were success stories, producing (in the case of the GDR) living standards in excess of several West European countries, and, in the case of the USSR itself, superior health and social services, and a high level of technological innovation.

Such a view was, of course, an absurdity in the eyes of any who had ever had practical experience of life in Soviet-style societies; but their experiences were dismissed, and their voices went unheard. It was to the credit of elements in the Soviet elite itself, rather than of any section of western opinion, that the evidences were at last made public that vindicated Hayek's analysis.

The revelations of the Soviet *glasnost*, and of the reunification of Germany, disclosed living standards in Russia, and in many parts of the Soviet Union, that were as low, or lower, than those in many Third World countries; an industrial plant that was decades, even generations, out of date; statistical and accounting techniques whose closest affinities were with the surreal worlds envisaged by Borges; worthless medical care, nonexistent social services, negligible provision for industrial safety or consequent disability, and catastrophic housing conditions; and a degradation of the natural environment that verged, in many parts of the Soviet Union, on the apocalyptic. To be sure, conditions varied somewhat, in different parts of the former Soviet bloc. In Russia, the picture was complicated by the fact that the strategic-military sector of the economy, which probably absorbed between forty and sixty percent of its resources, was markedly less inefficient than the civilian economy, sometimes yielding products—such as the MIG-29 aircraft—that were superior to anything that existed in the west. And, as Michael Polanyi had pointed out in his criticism of Hayek,[10] the epistemic impossibilities of central planning had everywhere resulted in economic institutions (even those of the planning bureaucracies) going their own way, reinventing markets (often barter markets) and thereby mimicking in rudimentary ways the market institutions of the west. In truth, central planning existed nowhere; but the attempt to impose it had everywhere the same result—economic ruin, moderated only by corruption, the re-emergence of markets and (in the Soviet strategic-military sector) the simulation of market institutions.[11]

Hayek's account of the epistemic functions of market institutions, and of the insuperable epistemic problems of central planning, built on the earlier analysis of Mises; and it was surpassed by the deeper account of Polanyi, who showed how the attempt to plan economic life as a whole resulted in a waste of the tacit knowledge embodied in market processes, just as the project of planning science resulted not in the growth of scientific knowledge, but in the depletion of the tacit knowledge on which such growth depends. Hayek's analysis is nevertheless an extraordinary achievement, well justifying his status as an intellectual hero in the post-communist lands. It provides a deep theoretical account of the failures of central planning, and it gave reasons for anticipating the eventual collapse of the planning institutions. This is not to say that Hayek's analysis of the epistemic functions of market institutions, and of the epistemic impossibilities encompassed in central economic planning, give any useful guidance in the post-communist transition period. I have indeed elsewhere argued the contrary: Hayekian prescriptions are in most post-communist lands worse than useless.[12] The theoretical question remains: How far, if at all, do Hayek's brilliant insights into the epistemic role of market institutions support his conception of a spontaneous social order?

*II. The idea of a spontaneous social order and the mirage of cultural evolution*

At the theoretical level, Hayek's critique of central planning is associated in this thought with a broader critique of constructivist rationalism, and with the idea of a spontaneous order in society. In his later work, the idea of spontaneous social order is linked, explicitly and systematically, with a theory of institutional Darwinism, or cultural evolution, in many respects reminiscent of Herbert Spencer's synthetic philosophy.[13] None of these conceptions survives critical scrutiny, especially when they are conjoined (as they are unequivocally in Hayek's later work) so as to compose a comprehensive world view. Consider the theory of cultural evolution in the later Hayek.[14] This is the theory that there is a sort of natural selection at work among human social groups according to their distinctive practices and traditions.

There is, for example, a natural selection of religions, whereby those prevail that have a Darwinian advantage in virtue of their attachment to the institutions of the family and of private property, which boost the numbers of their adherents. There are many difficulties in this later Hayekian theory of cultural evolution, some of them fatal. We do not know of any *mechanism* of cultural evolution analogous with that of the environmental selection of random genetic mutations in Darwinian biological theory. It may be true that religions which favor institutions that promote human fertility have a comparative advantage over others which do not; but in historical terms the decisive factor that explains the success of some religions and the failure of others is not their Darwinian properties but their skill or good fortune in acquiring access to the power of the state, and their ruthlessness in using it to extirpate their rivals. There is, in the history of religions, no detectable mechanism of cultural evolution, only the contingencies of political fortune. In this respect, as in others, the later thought of Hayek resembles Marxism in its neglect of historical contingency. Cleopatra's nose is a better guide to the vicissitudes of human history than Hayekian cultural evolution.

Not only does the theory of cultural evolution lack a mechanism: it fails to specify a *unit*. In neo-Darwinian biology, the unit is not the species, nor even the individual, but rather the gene, or its lineage. What is the corresponding unit in cultural evolution? Social groups, their practices and traditions, are notoriously difficult to individuate. There is a problem here for Hayek akin to that which confronts functionalism in social theory—the problem of individuating the social system. *Which* institutions or practices are constitutive of any social system? How are these to be determined, and, once determined, themselves individuated? Is widespread divorce, say, a symptom of the breakdown of the institution of marriage? Or is the popularity of remarriage after divorce evidence that the institution of marriage has renewed itself, albeit in a modified form? How are these questions to receive any disciplined answer? Their undecidability within funtionalist theories is a decisive argument against all varieties of functionalism, including Hayek's.

A social system may be theorized as a self-regulating, homeostatic, equilibrating whole, whose behavior is intelligible in terms of its self-regulating tendencies; and is so theorized by functionalists, including Hayek. But social systems break down, even as organisms perish; what is to count as an equilibrating modification of a social system, and what is a symptom of its disintegration? These are questions we can hope to answer only if we have already adequately specified the social system itself. This Hayek, along with every other functionalist, utterly fails to do.

What, in any case, is the *measure* of cultural evolution, and what is its *criterion*? Hayek seems not to distinguish between these two questions. He tells us that the success of a group, or of a set of institutions, is to be assessed by reference to the human population it sustains; but this is a very indeterminate standard of cultural evolution. Is the test the *actual size* of the human population sustained by a set of institutions, or its carrying capacity—the human population that *could* be supported by a given system of productive institutions? And over what time-period, and at what level of well-being? The market institutions of advanced industrial society may well be able to carry vast populations at high living standards, but—because of their ecological side-effects, or their virtuosity in producing weapons of mass destruction—many do so only for short periods; while the small populations of aboriginal cultures with Neanderthal technologies may be capable of reproducing themselves for tens or hundreds of millennia. Which best passes the Hayekian test? And what, indeed, is the population test meant to establish?

These questions, unanswerable in the theory of cultural evolution advanced in Hayek's later work, haunt the idea of spontaneous order itself. As it is used in the writings of latter-day classical liberals influenced by Hayek, the idea has no single, clear, or coherent sense, but is rather an eclectic confusion of a number of distinct theses, most of which are either questionable or else plainly false. It is necessary to separate out these distinct elements, before we can establish what, if anything, remains valid or useful in this conception. Let us begin with a simple observation.

In Hayek's later work, spontaneous orders are found not only in human societies but in the lives of other species, and among such natural phenomena as galaxies, magnetic filings, crystals, and so on. It is unclear what "order" signifies here, other than a self-replicating structure of some sort; but it is evident that the term "spontaneous order" is being deployed in a value-free way as an explanatory cipher for self-regulating systems of all kinds. If spontaneous order is a value-free idea, however, then spontaneous orders in human society may or may not be beneficent: they need only be undesigned, relatively stable, reproduce themselves over time, and so forth. Mafias as well as markets will qualify as spontaneous orders: a spontaneous order will come into being whenever conventions emerge which coordinate human activities, such that their regularity and predictability are enhanced. The emergence of conventions is a ubiquitous phenomenon in human interactions, occurring on battlefields, in prisons and concentration camps, in relations between criminal gangs and in price wars between rival enterprises. If the idea of spontaneous order is part of positive science, and has application whenever human activities are coordinated by the emergence of conventions rather than by human design, plan or will, then it is a morally empty idea, having no special affinity with the theory of a free society. It describes features of the social world that are universal and ubiquitous, as much elements in tyrannies as in liberal civil societies. Indeed, if the idea of spontaneous order is to be an element in any genuine social science, it has to have this character as a value-free explanatory cipher.

In Hayek's work, of course, the idea of spontaneous order is *not* used consistently as a value-neutral explanatory cipher, or as an aspect of a research program in positive social theory. It has a clear normative content. This derives from the Mandevillian insight that private vices may yield public benefits, and the Smithian perception that voluntary exchanges, especially when often repeated, are typically not zero-sum transactions, but exchanges in which all parties benefit. The implication is that, in circumstances in which economic life is conducted via a network of voluntary exchanges, the well-being of all will be enhanced. Further, the idea of spontaneous social order borrows here from Hayek's epistemic arguments against central planning in suggesting that the coordination of human activities that occurs in a network of voluntary exchanges will be superior to any that could be achieved via human design or rational, overall planning. It can be seen that the idea of spontaneous order is in this respect a cipher for the market process, that vast nexus of voluntary exchanges in which human activities are coordinated without the intervention of any planning authority.

We must note at once a crucial point, however: that market exchanges have the beneficent properties attributed to them in Hayek's conception of spontaneous order, only so long as their character as voluntary transactions is guaranteed by an undergirding structure of institutions—of private property, contractual liberty and the prohibition of extra-judicial coercion—that are enforced by law. It is the legal infrastructure of market institutions which defines and protects the conditions of voluntary exchange, that assures the beneficence of the spontaneous order of the market process. Without the matrix of law, of enforceable titles to property and the terms of contract, the market process is a spontaneous order no more likely to be beneficent than that of the Mafia.

The central error of Hayek's account of spontaneous social order, replicated in the uses made of it by his libertarian and classical liberal followers, is that it makes an illicit generalization from the beneficent properties of market processes as systems of voluntary exchanges enforced by the legal framework of market institutions to the supposed character of such legal frameworks as themselves spontaneous orders. The truth is precisely the contrary: *except* in the context of a legal framework that guarantees voluntary exchange, there is no reason whatsoever to suppose that spontaneous orders will be beneficent. Indeed, such rudimentary market processes as may exist without such legal framework are likely to be often exploitative and intimidatory as they are mutually beneficial to their participants.

Nor—and this brings us back to the errors of the Hayekian theory of cultural evolution—is there any reason to suppose that the unplanned evolution of legal systems will systematically favor market institutions as systems of voluntary exchanges. The historical evidence suggests the opposite, with legal rules—the rules of the game of the market—becoming themselves objects of political predators, and the legal framework of market institutions being shaped by the requirements of coalitions of collusive interest groups. The idea, suggested by Hayekian theory, that there is an evolutionary selection of legal rules, or of systems of such rules, that acts in favor of those which best promote the voluntaristic properties of market institutions, is an illusion, as groundless and as dangerous as the allied illusion that free societies must win out in competitions with unfree societies.

History suggests otherwise: that competition among jurisdictions, for capital and skills, is likely to be interdicted by the mortal rivalry of war; that war will thwart the mechanisms of emulation and migration, on which the Scottish School, and Hayek, rely for their belief that successful market economies will have a "demonstration effect" which will lead to their replication. So the darker side of the Scottish School, the civic republican fear that commercial society will weaken the martial spirit and render itself vulnerable to militant barbarism, which the passions unleashed by commercial civilization may as easily express themselves in destructive envy as in benign emulation—this darker prospect, foreshadowed in Ferguson and even in Smith, seems far closer to historical realities than the Panglossian harmonies of Hayekian theory.

*III. The idea of a spontaneous order and Hayek's conjectural history of market institutions*

What, then, remains of the idea of spontaneous order? On the negative side, it implies—what is surely correct—that any modern economy is bound to be polycentric, its activities coordinated principally by market institutions rather than by a comprehensive plan. As Polanyi always stressed,[15] the choice is not between market institutions and central planning, since the latter is an impossibility, and Soviet central planning was always an illusion; the choice is only between better or worse market institutions. It is *this* issue—the "systems debate" between central planning and market institutions—that has been resolved decisively by history.

This is *not* to say that market institutions are infallibly self-regulating, that discoordination in them is always the result of exogenous factors such as government intervention, as Hayek often seems to suggest. As G. L. S. Shackle has shown,[16] borrowing heavily from Keynes,[17] market processes are liable to endogenous discoordination, sometimes of massive proportions;[18] and macroeconomic policy by governments is in such circumstances unavoidably necessary. The "calculation argument" establishes the impossibility of successful central planning, *not* the inevitability, or superiority, of *laissez faire*. It demonstrates the inevitability, in a complex modern economy, of market institutions; it tells us nothing as to their varieties, or their limits. In other words, it tells us nothing as to *which* varieties of market institutions are to be adopted in which circumstances; and nothing as to the different limits of these diverse forms of market institutions. On the positive side, it suggests that any human society will be held together in its activities by the emergence of conventions, undesigned norms of conduct which confer a measure of predictability on human interactions. More speculatively, it suggests that the stability of all human institutions—insofar as they *are* stable—depends upon a subterranean nexus of adjustments and exchanges, not apparent on the visible surface of the institutions, but indispensable to their identity and stability nevertheless. This latter is an important truth, but it applies to all societies, not only (or especially) to free ones. If it supports any political philosophy, it is that of traditional conservatism, not classical liberalism, since it intimates that reformist social engineering—including that designed to transplant Western market institutions to societies in which command economies have hitherto supposedly prevailed—is certain to have unpredictable, and likely destabilizing consequences, whatever the societies or regimes to which it is applied.

Hayek's theory of market institutions reposes on what might be called a conjectural history of their origins. This conjectural history tells us that market institutions arise as the unplanned outcomes of human actions; like the institution of money in the Mengerian account of it, they are emergent properties of human interactions, not the results of human design or intention. This is true, however, only of markets in their most rudimentary forms. The market institutions of any modern economy have not so arisen, but are the artifacts of law and government. Hayek's analysis of market institutions betrays here another illicit generalization—from the English experience, in which market institutions *did* emerge largely through the unplanned development over centuries of the common law, to market institutions everywhere. Now, in every case other than the most primitive, market institutions are creatures of law: the content of property rights, the conditions and limits of contractual liberty, are never natural facts, but artifacts of the legal system. But only in the English case, and in those countries to which English institutions were exported, were market institutions shaped by the slow evolution over centuries of common law. In Scotland, they were moulded, not by common law, but by Roman law, itself imposed by fiat; in post-revolutionary France, and its departmental and colonial extensions (including the State of Louisiana) by the Napoleonic code; in Attaturkist Turkey by the autocratic imposition of the Swiss civil code; and so on. In truth, contrary to Hayek, the English experience of the emergence of market institutions through the slow evolution of common law is a limiting case, not a paradigmatic exemplar.

The Hayekian model of the unplanned emergence through centuries of gradualist legal evolution of market institutions is a grand and wholly unwarranted generalization of their development in one country—England. Its limitations are a warning against the dangers of the method of conjectural history, as applied to the development of institutions, especially the danger of over-reliance on narrow historical examples. Nor are these dangers purely intellectual in character: they also threaten sober policy-making in contexts where market institutions are under construction, for example in post-communist states. The legal infrastructure of a market economy, wholly lacking in most of the post-communist states, can be created in them only by constructivist legislation. At present, with the partial exception of the fledgling Czech Republic, none of them has a law of property, a law of contract, a banking system, or a genuine capital market. If a policy of legislative quietism is pursued in the post-communist countries, inspired by Hayekian ideas of spontaneous order, then we may expect a replication in most of them of the Russian experience to date—namely, an outbreak of "wild," "spontaneous," or "Hayekian" privatization, that is in fact merely the latest episode in *nomenklaturist* rent-seeking, in the context of an economic order best characterised as an anarcho-capitalism of the Mafia. Such a development is very unlikely to be politically stable. It will reinforce popular suspicion—itself well founded in terms of actual experience of *nomenklatura*-controlled markets—that market exchanges are typically exploitative, zero-sum transactions, and it will evoke a political backlash to market reform that is syndicalist, *dirigiste* or autarchic in character. The likely upshot of Hayekian policy in most of the transitional post-communist states will not be the transposition of Western market institutions but the emergence of hybrid economic institutions, constituted partly by lawless market processes and partly by *nomenklaturist*-controlled forms of *dirigisme*, in political contexts of weak and tyrannous governments which rely for their legitimacy on embodying pre-communist national and ethnic traditions. Contrary to the triumphalist expectations of Fukuyama, "democratic capitalism" on the Anglo-American model will be established in none of the post-communist countries.

The limitations of the Hayekian conjectural history of market institutions, arising from its dependency on narrowly Anglo-American historical examples, can be illustrated in another way. Both civil societies and market institutions come in many varieties; there is no single, ideal-typical form of either of them. Further, they do not always come together. Civil societies have been, and are, sheltered by a diversity of political regimes, more commonly authoritarian than democratic: there is no necessary or systematic connection between the institutions of a civil society and political democracy. They can happily coexist with many forms of government. By civil society, I mean here that structure of autonomous institutions, standing between individuals and the state but whose shape is defined and protected by law, in which persons and communities with different purposes and world views can coexist in peace and equality under a rule of law.[19] In all civil societies, the bulk of economic life is transacted in market institutions. It is civil society, not liberal democracy, that is the real negation of totalitarianism—which is a *weltanschauung-state* in which the polity and the economy are fused.

Totalitarianism is in our time, however—since the Soviet collapse—no longer the chief enemy of civil society; its principal rival is now fundamentalism, not only the universalist and imperialist fundamentalism that has arisen within some sections of Islam, but also other species of fundamentalism, such as the particularistic Hindu fundamentalism that is currently being built up in the ruins of the secular Indian state. Those who think that the chief rival of civil society must be species of totalitarianism animated by Westernizing ideologies have not understood that the collapse of the Soviet system is also the eclipse of the Occidental ideologies—liberal as well as Marxist—that were spawned by the Enlightenment project. They will find it hard to grasp that the rejection of civil society comes in our time not from secular European ideologues but from fundamentalist religions. They will find it even harder to understand—indeed, we may be sure that they will deny—that market institutions are being constructed in various parts of the world, and particularly in parts of East Asia, which promise to be stable and successful over significant periods of time without generating, or being accompanied by, anything resembling a Western-style civil society. In this the followers of Hayek, of Fukuyama and of Marx are at one in clinging to the whiggish philosophy of history that moulded most of the theorists of the Scottish Enlightenment, with the significant (but partial) exception of Hume.

Hayekian conjectural history tells us nothing, or little, about the diversity of civil societies or of market institutions, of their limits or of their complex historical and contemporary relations. Market institutions, like civil societies, come in many varieties, of which there is no single ideal type. The market institutions of Anglo-American capitalism differ profoundly from those in the

German (and Austrian) social market economy, from Italian and French market institutions and, even more, from the distinctive marked institutions of East Asia, especially those of Japan, Taiwan, Singapore and south Korea. They differ in the fact that they are not animated by an individualist morality, and they do not depend upon the legalist culture, that permeate Anglo-American market institutions, especially in the United States. They differ from "democratic capitalism," especially in its American version, also in the incontestable fact—nonetheless universally denied by Western neo-liberals—that the strategic involvement of government in these economies is decisive and pervasive.

It is not insignificant that the avowed models for market reform in mainland China are not Western models, but those of Singapore and South Korea. This should lead us to the insight that the connection between flourishing market institutions on the one hand, and an individualist morality and a civil society on a Western model on the other hand, which the Scottish thinkers—and, for that matter, Hayek—took to be necessary and universal, is instead an historical accident, a singularity—and perhaps a short-lived one at that. It is no less important to grasp that market institutions can exist, and even flourish, in the absence of a civil society. Saudi Arabia is not a civil society, on any conception of what that means: but who will deny that its economic life is governed by market institutions? And are we ready to rule out *a priori* the possibility that a flourishing market economy can coexist with some varieties of fundamentalism—in the context, say, of a Hindu regime in India, always supposing that the present Indian state, or something like it, survives over the coming years?

It is true that well-developed market institutions presuppose private property and the price mechanism, and the protection of economic liberties by law; they do not presuppose that the society in which market institutions are embedded be a civil society. A flourishing market economy may exist, and has existed, in societies having an established religion, lacking anything akin to equality before the law, or most of the civil liberties. The idea that market institutions will flourish only in a civil society is as unhistorical as the notion that civil societies always go with, or issue in, liberal democracies. We need only think of the Moorish civilizations to think of market institutions flourishing in the absence of civil society; or, in our own days, of Singapore. If the current project of market reform in China is even halfway successful, we will have a world-historical example of flourishing market institutions which have no dependency on the institutions of civil society.

These apparently abstruse theoretical and historical considerations are, in fact, of the closest practical relevance to policy—for example, in the post-communist societies. The essential truth to grasp is that policies of privatization and marketization on any Western model are bound to fail in most of the post-Soviet economies, even as *perestroika* failed,[20] their failure carrying with them the ruin of the reformist governments that sponsor them. If there are Western models for the post-communist economies, the most appropriate may be that of post-war Germany, where it was recognized—in very unHayekian spirit—that the recreation of a market economy demanded constructivist legislation by government.[21] Even the German model is not exportable, and may not indeed be renewable in Germany in its historic form, since it depended on a contingent political settlement, involving a compromise between the traditions of *Ordoliberalism* and of Catholic social theology, which events—including the unification of Germany and the undoing of the postwar settlement in Europe—have rendered anachronistic and untenable. This example should teach us a truth—intensely disagreeable to classical liberal ideologues, if indeed it is intelligible to them—of the first importance: that the stability of market institutions, and the viability of civil societies, never depends on the niceties of constitutional design, or indeed on the application of any set of principles, but on contingent political settlements, constantly renewed against the background of the diverse cultural traditions of the peoples who are their bearers.

*IV. Homo economicus, liberal legalism and the illusion of spontaneous social order*

The overriding error of the Hayekian model of the spontaneous emergence of market institutions is that its original exemplar, the English case, was a settled society and polity for centuries, in which property titles and contractual liberties were given content by the slow evolution of the common law. As against the Hayekian model, the Virginia School[22] correctly perceives the necessity of contructivist legal activism in the development of market institutions in all those countries where such slow evolution of common law has not occurred and is not to be expected. The Virginia School, like the other dominant schools of liberal theory, errs in its legalism: in particular it errs in its faith in constitutional contract as a vehicle for the generation of political legitimacy. This is partly because, again in common with the conventional schools of liberal theory, the Virginia School has at its centre, not any conception of human behavior that can be squared with human history, but an unhistorical cipher; in the Virginia School, not the disembodied subject of Kantian philosophy which haunts the pages of Rawls, but *homo economicus*, the illegitimate offspring of Hobbesian theory.

The objection to both of these theoretical conceptions is *not* that they are abstractions—What else could they be?—but that they incapsulate a philosophical anthropology from which all the historical contingencies whereby human beings acquire particular identities have been erased. For the philosophical anthropology that informs these standard liberal theories it is only an accident that human beings have the histories they do. Such liberal theories, insofar as they are embodied in projects of positive science, model human behavior on conceptions of rational choice, for which the contingent histories of human beings are not constitutive of their identities. Such liberal theorizing will find it impossible, except by a sleight of hand, to explain why ethnic and religious allegiance so often have pre-eminence in political behavior over economic self-interest; and it will be constantly confounded by events, as it was when— entirely predictably, for anyone familiar with the larger outlines of European history—plans for European federalism ran aground on the reef of national sentiment and allegiance. The rationalist anthropology of standard liberal theory is faithful to its origins in the Enlightenment project—French or Scottish—in system-atically underestimating the significance of cultural difference, and its ramifications in political behavior.

Now it will undoubtedly be objected that, whereas these criticisms may have considerable force against standard versions of liberalism, they have far less against Hayek, whose thought contains a powerful critique of constructivist rationalism, and whose model of human behavior is not that of rational choice but of rule-following.[23] This objection is not altogether without merit but it understates the affinities between Hayek's thought and the standard positions in liberal political philosophy. In the first place Hayek's critique of rationalism is insufficiently radical. It amounts to the claim that, since social rules or conventions are embodied knowledge not of one but of many generations of human beings, we are justified in following them uncritically, varying them at the margin perhaps, but not in attempting to subject them to rational scrutiny. This is an instrumentalist view of the function of rules which, if it is to be fully defensible, probably needs the support of the whole dubiously coherent functionalist social theory we have earlier criticized, and cer-tainly has defects analogous to those that are fatal to Hayek's conception of cultural evolution.

The claim that rules or conventions are embodied knowledge inaccessible to any one man or generation of men, and thus merit uncritical obedience, also neglects the real possibility—indeed, the commonplace fact—that inherited rules embody tacit ignorance and error as often as they embody tacit knowledge. When they do, blind obedience to them can be fatal. This possibility is neglected in Hayek, perhaps because in the evolutionary epistemology he has in common with Popper it is reasonable to suppose that the tacit knowledge or theories inherited and embodied in our sense-organs must track or mirror the world sufficiently for us to have survived over long stretches of evolutionary time. There is a disanalogy, however, between the knowledge or theories that are inherited along with our genetic constitution and the beliefs or expectations that are embodied in inherited social rules or conventions. This disanalogy arises from the fact that abrupt and drastic changes in human society occur frequently enough for our inherited expectations, as embodied in traditional rules, to be often very poor mirrors of social reality. Historical discontinuities are too common for a policy of uncritical reliance on the beliefs embodied in inherited social rules to be effective or prudent. Consider those European Jews, for whom the thought that the Final Solution could be a serious project of Hitler's violated the tacit knowledge and the unarticulated commonsense embodied in their traditions, even when these traditions were formed partly by the immemorial experience of pogroms; such Jews, like others for whom the Nazi project was beyond the bounds of commonsense imagination, paid for their reliance on inherited tacit knowledge with their lives.[24]

This limitation of inherited tacit knowledge may be put another way. There is in human history and society no error-elimination mechanism, no filter device, analogous to bankruptcy in market processes, whereby the erroneous expectations embodied in inherited rules are corrected, as the false entrepreneurial conjectures of business organizations are corrected in the market according to those economists who model market processes on evolutionary processes.[25] Analogies to the punctuated equilibria of evolutionary biology are commonplaces in human history, as Hume recognized when he attached the whiggish historiography of incremental change, and reminded his readers of the frequency of catastrophic transformations in regimes, institutions and conventions. The conception of rules as vehicles or bearers of inherited tacit knowledge, as transmitters of unarticulated experience across the generations, which is a key element in Hayek's conception of spontaneous social order and in his critique of constructivist rationalism, breaks down when it is realized how common are the occasions when the beliefs and expectations so transmitted prove erroneous.

This criticism of Hayek's conception of the function of social rules is also a criticism of Polanyi's epistemology of tacit or personal knowledge, and to that extent may be thought to endorse Popperian or Millian fallibilism as alternatives to Hayek's epistemology. No such endorsement is intended.[26] Rather, the very idea of rule-following in Hayek is a vestige of rationalism, of which his familiarity with Wittgenstein's philosophy should have cured him.[27] It is in this, and related aspects, that Hayek's critique of rationalism is less than radical: he fails to recognize that judgement, not rule-following, is primordial in human action, and that rules are abridgements or distillates of practices, upon which they depend both for their authority and for their very meaning.[28] The radical critique of rationalism that is to be found in Wittgenstein and Oakeshott treats practical reasoning as referring always to particular forms of life, of which rules and principles are only shorthand versions. Hayek came closest to this view in the radically subjectivist account of social objects he developed in *The Counter-Revolution of Science*,[29] which, if he had applied it consistently, would have disallowed any naturalistic conception of rule-following. In fact, Hayek soon fell back on the scientistic account of human behaviour, in which a natural selection of rules is central, which is contained in his conception of cultural evolution. When coupled with his instrumentalism about rules, this perspective of Hayek's is little different from the account of human action, found in its starkest form in the work of Gary Becker, in terms of the rational choice model of *homo economicus*. For all its weak traditionalism, Hayek's political philosophy for this reason belongs to the same family of rationalist liberal philosophies of which those of Rawls and Buchanan are also members, and shares with them common limitations and disabilities, in particular the combination of legalism with economism by which the idea of rational choice is given content.

This is not to say that Hayek's rationalism is a doctrine that is all of one piece, since it attempts a synthesis of two rationalisms, Kantian and Humean, that are not ultimately reconcilable. Whereas Kant's metaphysical conception of the human subject as a noumenal self dispossessed of the constitutive contingencies—of language, lineage and cultural tradition—that give human beings their particular identities in historical practice does support the rationalist universalism of doctrinal or fundamentalist liberalism, such a conception of the subject is not an option for Hayek—or for anyone touched by empiricism. Hume's sceptical naturalism, on the other hand, supports liberal norms, only on very implausible assumptions about the constancy, across cultures and over long stretches of history, of human nature. Such assumptions are precisely those that are made, from Hobbes onwards, in political theories in which rational choice is central and fundamental, both as a general explanation of human behaviour and as an account of the origins of political allegiance. There is an unresolved, and likely irresolvable tension, both in Hume and in Hayek, between the particularism and historicism which a truly skeptical and naturalistic approach to human society supports, and in which liberal practices are simply one form of life among others tried out by a highly inventive species, and the universalistic rationalism in which a liberal regime is conceived as the normal form of civilized life for mankind. There can be no reasonable doubt that Hayek resolves this tension by abandoning scepticism for rationalism—a move that should teach us something about the prospects of those varieties of fundamentalist or classical liberalism that, despairing (rightly) of constructing foundations in a comprehensive moral theory, seek instead for the foundations of liberalism in epistemology.

The fate of Hayek's attempt at a comprehensive liberal political philosophy turns on *naivetes* in his philosophical anthropology, and in his philosophy of history, that are closely intertwined. His philosophy of history, though it is free of the ignorant vulgarity and innocent parochialism that inform Fukuyama's historiosophical speculations, is at one with it in anticipating universal convergence, if not on the institutions of "democratic capitalism," then at any rate on the practices of liberal civil society. On all such expectations Stuart Hampshire has written the definitive epitaph, when he alludes to "the belief in a positivist theory of modernization," a theory that is traceable to the French Enlightenment. The positivists believed that all societies across the globe will gradually discard their traditional attachments to supernatural forces because of the need for rational, scientific and experimental methods of thought which modern industrial economy involves. This is the old faith, widespread in the nineteenth century, that there must be a step-by-step convergence on liberal values, on 'our values'." Of this old faith Hampshire concludes: "We now know that there is no 'must' about it and that all such theories of human history have a predictive value of zero."[30] Hayek's philosophy of history, which is a sort of Darwinian secularization of Burkean providentialism, is a prime exemplar of the old faith, which is the fundamentalist faith in the Enlightenment project, to which Hampshire refers.

*Conclusion*

The upshot of our examination of the idea of spontaneous order, as it is found in Hayek, is that it is a farrago, which ought to be removed from social theory. It is also an illusion in political philosophy, and a danger in policy. It is an illusion in political philosophy because it reinforces the liberal fantasy that political allegiance can be to abstract rules, or to the terms of a constitutional contract, rather than to the particular forms of common life and culture that—in the real world of human history— sustain liberal practices. It is noteworthy that nowhere in Hayek's voluminous writings, apart from a few scattered references to federalism, does he ask, or answer, the question, What is the political unit by which liberal practices are to be governed?; and that nowhere does he recognize the close historical links between classical liberalism and nationalism, or the decisive role that classical liberals played in the construction of the modern European nation-state. Equally notable is the absence in Hayek's work of any serious consideration of the relations of religion and liberty, apart from occasional Voltairean asides on the social utility of superstition, and embarrassing speculations on the natural selection of faiths. These are lacunae in Hayek's liberal political philosophy that cannot be remedied; rather, they are integral to it as a species of the Enlightenment project, and they entail its undoing.

At the back of Hayek's extraordinary neglect of the real sources of allegiance to a liberal state there lies the magnificent anachronism of the Habsburg Empire, which he was just old enough to have known, and indeed to have fought for; it is this exemplar of liberal imperialism which probably embodies his real ideal of a liberal polity. Its utter unreality in our time, like the unreality of liberal schemes for constitutional contract and for federalism, should caution us as to the dangers for policy of Hayekian ideas of spontaneous order. The Hayekian idea of the

Great Society, of a social order held together only by a calculus of exchanges conducted against a background of common legal rules, which is the political embodiment of his conception of spontaneous order, is only another exercise in utopian liberal ideology, which in our circumstances is the merest folly. For us, the future of market institutions and the prospects of civil society depend, as always, on statecraft and the political arts, with *all* their attendant vicissitudes and tragedies, not upon constitution-making or theorizing. It is an infantile absurdity to suppose, for example, that the post-communist states will succeed, where all other have failed, in constructing a neo-liberal utopia. For them, as for us, achieving a liberal form of life is a matter, not of decades, but of centuries of laborious institution-building, often entailing the use of political coercion, as a result of which liberal practices at last take root in the soils of common life. For both the Western countries and the emerging post-communist states, a liberal society will be stably renewed across the generations, only if it is embedded in particular common cultures to which popular allegiance is deep and strong. Such common cultures are, in our historical context, inescapably those of nations. Neglect of this truth condemns liberal political philosophy in all of its standard forms, including that of Hayek, to sterility and shallowness. Neglect of the political necessity, for any liberal state, of a common national culture that is richer and deeper than any that can be captured by the banal abstractions of liberal economism and legalism, condemns liberal polities to dissolution and extinction.

## ENDNOTES

1. See my book, *Post-liberalism: Studies in Political Thought*, New York and London, Routledge, 1993, Chapter 5, "Buchanan on Liberty", pp. 47-63.
2. For a systematic statement of Rawls's later thought, see his book, *Political Liberalism*, New York: Columbia University Press, 1993. I have criticized Rawls's

later thought in my book, *Liberalisms: Essays in Political Philosophy*, New York
and London: Routledge, 1989, Chapter 10.

3. Notable exceptions to it are Joseph Raz, *The Morality of Freedom*, Oxford:
Oxford University Press, 1986; and the liberal thought of Isiah Berlin. On the
latter, see my *Berlin*, New York and London: Harper Collins, Fontana Modern
Master, 1994, and my article, "Agonistic liberalism," forthcoming in *Social
Philosophy and Policy*.

4. I have argued this in my *Hayek on liberty*, Oxford and New York: Basil
Blackwell, Second Edition, 1986.

5. The failure of *perestroika*, and the revolutionary implications of its failure for
the Soviet system, did not go altogether unpredicted, though they ran counter to
the conventional wisdom of generations of Western Sovietologists. For statements in 1989 that the Soviet Union was at that time in a pre-revolutionary
situation, see my *Post-liberalism, op. cit.*, Chapters 8 and 12.

6. F. A. Hayek's *Individualism and Economic Order*, London and Henley,
Routledge and Kegan Paul, 1976, Chapters II, IV, VII-IX.

7. Mises's contribution to the calculation debate is well surveyed in D. Lavoie,
*Rivalry and Central Planning: the Socialist Calculation Debate Reconsidered*,
Cambridge: Cambridge University Press, 1985.

8. I have analyzed and assessed the calculation argument in a more systematic and
extended way in my book, *Beyond the New Right: markets, government and the
common environment*, New York and London: Routledge, 1993, Chapter Three.

9. Joseph Schumpeter, *Capitalism, Socialism and Democracy*, London, 1954.

10. Michael Polanyi, *The Logic of Liberty*, Chicago: University of Chicago Press,
1951, "The Span of Central Direction." Polanyi's analysis is developed in Paul
Craig Roberts, *Alienation and the Soviet Economy: the Collapse of the Socialist Era*,
2nd Edition, New York and London: Holmes and Meier, 1990.

11. I have discussed this simulation of market institutions in the Soviet strategic-
military complex in my monograph *The Strange Death of Perestroika: Causes and
Consequences of the Soviet Coup*, European Security Studies no. 13, London:
Institute of European Defence and Strategic Studies, 1991.

12. See my paper, "From Post-Communism to Civil Society: The Reemergence
of History and the Decline in the Western Model" in *Social Philosophy and Policy,
Liberalism and the Economic Order*, vol.10, Number 2, Summer 1993, pp. 26-50.

13. It is, perhaps, of more than historical interest that the expression "spontaneous order" finds some of its earliest uses in the writings of Michael Polanyi. It is
found there no later than the papers reprinted in Polanyi's *The Logic of Liberty*
(1951). The point of intellectual or philosophical interest is not whether Hayek—
who overlapped with Polanyi at the University of Chicago in the Fifties—owes
the expression to Polanyi; that historical question can be settled, if at all, only by
a detailed study of Hayek's writings of the Thirties and early Forties, and does
not concern the purposes of this paper. The point of philosophical interest is that
the idea of spontaneous order in Polanyi, whatever its other difficulties, is not
coupled with the incoherent conception of cultural evolution with which it is
conjoined in Hayek. The explanation for this is probably in the fact that Polanyi
was never under the influence of the positivist and scientistic philosophers, such
as Mach and Ehrenfeld, who dominated Viennese intellectual life at the turn of

the century, and who were profoundly important in Hayek's intellectual forma-tion; and, partly as a consequence of this, was never captivated by the simplicities of evolutionary epistemology, which Hayek embraced in his *Sensory Order* (1952), and to which his attachment was strengthened by his long friendship with Popper.

14. Hayek's theory of cultural evolution is set out most explicitly in his last book, *The Fatal Conceit*. There are, however, many anticipations of the theory of group selection in Hayek's earlier work, particularly in his greatest book, *The Constitu-tion of Liberty* (1960). It is because evolutionist and functionalist conceptions run through most of Hayek's work that any simple periodization of his intellectual life is indefensible.

15. See Polanyi, *Ibid.*, endnote 10 above.

16. See especially, G. L. S. Shackle, *Epistemics and Economics*, Cambridge: Cambridge University Press, 1972.

17. For a superb intellectual reconstruction of Keynes's work, see Robert Skidelsky's magnificent biography, especially volume two, which examines the relations between Keynes's economic theories and philosophy of practice those of Hayek and Shackle. The sections on Keynes's philosophy of probability, and its connections with the dissolution of rational expectations wrought by the destruction of the conventions of social order that occurred as a side-effect of the First World War—a dissolution grasped by Keynes and Shackle, but not by Hayek—are particularly noteworthy.

18. That the price mechanism does not transmit effectively all relevant informa-tion to market participants, even where there are not large-scale discoordinations, is shown by the existence of arbitrators, who make a living by spotting and exploiting price discrepancies.

19. I have discussed totalitarianism and civil society in my article, "Totalitarian-ism, reform and civil society," in *Totalitarianism at the Crossroads*, ed. E. F. Paul, New Brunswick and London, 1990. This paper is reprinted in my book, *Post-liberalism: Studies in Political Thought*, London: Routledge, 1993, Chapter 12.

20. I earlier forecast the failure of *peristroika*. In the *Times Literary Supplement* of July 27, 1989, I wrote: "Whatever the immediate outcome of current negotiations, it is safe to assert that neither the division of Germany in its present form, nor West Germany's current relationship with NATO, can be sustained for long. As it stands, the political and military posture of West Germany disregards both the realities of history and legitimate German aspirations for unification; and the pressures for a separate settlement between West Germany and the Soviet Union are probably irresistible.... The darker side of the dissolution of the post-war settlement is in the prospect of... West Germany pried loose from NATO only to inherit the rusting industries and indigent pensioners of the GDR." I wrote in *The Financial Times*, London, 13 September, 1989: "The danger is that the decay of the totalitarian system build up by Stalin and Lenin will result not in the reconstitution of a stable civil society, but in mounting chaos and economic collapse.... If this is so, then what we are witnessing in the Soviet Union is not the middle of a reform, but the beginning of a revolution whose course no-one can foretell." In October, 1989, in *Totalitarianism at the Crossroads, Ibid.*, p. 134, I wrote: "....classical Communist totalitarianism is already showing signs of

weakness (as in Bulgaria) and even Romania may not prove immune to change or collapse.... The model for such a prospect...may be contemporary Yugoslavia, with its intractable ethnic conflicts, profound economic problems, weak populist governments, and chronic tendencies toward political disintegration." In the London *Times*, December 28, 1989, I wrote: "The aftermath of totalitarianism will not be a global tranquilization of the sort imagined by American triumphalist theorists of liberal democracy. Instead, the end of totalitarianism in most of the world is likely to see the resumption of history on decidedly traditional lines: not the history invented in the hallucinatory perspectives of Marxism and American liberalism, but the history of authoritarian regimes, great-power rivalries, secret diplomacy, irredentist claims and ethnic and religious conflicts. It is to this world, harsh but familiar, that we are now returning, and for whose trials we should not be preparing." These warnings were widely dismissed as alarmist.
21. As T. W. Hutchison remarks of Eucken: "The launching of the Social Market Economy was and had to be an explicitly constructivist act." And as Eucken himself put it: "The economic system has to be consciously shaped." See T. W. Hutchison, *The Politics and Philosophy of Economics: Marxists, Keynesians and Austrians*, Oxford: Basil Blackwell, 1981, p. 17.
22. For the best statement of the theoretical perspective of the Virginia School of Public Choice, see James Buchanan, *The Limits of Liberty: Between Anarchy and Leviathan*, Chicago: University of Chicago Press, 1975.
23. This rule-following conception of human conduct is most clear in Hayek's paper, "Rules, Perception and Intelligibility," in his *Studies in Philosophy, Politics and Economics*, London: Routledge and Kegan Paul, 1967.
24. I owe this example to conversations with Ernest van den Haag. Its use in my argument is my responsibility alone.
25. I refer in particular to the fascinating work of Armen Alchian.
26. I set out the place of Mill's fallibilistic account of knowledge in his broader liberal doctrine in my book, *Mill On Liberty: A Defence*, London and New York: Routledge, 1983. I criticised Millian and Popperian fallibilism as epistemological foundations for liberalism in my *Liberalisms: Essays in Political Philosophy, op. cit.*, "Postscript," pp. 241-249.
27. For the best statement of Wittgenstein's devastating argument for rule-scepticism, see Saul Kripke, *Wittgenstein on Rules and Private Language*, Oxford: Basil Blackwell, 1982.
28. The idea of rules as abridgements of practices is, of course, central in the thoughts of Michael Oakeshott. The most explicit statement of Oakeshott's conception of a practice occurs in his book, *Human Conduct*, Oxford: Clarendon Press, 1975.
29. F. A. Hayek, *The Counter-Revolution of Science: Studies on the Abuse of Reason*, Glencoe, Illinois: The Free Press, 1952. The first two sections of this study appeared as articles in the journal *Economica*, 1941-44.
30. Stuart Hampshire, *Justice is Strife*, Presidential Address, 1991 Pacific Division Meeting, American Philosophical Association, printed in *Proceedings and Addresses of the American Philosophical Association*, vol. 65, no. 3, November 1991, pp. 24-5.

# About the Contributors

*William B. Allen* received his Ph. D. in Government at Claremont Graduate School, and is currently Dean and Professor of James Madison College of Michigan State University. His interests include political philosophy, American government, jurisprudence, and political economy. Dean Allen taught formerly at Harvey Mudd College in Claremont, California, and he has been a Kellogg National Fellow, Fulbright Fellow, a member of the National Council on the Humanities, a member and Chairman of the U.S. Commission on Civil rights (1987-92), and has received the international Prix Montesquieu. He recently published *Let the Advice Be Good: A Defense of Madison's Democratic Nationalism.* He has edited several collections, including *George Washington: A Collection,* and the *Essential Antifederalist,* and has authored many essays on American political thought and similar topics. Born in Fernandina Beach, Florida, Dean Allen is married to Susan A. Macall, and they have two children, both adult.

*George W. Carey* is Professor of Government at Georgetown. He is editor of *The Political Science Reviewer.* Professor Carey's works include *Basic Symbols of the American Political Tradition* with the late Willmoore Kendall; *The Federalist: Design for a Constitutional Republic;* and *In Defense of the Constitution.* He is editor, with James McClellan, of a definitive student edition of *The Federalist.*

*J. Rufus Fears* is Professor of Classics and holds the G. T. and Libby Blankenship Chair in the History of Liberty at the University of Oklahoma, where he is Director of the Center for the History of Liberty. Professor Fears is internationally recognized for his scholarship and teaching in ancient history. He has been a Fellow of the American Academy in Rome, a Guggenheim Fellow, and twice a Fellow of the Alexander von Humboldt Foundation. On eight occasions he has received awards for outstanding teaching. In 1996, he was named University of Oklahoma Professor of the Year. In addition to numerous books, monographs, articles and reviews in ancient history, Professor Fears has edited a three volume edition of the writings of Lord Acton.

*Timothy Fuller* is Professor of Political Science and Dean of the Faculty and of the College at Colorado College. Among his special interests is the history of British political thought from Thomas Hobbes to Michael Oakeshott. He is editor of the *Hobbes Newsletter* and editor of the papers of Michael Oakeshott for the Yale University Press, in which series four volumes have so far been published. The most recent is *The Politics of Faith and the Politics of Skepticism*, published by Yale in the Spring of 1996.

*John Gray* was educated at Exeter College, Oxford University, where he read Philosophy, Politics and Economics and received his B.A., M.A., and D. Phil. degrees. Since 1976 he has been a Fellow of Jesus College, Oxford University. He has held numerous visiting appointments, including: Professor of Government, Harvard University; Visiting Distinguished Professor in Political Economy at the Murphy Institute, Tulane University; Stranahan Distinguished Research Fellow at the Social Philosophy and Policy Center, Bowling Green State University, Ohio; and Olmsted Visiting Distinguished Professor at Yale University. His books include: *Mill on Liberty: a Defence; Hayek on Liberty; Liberalism; Liberalisms: Essays in Political Philosophy; Post-liberalism: Studies in Political Thought; Beyond the New Right: Markets, Government and the Common Environment.* Two of his recent monographs are:

*The Post-Communist Societies in Transition* and *The Undoing of Conservatism* (Social market Foundation, London, 1994). His most recent books, *Isaiah Berlin* and *Enlightenment's Wake: Politics and Culture at the Close of the Modern Age*, were published in 1995.

*Leonard P. Liggio* is Distinguished Senior Scholar at the Institute for Humane Studies, George Mason University and Research Professor at the Law School. He is Executive Vice President of the Atlas Economic Research Foundation, and Chairman of the Advisory Council of the Salvatori Center for Academic Leadership at the Heritage Foundation. He was President of the Philadelphia Society from 1992 to 1995; member of the Program Committee for the Mt. Pélerin Society in 1994 and of the American Catholic Historical Association in 1992. He has been a Visiting Professor at the Francisco Marroquin University and at the University of Aix-en-Provence. He formerly taught at City College of New York and the State University of New York at Old Westbury. He is former editor of *Literature of Liberty*, and his most recent publication is "Law and Legislation in Hayek's Legal Philosophy," in the *Southwestern University Law Review*.

*George B. Martin* received his undergraduate degree from Wofford College, his graduate degrees from the University of Georgia (M.A.), and the University of Manchester, England, (PhD). He has taught at the University of Georgia, and at Wofford College, Spartanburg, S.C., until January 1996, when he became president of Liberty Fund, Inc.

*Ralph McInerny* received his Ph. D. at Laval University. He is currently Michael P. Grace Professor of Medieval Studies and Director of the Jacques Maritain Center. He is the author of *The Logic of Analogy; Thomism in an Age of Renewal; St. Thomas Aquinas; Ethica Thomistica; A First Glance at St.*

*Thomas Aquinas: A Handbook for Peeping Thomists; Boethius and Aquinas; Aquinas on Human Action; The Question of Christian Ethics;* and *Aquinas Against the Averroists.* He is also a novelist, and author of the Father Dowling mysteries. He has been the recipient of various fellowships—Fulbright, NEH and NEA—and is a fellow of the Pontifical Academy of St. Thomas Aquinas. He is past President of the Fellowship of Catholic Scholars, the American Metaphysical Society, and the American Catholic Philosophical Association. He edited *The New Scholasticism* for many years, and is the founder/ publisher of *Catholic Dossier;* and co-founder (with Michael Novak) of *CRISIS: A Journal of Lay Catholic Opinion.* Under his general editorship, the Maritain Center is about to launch a 20-volume edition of the *Works of Jacques Maritain.* He is also publishing a 6-volume edition of *Aquinas's Commentaries on Aristotle.*

*Edward B. McLean* holds the Eugene N. and Marian C. Beesley Chair in Political Science at Wabash College. He served nineteen years as Deputy Prosecutor in Montgomery County, Indiana. He received his J.D. and Ph.D degrees from Indiana University. Professor McLean recently published *Law and Civilization: The Legal Thought of Roscoe Pound,* and edited *Derailing the Constitution: The Undermining of American Federalism.*

*Jeffrey D. Wallin* received his Ph.D. and M.A. from the Claremont Graduate School, and his B.A. from Pepperdine University and is currently President of the American Academy for Liberal Education. He is a former Director of the Division of General Programs at the National Endowment for the Humanities where he also served as director of the Office of the Bicentennial of the U.S. Constitution. Dr. Wallin has taught at the University of Dallas and the University of California, Santa Barbara, and has lectured on liberal education, U.S.

Constitutional Law, and national security affairs in the United States, Europe, and Latin America. He has been Director of Program at the Robert M. Hutchins Center for the Study of Democratic Institutions in California, and at the Liberty Fund in Indianapolis, as well as Senior Fellow at the Institute for Foreign Policy analysis in Cambridge and Washington. Dr. Wallin was associate editor of Praeger's series *Democracy in the World*. He is the author of *By Ships Alone: Churchill and the Dardanelles*, and co-editor of *Rhetoric and American Statesmanship*. He has recently published in *Notes et Documents*, and *The Aspen Institute Quarterly*.